Olivier Messiaen's *Catalogue d'oiseaux*

Roderick Chadwick and Peter Hill give a detailed account of the evolution of Olivier Messiaen's *Catalogue d'oiseaux* for piano solo, from its initial conception in the Black Forest in 1953 to its completion and premiere in the Parisian 'Concerts du Domaine musical' at the end of the decade. Through close examination of the composer's birdsong *cahiers* they demonstrate how Messiaen translated nature into music in a way that had a major impact on his later work. They also consider issues of performance, and Messiaen's artistic relationship with his dedicatee and wife-to-be, Yvonne Loriod, including the significance of her two recordings of the cycle. This book illuminates the *Catalogue* from a variety of angles: its historical significance, as a study of how mimicry of nature can be transformed into music of mesmeric originality, and as a guide that offers a wealth of fresh insights to listeners and performers.

RODERICK CHADWICK is Reader in Music at the Royal Academy of Music and is a frequent performer of Messiaen's music. He has also produced critically acclaimed recordings of works by Stockhausen, Gloria Coates and Finnissy amongst others, and his writing has been included in Christopher Dingle and Robert Fallon (eds.), *Messiaen Perspectives 2* (2013).

PETER HILL is Professor Emeritus at the University of Sheffield, and his recording of Messiaen's complete piano works won praise from critics as well as from the composer himself. In 2005 he published a groundbreaking biography, *Messiaen*, and in 2008 his work on Messiaen was recognised with the award of the annual prize for musical scholarship by the Académie des Beaux-Arts in Paris.

MUSIC IN CONTEXT

Series editors

J. P. E. Harper-Scott
Royal Holloway, University of London

Julian Rushton
University of Leeds

The aim of Music in Context is to illuminate specific musical works, repertoires or practices in historical, critical, socio-economic or other contexts; or to illuminate particular cultural and critical contexts in which music operates through the study of specific musical works, repertoires or practices. A specific musical focus is essential, while avoiding the decontextualisation of traditional aesthetics and music analysis. The series title invites engagement with both its main terms; the aim is to challenge notions of what contexts are appropriate or necessary in studies of music, and to extend the conceptual framework of musicology into other disciplines or into new theoretical directions.

Books in the series

Simon P. Keefe, *Mozart's Requiem: Reception, Work, Completion*
J. P. E. Harper-Scott, *The Quilting Points of Musical Modernism: Revolution, Reaction, and William Walton*
Nancy November, *Beethoven's Theatrical Quartets: Opp. 59, 74, and 95*
Rufus Hallmark, *'Frauenliebe und Leben': Chamisso's Poems and Schumann's Songs*
Anna Zayaruznaya, *The Monstrous New Art: Divided Forms in the Late Medieval Motet*
Helen Deeming and Elizabeth Eva Leach, *Manuscripts and Medieval Song: Inscription, Performance, Context*
Emily Kilpatrick, *The Operas of Maurice Ravel*

Olivier Messiaen's *Catalogue d'oiseaux*

From Conception to Performance

RODERICK CHADWICK
Royal Academy of Music, London

PETER HILL
University of Sheffield

CAMBRIDGE
UNIVERSITY PRESS

University Printing House, Cambridge CB2 8BS, United Kingdom

One Liberty Plaza, 20th Floor, New York, NY 10006, USA

477 Williamstown Road, Port Melbourne, VIC 3207, Australia

314-321, 3rd Floor, Plot 3, Splendor Forum, Jasola District Centre, New Delhi - 110025, India

103 Penang Road, #05-06/07, Visioncrest Commercial, Singapore 238467

Cambridge University Press is part of the University of Cambridge.

It furthers the University's mission by disseminating knowledge in the pursuit of education, learning and research at the highest international levels of excellence.

www.cambridge.org
Information on this title: www.cambridge.org/9781009247672
DOI: 10.1017/9780511843679

© Roderick Chadwick and Peter Hill 2018

This publication is in copyright. Subject to statutory exception and to the provisions of relevant collective licensing agreements, no reproduction of any part may take place without the written permission of Cambridge University Press.

First published 2018
First paperback edition 2022

A catalogue record for this publication is available from the British Library

Library of Congress Cataloging in Publication data
Names: Chadwick, Roderick, author. | Hill, Peter, 1948– author.
Title: Olivier Messiaen's *Catalogue d'oiseaux* : from conception to performance / Roderick Chadwick, Peter Hill.
Description: Cambridge, United Kingdom ; New York, NY : Cambridge University Press, 2018. | Series: Music in context | Includes bibliographical references and index.
Identifiers: LCCN 2017037841 | ISBN 9781107000315 (hardback)
Subjects: LCSH: Messiaen, Olivier, 1908– 1992. Catalogue d'oiseaux.
Classification: LCC ML410.M595 C53 2018 | DDC 786.2/156–dc23
LC record available at https://lccn.loc.gov/2017037841

ISBN 978-1-107-00031-5 Hardback
ISBN 978-1-009-24767-2 Paperback

Cambridge University Press has no responsibility for the persistence or accuracy of URLs for external or third-party internet websites referred to in this publication, and does not guarantee that any content on such websites is, or will remain, accurate or appropriate.

Contents

List of Illustrations [*page* vi]
List of Music Examples [vii]
List of Tables [x]
Acknowledgments [xi]
List of Abbreviations [xii]

Introduction [1]

1 Content and Context [8]

2 Birdsong and the Genesis of *Catalogue d'oiseaux* [16]

3 Beyond the Birdsong of *Catalogue d'oiseaux* [57]

4 The First Wave of Composition [71]

5 The Second Wave of Composition [125]

6 Performance [178]

7 Postlude [202]

Bibliography [225]
Index [229]

Illustrations

2.1 Jacques Delamain's house   [*page* 23]
4.1 The Meije glacier viewed from La Grave   [73]
5.1 The Charenton   [128]
5.2 The coastline at Banyuls   [135]
5.3 The Cirque de Mourèze   [161]
5.4 'The Sphinx'   [165]
5.5 Max Ernst, *Au rendez-vous des Amis*   [168]

Music Examples

2.1 'La Colombe' [*page* 17]
2.2 (a) *Turangalîla*: 'Jardin du sommeil d'amour'; (b) *Cantéyodjayâ*;
     (c) *Le Merle noir*; (d) 'La Rousserolle effarvatte' [20]
2.3 (a) Nightingale, 14 May 1952; (b) Nightingale, 27 April 1953 [25]
2.4 Tawny owl, 6 October 1953 [29]
2.5 Wood thrush, from *Oiseaux exotiques* [34]
2.6 Nightingale, from *More Songs of Wild Birds* [36]
2.7 Reed warbler, from *Songs of British Birds* [36]
2.8 Woodlark, from *More Songs of Wild Birds* [38]
2.9 Waves off the Brittany coast [41]
2.10 (a) Red-backed shrike; (b) Red-backed shrike harmonised [43]
2.11 (a) Blackcap; (b) its realisation in 'La Bouscarle' [43]
2.12 Reed warbler notated from the Swedish discs and as realised in
     'La Rousserolle effarvatte' [45]
2.13 Sketch for 'L'Alouette lulu': the numbers in brackets indicate the
     order of phrases in the finished score [51]
2.14 Woodlark from the Forez, 14 July 1956 (facsimile) [53]
2.15 Opening of 'L'Alouette lulu' [55]
3.1 The 'tragic cry' of the Alpine chough in the *cahier* (a) and in the
     score (b) [60]
3.2 'Le Courlis cendré', b. 1 [62]
3.3 Richard Wagner, *Tristan und Isolde*, Act III, bb. 1–4 [63]
3.4 Maurice Ravel 'Oiseaux tristes', b. 29 [63]
3.5 The first planned ending of 'Le Courlis cendré' (23044, p. 19) [63]
3.6 'Le Loriot', p. 2, b. 3 [64]
3.7 Claude Debussy, *Pelléas et Mélisande*, Act IV, Scene 4 [65]
3.8 'Le Merle de roche', p. 2, b. 10 [65]
3.9 Claude Debussy, 'Clair de lune', bb. 13–14 [65]
4.1 (a) 'Le Chocard des Alpes': the 'majestic flight of the golden eagle';
     (b) Richard Wagner, *Tristan und Isolde*, prelude to Act III [74]
4.2 High peaks of the Cirque de Bonne-Pierre [75]
4.3 Simhavikrama and candrakalâ-lakskmîça [76]

4.4 Memorable bars in the opening Strophe of 'Le Chocard des Alpes' [77]
4.5 (a) Igor Stravinsky's 'Augurs of spring' chord; (b) the 'Golaud' chord from Claude Debussy, *Pelléas et Mélisande* [80]
4.6 Notation of a golden oriole, 13 June 1952 [83]
4.7 Notation of a golden oriole, 15 June 1953 [84]
4.8 Notation of the golden oriole with harmonies, 7 May 1956 [85]
4.9 (a) Golden oriole from the Brittany *cahier*; (b) the opening to 'Le Loriot' [86]
4.10 Robin from 'Le Loriot' [88]
4.11 Midday [90]
4.12 The 'memory of gold and rainbow' in 'Le Loriot' [91]
4.13 Possible hand distribution on p. 4 of 'La Chouette hulotte' [95]
4.14 Opening of 'L'Alouette calandrelle' [98]
4.15 Notations for 'L'Alouette calandrelle', including the short-toed lark, skylark and quail (facsimile) [100]
4.16 Skylark [102]
4.17 Notation of a curlew from *More Songs of Wild Birds* (Ludwig Koch) [105]
4.18 (a) The curlew harmonised; (b) the redshank; (c) the opening of the curlew's song in the score; (d) the redshank in the score [107]
4.19 (a) *Turangalîla* material in *La Transfiguration de Notre-Seigneur Jésus-Christ*; (b) opening of *La Fauvette des jardins* [114]
4.20 Notation of a bittern from the Swedish discs (23045, p. 50) [116]
4.21 The source of the first reed warbler solo in 'La Rousserolle effarvatte' (23045, p. 22) [117]
4.22 Notation of the grasshopper warbler from the Swedish discs (23045, p. 27) [118]
4.23 'La Rousserolle effarvatte' p. 18, bb. 7–9 [119]
4.24 The opening of 'La Rousserolle effarvatte' [121]
4.25 'La Rousserolle effarvatte', p. 25, bb. 11–14 [123]
5.1 Birdsongs for 'La Bouscarle' (facsimile) [127]
5.2 Kingfisher [130]
5.3 Part of Messiaen's sketch for the reflections, from 23056(2), p. 7 [130]
5.4 'La Bouscarle': 'The water reflects the willows and poplars' [131]
5.5 The river [133]
5.6 (a) Ortolan bunting (*bruant ortolan*); (b) Thekla lark (*cochevis de Thékla*); (c) black-eared wheatear (*traquet stapazin*); (d) spectacled warbler (*fauvette à lunettes*); (e) Thekla lark; (f) spectacled

	warbler; (g) goldfinch (*chardonneret*); (h) rock bunting (*bruant fou*); (i) Thekla lark; (j) spectacled warbler (facsimile) [137]
5.7	(a) Harmonies from the first two bars; (b) wheatear (right hand); (c) ortolan bunting with introductory harmonies; (d) spectacled warbler with introductory harmonies; (e) herring gull and raven [142]
5.8	Harmonic progression, sunrise to sunset [145]
5.9	'La mer bleue' [149]
5.10	Thekla larks in 23057, p. 37 (a); p. 40 (b) [151]
5.11	Opening of the first Thekla lark duet in 'Le Merle bleu', p. 10 [152]
5.12	The mistle thrush in 23051, p. 6 (a); as realised in the score, p. 5 (b) [156]
5.13	'Le Merle de roche' p. 9, bb. 1 and 2 [163]
5.14	Idealisation of the rock thrush [163]
5.15	*Cahier* 23060, p. 7 (facsimile) [164]
5.16	'Le Traquet rieur', bb. 1–4 [171]
5.17	The last black wheatear solo in 'Le Traquet rieur' [173]
5.18	The black wheatear's last call on p. 19 of 'Le Traquet rieur' [175]
5.19	The 'gust of wind over the sea' (p. 17, b. 3) [176]
5.20	'Silvery sun sprinkled over the sea' (p. 18, b. 9) [177]
7.1	*La Fauvette Passerinette* (facsimile) [206]
7.2	The blackcap, from 23101, p. 18 [209]
7.3	*La Fauvette des jardins*, p. 49, bb. 10–12 [211]
7.4	*La Fauvette des jardins*, p. 55, bb. 14–17 [211]
7.5	(a) *Cahier* 23104, p. 13; (b) *La Fauvette des jardins* p. 26, line 2 [214]
7.6	Long garden warbler solo, 23 July 1967 (23022, p. 12) [215]

Tables

4.1 Rhythms of the opening 'Meije glacier' section of 'Le Chocard des Alpes' [*page* 77]
4.2 Pitches and dynamics in the 'mode' of 'La Chouette hulotte' [94]
4.3 The two versions of 'La Rousserolle effarvatte' [113]
5.1 The strophic structure of 'Le Merle bleu' [148]
5.2 The tonal structure of Book 7 [157]
5.3 The form of 'Le Merle de roche' [166]
5.4 The left hand of 'Le Traquet rieur' [176]
5.5 Twelve-note groupings in 'silvery sun sprinkled over the sea' [177]

Acknowledgments

We owe a great debt of gratitude to a large number of people. Foremost among these are Christopher Dingle, Julian Rushton and J. P. E. Harper-Scott, who read our drafts and gave invaluable support and advice. Important support was also given by Timothy Jones and Neil Heyde of the Royal Academy of Music. Among many who shared insights with us we should particularly like to thank Julian Anderson, James Good, Alex Hills, Roy Howat, Robert Keeley, Daniel-Ben Pienaar, Caroline Rae, John Rink, Peter Sheppard Skaerved, Robert Sholl and Jeremy Thurlow, together with Halusia Good, Richard Stokes and Roger Nichols for their help with translations, and Gerardo Gozzi and Gareth Moorcraft for their expertise in preparing the numerous music examples. We are also grateful to the late Yvonne Loriod-Messiaen (who first encouraged Peter Hill to study the birdsong *cahiers*) and to the staff of the Département de la musique of the Bibliothèque nationale de France, and for permission to quote from and to reproduce the *cahiers* our thanks go to the Fondation de France and to the Fondation Messiaen. All unattributed sayings of Messiaen are from his discussions with Peter Hill in the years 1986–1992. All translations are by us unless otherwise stated. The cover illustration of the golden oriole (*loriot* in French) is by the nineteenth-century bird illustrator John Gould. We should like to thank most warmly Kate Brett and her colleagues at Cambridge University Press for their enthusiastic support, and are particularly grateful to Robert Whitelock for his rigorous scrutiny of the text. Last, our thanks go to our friends and families, and in particular to our wives, Jane and Charlotte, for their unfailing patience and encouragement.

Abbreviations

OMR   Yvonne Loriod-Messiaen, 'Olivier Messiaen: Relevé des concerts, des classes et des évènements de la vie d'Olivier Messiaen notées au jour le jour sur ses agendas depuis 1939' (unpublished)

PH/NS   Peter Hill and Nigel Simeone, *Messiaen* (New Haven and London: Yale University Press, 2005)

Introduction

In March 1948 Olivier Messiaen gave an interview to the newspaper *France-Soir*. He seemed at ease with life and, with the *Turangalîla-Symphonie* about to be finished, he spoke of his plans for an opera with a freedom unthinkable in later years, when he would become cautious and secretive about work in progress. When asked which musicians had most influenced him the conversation took an unexpected turn:

The birds.
Excuse me?
Yes, the birds. I've listened to them often, when lying in the grass pencil and notebook in hand.
And to which do you award the palm?
To the blackbird, of course! It can improvise continuously eleven or twelve different verses, in each of which identical musical phrases recur. What freedom of invention, what an artist![1]

In the event there was to be no opera, at least not for another thirty-five years. Instead, Messiaen went through a period of experiment, prompted initially by a desire to develop his own version of serialism. The transformation of his music moved into a second phase from 1952 when, taking his cue from the *France-Soir* interview, he embarked on a decade in which almost all his music was inspired by the study of birds and birdsong. Messiaen's belief that birdsong is music gave him a sense of mission to bring that music within the scope of human understanding. A trio of works followed one another, each with 'birds' in the title: *Réveil des oiseaux* (1952–1953) and *Oiseaux exotiques* (1955–1956), both for orchestra with solo piano; and the most ambitious of the three, the *Catalogue d'oiseaux* (1956–1958), a vast cycle of thirteen pieces for solo piano portraying the birdsongs of France in their natural settings.

The years of renewal that followed the extraordinarily prolific decade of the 1940s form arguably the most fascinating time in Messiaen's life, of which

---

[1] Robert de Saint-Jean, 'C'est le merle noir et non le rossignol qui inspire Olivier Messiaen: à quarante ans, le musicien se prépare à écrire l'opéra dont il rêve depuis son enfance', *France-Soir*, 28–29 March 1948.

the *Catalogue d'oiseaux* is the crowning achievement. Despite this, the work has, in the past, struggled to win the admiration given to Messiaen's earlier piano cycle, *Vingt Regards sur l'Enfant-Jésus* (1944). This is in part due to a misunderstanding. Messiaen's research into birdsong was carried out with characteristic thoroughness, and he was always proud of what he regarded as the accuracy of the birdsong in his music. By stressing this, however, Messiaen gave the impression that the *Catalogue* is a work as much of ornithology as it is of music, an impression perhaps reinforced by the work's matter-of-fact title. The result was that the *Catalogue* acquired a false reputation. Pianists who were eager to take on the challenge of the *Vingt Regards* looked on the *Catalogue* as the product of a private obsession, leaving the work to a small number of Messiaen specialists, led by Yvonne Loriod, the work's dedicatee.[2] Today the situation could not be more different. Loriod's pioneering recordings (made in 1959, the year of the *Catalogue*'s premiere, and in 1970) have been joined by versions made by a number of other pianists, while a younger generation regards the *Catalogue* as standing with works such as the Ligeti *Etudes* as pinnacles of the piano repertoire from the second half of the twentieth century.

Catalogue d'oiseaux unites two characteristics that stem from Messiaen's childhood: a love of nature (influenced by the poetry of his mother, Cécile Sauvage) and of drama, through his enactments with his younger brother Alain of the plays of Shakespeare (Messiaen's father, Pierre, would later translate Shakespeare into French). For Messiaen the natural world would become the supreme resource: 'ever beautiful, ever great, ever new, Nature, an inextinguishable treasure-house of sounds and colours, forms and rhythms, the unequalled model for total development and perpetual variation'.[3] Birds, in particular, fascinated him from an early age,[4] and as a teenager he made his first attempts to copy down birdsong in musical notation.[5] During his student years at the Paris Conservatoire (1919–1930) he took to heart the dictum of his composition teacher Paul Dukas: 'Listen to the birds, they are great masters.'[6]

---

[2] The *Catalogue* is dedicated both to Yvonne Loriod and to the birds.
[3] Olivier Messiaen, *Conférence de Bruxelles, prononcée à l'Exposition Internationale de Bruxelles en 1958* (Paris: Alphonse Leduc, 1960), p. 14.
[4] Brigitte Massin, *Olivier Messiaen: une poétique du merveilleux* (Aix-en-Provence: Editions Alinéa, 1989), p. 24.
[5] Claude Samuel, *Music and Color: Conversations with Claude Samuel*, trans. E. Thomas Glasow (Portland: Amadeus, 1994) from Claude Samuel, *Olivier Messiaen: musique et couleur. Nouveaux entretiens avec Claude Samuel* (Paris: Pierre Belfond, 1986).
[6] Quoted by Olivier Messiaen, *The Technique of My Musical Language*, trans. John Satterfield, 2 vols. (Paris: Alphonse Leduc, 1956), Vol. I, p. 34; single vol. edn (Paris: Alphonse Leduc, 2001), p. 38.

As a devout Catholic, Messiaen regarded birds as having a special purpose in God's creation as 'the greatest musicians on our planet', illustrated by the 'Regard des Anges' from *Vingt Regards*. The piece, as Messiaen explained it, is a battle between the angels and the birds; the cadenza of birdsong shortly before the end is a whoop of triumph as the birds realise that it is they, not the angels, who have been blessed with the gift of music. Throughout Messiaen's early music birdsong runs as a symbolic thread, with flights of song winging free from earthly existence.

During the 1930s and 1940s Messiaen's musical approach made little distinction between sacred or secular subject matter; one could point to the striking similarity between the love theme of *Vingt Regards*, representing divine love, and the portrayal of human, erotic love in *Turangalîla*. Another example is *Poèmes pour Mi* (1936), in which divine love is reflected in the love of husband and wife. In a second song cycle, *Chants de terre et de ciel* (1938), Messiaen's poems interleave scenes from infancy and the life of the family with religious reflections that culminate in an ecstatic paean of praise to Easter (a reference to Messiaen's son Pascal, born in 1937). Defending his approach, Messiaen argued that religious art is by its very nature diverse: 'Why? Because it expresses ideas about a single being, who is God, but a being who is ever-present and who can be found in everything, above everything, and below everything. Every subject can be a religious one on condition that it be viewed through the eye of one who believes.'[7]

The interview with *France-Soir* hinted at a new ambition for birdsong, and there are signs of this in the two works for organ from the early 1950s, *Messe de la Pentecôte* and *Livre d'orgue*, in which birdsong is associated symbolically with the central mysteries of the Catholic faith, Communion and Easter.[8] Nonetheless, the complete immersion in birdsong from 1952 was a decisive change. From now on Messiaen sought the company and advice of leading ornithologists, and he began compiling his notations of birdsong in specially designated notebooks. These *cahiers* take us deep into the heart of Messiaen's private musical world, a world that despite everything Messiaen said publicly about his music – in books, essays, lectures and interviews – he was at pains to keep private.

The *cahiers* are an indispensable source for understanding the development of Messiaen's music in the 1950s and beyond.[9] No Messiaen

---

[7] Olivier Messiaen, 'Autour d'une parution', *Le Monde musical*, 30 April 1939, p. 126. Quoted in PH/NS, p. 80.
[8] See Christopher Dingle, *The Life of Messiaen* (Cambridge: Cambridge University Press, 2007), p. 139.
[9] Some 203 of Messiaen's *Cahiers de notations des chants d'oiseaux* survive; the last entry came in the summer of 1991, a year before Messiaen's death. See Peter Hill, 'From *Réveil des oiseaux* to *Catalogue d'oiseaux*: Messiaen's *Cahiers de notations des chants d'oiseaux*, 1952–59', in

documents demonstrate better than the *cahiers* the extremes in Messiaen's character, the way he balanced relentless pursuit of detail and soaring imagination. Messiaen spoke about music in terms that were by turns technical and poetic, a trait that inevitably influences the way his music is discussed. For the *Catalogue* the *cahiers* show not only how he evolved the parallel language with which he translated birdsong into his music, but also the evolution of his thinking as he worked to solve the musical and structural problems in his path. At the heart of these was the tension between Messiaen the ornithologist – with his passionate admiration for birdsong – and Messiaen the composer. Messiaen's difficulty was that he regarded birdsong as music – and (as we have seen) God-given music at that – not simply as a source of sounds and patterns of which a composer might make use. As a result it was essential that the birdsong in his music, necessarily adapted to the limitations of human musical instruments, should be as authentic as possible. All this accounts for the very literal approach Messiaen took in *Réveil des oiseaux*, the first major work after the inception of the *cahiers*. As Messiaen's knowledge of birdsong deepened, however, his approach started to change, so that his birdsong became less a transcription and more an imaginative response. At the same time he started to select and edit the birdsongs he had collected so that by the time he came to compose the *Catalogue* they interact, almost like protagonists in a drama.

Messiaen, it should be remembered, approached birds as a musician, not a scientist, seeing them as singers with the ability to express human emotions. Here he describes the nightingale's song to his interviewer, Claude Samuel:

MESSIAEN: Most nightingales alternate five or six themes common to all, with changes in intensity and feeling. The nightingale performs a volte-face from sadness to joy –

CLAUDE SAMUEL: What *we* call 'sadness' –

MESSIAEN: Yes, you'll excuse my use of human terms: being anthropomorphic despite myself. Let's say that the nightingale seems to be passing brusquely from sadness to joy, from anger to renunciation, from rancour to forgiveness, or from supplication to victory; and it really goes from a slow tempo into a fast one, from a *pianissimo* nuance to *fortissimo*, with brusque and obvious contrasts.[10]

Christopher Dingle and Robert Fallon (eds.), *Messiaen Perspectives 1: Sources and Influences* (Farnham: Ashgate, 2013), pp. 143–171.

[10] Samuel, *Music and Color*, pp. 88–89.

The *Catalogue d'oiseaux* – and this is another misleading aspect of the title – is also as much about the landscapes of France as the birds that inhabit them. For the first time in Messiaen's music birds are set in their habitats, and these inspire many of the work's most memorable images – the veiled light of dawn, the sunset staining the sky shades of pink and violet, silvery-grey foliage reflected in water, and the peaks and chasms of the Alps, which had impressed Messiaen during his boyhood years in Grenoble. On his trips to Brittany in 1955 and 1956 Messiaen devoted pages of his *cahier* not only to the cries and calls of the birds but also to musical studies of the sounds and movement of the sea, leading eventually to the *Catalogue*'s shattering finale, in the final piece 'Le Courlis cendré' (curlew), as the Atlantic shoreline, smothered in sea-fog, disappears into the darkness.

The *cahiers* enable us to follow in great detail the progress of Messiaen's thinking during the long gestation of the *Catalogue* (from the summer of 1953) and its composition (between September 1956 and December 1958). Each piece in the *Catalogue* imagines a fresh relationship between birds and their habitat, and at the same time shows a fresh relationship between Messiaen and his birdsong material. In broad terms, the composition of the *Catalogue* divides into two: the seven pieces composed over the autumn and winter of 1956–1957, and the six further pieces written in the summer of 1957 and the following year. The earlier pieces were composed on the basis of notations made earlier from nature or from recordings. By the summer of 1957, however, the *cahiers* show that Messiaen's approach had moved on, with birdsong now an instantaneous trigger to his composer's imagination, so that increasingly the act of writing down birdsong becomes the act of composition.

A desire to trace the progress of Messiaen's thought influences the shape of the book, which follows a chronological order wherever possible; in particular, we decided to discuss the individual pieces of the *Catalogue* in the order in which Messiaen composed them, in so far as this is known, rather than the order in the score. The order of the thirteen pieces of the *Catalogue* in the printed score is given in Chapter 1 (pp. 9–10). The order in which we consider the pieces (reflecting the order of composition) is as follows:

'L'Alouette lulu' (composed in September 1956); 'Le Chocard des Alpes', 'Le Loriot', 'La Chouette hulotte', 'L'Alouette calandrelle', 'Le Courlis cendré', 'La Rousserolle effarvatte' (composed between September 1956 and February 1957 – 'La Rousserolle effarvatte' was substantially revised later in 1957); 'La Bouscarle', 'Le Traquet stapazin', 'Le Merle bleu', 'La Buse variable' (composed during the summer of 1957); 'Le Merle de roche' and 'Le Traquet rieur' (composed in 1958).

The first three chapters set the scene in different ways. We start by introducing the *Catalogue* and its characteristics as a whole. Chapter 2 examines the uses of birdsong in Messiaen's earlier music, before tracing the evolution of his *style oiseau* in the 1950s, following his researches up to the point where he began composing the *Catalogue*; the chapter ends with the first piece to be written, 'L'Alouette lulu'. Chapter 3 considers a number of specifically musical influences on the *Catalogue*, including Messiaen's own earlier music and the music of his contemporaries.

Chapter 4 resumes where we left off at the end of Chapter 2 by considering the remaining six pieces written over the winter of 1956–1957 (five of these are given in the order they appear in the score, for lack of better evidence). On 30 March 1957 Loriod performed six pieces in a recital billed as 'Extracts from the *Catalogue d'oiseaux*'; she omitted 'La Rousserolle effarvatte', which she was given too late for her to learn, and which in any case was considerably enlarged later in the year. Loriod's recital marks the division between the earlier pieces and those composed later that summer and in the following year. With the second wave of composition (Chapter 5) the order of composition is much clearer. 'La Bouscarle' was conceived during a trip to south-west France in April, 'Le Traquet stapazin' and 'Le Merle bleu' were inspired by a visit to the Mediterranean coastline in late June, while 'La Buse variable' is based on notations made in the Alps of the Dauphiné in July. The last two pieces – 'Le Merle de roche' and 'Le Traquet rieur' – were based largely on notations made in the summer of 1958 and were completed later that year.

Both authors are pianists who perform the *Catalogue*, so that reflections on performance and interpretation feature throughout our discussions of the music. Chapter 6, however, is specifically devoted to performance. First we explore the early performances given by Yvonne Loriod, and in particular her two recordings of the work. Next Peter Hill recalls his time working on the *Catalogue* with Messiaen when preparing his own recording. Lastly, we consider the different approaches taken by a number of pianists in their recordings; this is not in any sense a review, but a comparison of different approaches to interpreting the music.

In the final chapter, the Postlude, we consider the influence of the *Catalogue* on Messiaen's later music, especially the works for solo piano. These are *La Fauvette des jardins* (1970), which returns to the location of

'La Buse variable' from the *Catalogue*, the scene in front of Messiaen's summer retreat at Petichet in the French Alps; and the late birdsong 'sketches', the *Petites Esquisses d'oiseaux* (1985). Also discussed is a recently discovered work from 1961, *La Fauvette passerinette*, which proves to be a significant missing link in the development of Messiaen's later birdsong style and which was almost certainly intended by Messiaen as the start of a second 'Catalogue'.

1 | Content and Context

The *Catalogue d'oiseaux* received its first performance from Yvonne Loriod on 15 April 1959 at a Domaine musical concert held as a belated tribute to Messiaen's fiftieth birthday, which had fallen on 10 December 1958. The reaction to Loriod's performance, given from memory and with just a single interval, was astonishment. One reviewer pointed to the coincidence of the pianist's surname with one of France's most spectacular songbirds, the *loriot*: 'Dressed like the brilliant golden oriole, her near homonym, gold with black wings, Yvonne, with her amazingly accurate fingers, chatters, strokes, chirps and teases the piano from its twittering heights down to its booming depths.'[1]

Loriod's feat of playing the entire work at a single concert is rarely attempted, understandably given the scale of the *Catalogue*: longer by thirty minutes or so than Messiaen's earlier piano cycle *Vingt Regards sur l'Enfant-Jésus* and (at around 2 hours 40 minutes) far exceeding any other composition by Messiaen, apart from the opera *Saint François d'Assise*.

The overall design makes it clear, nonetheless, that Messiaen intended *Catalogue d'oiseaux* to be understood as a single entity. Each of the thirteen pieces features a bird encountered in the French countryside, portrayed through its song, and placed alongside other birds present in its habitat, framed by evocations of the surrounding scenery. The pieces are grouped into seven books, each containing one, two or three pieces, and arranged in a symmetrical order: 3 1 2 1 2 1 3. The central and longest piece, 'La Rousserolle effarvatte' (reed warbler), is itself a symmetry that follows the cycle of a complete day, with the passing of time marked by various signals including a sunrise and sunset. Successive pieces tend to be sharply contrasted, so that the next piece, 'L'Alouette calandrelle' (short-toed lark), is the shortest as well as the most economical. Set in the torrid heat of Provence in July, 'L'Alouette calandrelle' complements its neighbour in Book 5, 'La Bouscarle' (Cetti's warbler), which evokes an April day of dappled light and shade.

---

[1] Suzanne Demarquez, 'Le *Catalogue d'oiseaux* d'Olivier Messiaen', *Guide du concert* 233 (1 May 1959), 42.

While these two pieces in Book 5 are linked by their concern with different qualities of light, they are balanced (on the other side of the central piece) by Book 3, which consists of a pair of nocturnes. Again, these pieces are opposites: in 'La Chouette hulotte' (tawny owl) darkness is evoked by a return to the jagged serial technique that Messiaen had developed in the piano pieces of 1949, *Cantéyodjayâ* and *Mode de valeurs et d'intensités*, while in 'L'Alouette lulu' (woodlark) night is serene, represented by a calm chorale. Book 2 consists of a single piece, 'Le Traquet stapazin' (black-eared wheatear), which follows the events of a brilliant summer day beside the Mediterranean; its symmetrical counterpart, in Book 6, is 'Le Merle de roche', in which the soloist, the rock thrush, sings apparently oblivious to its nightmarish setting, the surreal shapes formed by the rocks of the Cirque de Mourèze. Book 7 is a recapitulation, returning to two of the landscapes from Book 1, and completing the journey across France from the Alpine setting that opens the *Catalogue*, 'Le Chocard des Alpes' (Alpine chough), to end in 'Le Courlis cendré' (curlew) at the western extremity of Brittany.

Book 1

'Le Chocard des Alpes' (Alpine chough) – set in the Alps of the Dauphiné;
'Le Loriot' (golden oriole) – Charente and Loir et Cher;
'Le Merle bleu' (blue rock thrush) – the Mediterranean coastline near Banyuls (Roussillon).

Book 2

'Le Traquet stapazin' (black-eared wheatear) – among vineyards near Banyuls.

Book 3

'La Chouette hulotte' (tawny owl) – the forests around Orgeval on the western edge of Paris, and between Petichet and Cholonge (south of Grenoble);
'L'Alouette lulu' (woodlark) – near St-Sauveur-en-Rue, in the mountainous Forez region near St-Etienne.

Book 4

'La Rousserolle effarvatte' (reed warbler) – the lakes and marshes of the Sologne district, near Orléans.

Book 5

'L'Alouette calandrelle' (short-toed lark) – near Les Baux, Provence;
'La Bouscarle' (Cetti's warbler) – beside the River Charente between Jarnac and Cognac.

Book 6

'Le Merle de roche' (rock thrush) – the Cirque de Mourèze, a rocky landscape north-west of Montpellier.

Book 7

'La Buse variable' (buzzard) – the Alps of the Dauphiné, at Petichet, Messiaen's summer home;
'Le Traquet rieur' (black wheatear) – the Roussillon coast;
'Le Courlis cendré' (curlew) – the Atlantic coast of the Ile d'Ouessant (Ushant), Finistère.

The *Catalogue* was composed rapidly, probably as a result of its long gestation. As Messiaen says in his preface to the score: 'The journeys and repeated stays necessary for the notation of each bird were sometimes long in advance of the composition. Thanks to the precision of the notations the composer was able without difficulty to reawaken old memories, whether from a few hours or several years ago.'[2]

After the first wave of composition and Loriod's March 1957 recital, the next four pieces, written that summer, were all inspired by landscapes in southern France: the River Charente, the Mediterranean coastline of Roussillon near the border with Spain, and Petichet, which had been Messiaen's Alpine summer retreat since the mid-1930s. The last two pieces, added the following year, are also set in southern France: 'Le Merle de roche' in the Hérault region, and 'Le Traquet rieur', a return to the Roussillon coast. Messiaen dated the completion of the cycle to 1 December 1958.[3]

The success of the *Catalogue*'s premiere must have been especially satisfying for Messiaen after a decade that had been difficult and in some ways agonising. Messiaen had his doubts about his own role in setting the direction of the post-war avant garde, and when beset by argumentative students in his class

---

[2] Preface to the score: Olivier Messiaen, *Catalogue d'oiseaux*, 7 vols. (Paris: Alphonse Leduc, 1964). All further citations to the score are to this edition.
[3] Ibid.

at the Conservatoire would lapse into gloomy silence; and he was accustomed to having his passion for birdsong received with scepticism and, among his students, some hilarity. At the same time he was haunted by the decline of his wife Claire, the tragedy of her early dementia casting a shadow over the lives of Messiaen, their teenage son, Pascal, and Yvonne Loriod, who had become indispensable to Messiaen's musical and personal life since 1941 when, as a seventeen-year-old student, she joined his harmony class at the Conservatoire. All this is reflected in the essay Messiaen wrote in advance of the premiere of the *Catalogue*, in which he permitted himself a rare public confession of self-doubt:

In dark times, when my uselessness is brutally apparent to me, when all musical languages – classical, exotic, ancient, modern and ultramodern – seem no more than the result of patient research, with nothing behind the notes to justify so much effort, what is there to do but to seek again the true face of music, forgotten somewhere in the forest, the fields, the mountains, by the seashore, among the birds?[4]

Messiaen's decision, from 1952, to devote himself to the study of birdsong as the source for his music was an extraordinary step for a composer in his mid forties and at the height of his powers, just two years after the French premiere of his most ambitious work to date, the *Turangalîla-Symphonie*.[5] But birdsong was part of a conscious desire to renew his language after the triumphs of the 1940s, which had begun in the prisoner-of-war camp, in the bitter winter of 1940–1941, with the *Quatuor pour la fin du Temps*, and reached a climax with *Turangalîla*, first performed in 1949 by the Boston Symphony Orchestra under Leonard Bernstein. The works composed between 1949 and 1952 turned away from large forces, being for piano or organ, the instruments that Messiaen played himself. In *Cantéyodjayâ* and the *Quatre études de rythme* (for piano), together with the organ cycles *Messe de la Pentecôte* and *Livre d'orgue*, Messiaen developed various types of rigorous process, among them his own version of serialism, which had been occupying his thoughts during the latter half of the 1940s.[6]

Then in 1952 Messiaen answered a commission from the Conservatoire with a short piece for flute and piano, *Le Merle noir*, which showed a marked advance in realism over his previous uses of birdsong. The direction of

---

[4] Olivier Messiaen, 'La Nature, les chants d'oiseaux', *Guide du concert* 229 (3 April 1959), 1093–1094.
[5] *Turangalîla* was first performed in France on 25 July 1950. The premiere of the work had taken place in Boston on 2 December 1949.
[6] Messiaen's approaches to serialism are discussed later in Chapter 3 (pp. 66–70).

Messiaen's music suddenly altered course. He sought the advice of a leading ornithologist, Jacques Delamain, and the upshot was a second phase of experiment, this time with birdsong as the source for a further renewal and enrichment of his music. Messiaen was a man obsessed, devoting to birdsong every moment that could be spared from his duties teaching at the Conservatoire and as organist of the Church of the Trinité in central Paris.

The first fruit of Messiaen's researches, *Réveil des oiseaux*, aimed to translate a dawn chorus into human music – scored for piano and orchestra – with the minimum of intervention. Whole swathes of Messiaen's notations in the *cahiers* were transferred into the score virtually unmodified. The weakness of the experiment, as Messiaen must have realised, was that the notations were birdsong as Messiaen heard it, filtered through his musical sensibility. The result was that in the next work, *Oiseaux exotiques* (again for piano and orchestra) the pendulum swung sharply the other way, with the musician gaining the upper hand over the ornithologist.

With the *Catalogue* there was the additional difficulty of writing birdsong music for solo piano. The ambition to write a cycle of piano pieces may well have been Messiaen's intention when he began the birdsong *cahiers* in 1952. The first mention of piano pieces comes in a jotting made in July 1953. Later that year, in October, Messiaen drew up a list that included twenty-two species of birds grouped according to habitat: birds of the high mountain, birds of the vineyards, birds of the reeds and ponds, and so on, under the heading, 'Ecrire pour piano'. But why solo piano? Part of the answer was that in 1953 Messiaen lacked a commission for an orchestral work (this was before the approach from Boulez for *Oiseaux exotiques*, which arrived probably in early 1955). But in any case the piano had been at the centre of Messiaen's composing since Loriod came into his life: from 1941 onwards every work has an important piano part, apart from the organ works, and *Cinq Rechants* (1949) for twelve solo voices, which expresses Messiaen's feelings for Loriod in surrealist love poetry.[7] The piano had been the instrument for experiment, in *Cantéyodjayâ* and the *Quatre études*. Then, more recently, Loriod had given further proof of her dazzling abilities when in September 1953, a month before Messiaen drew up his outline of the *Catalogue*, she had mastered and memorised the solo part of *Réveil des oiseaux* at short notice, in just a week.

Besides all this, Messiaen had come to see the piano as the ideal instrument for expressing birdsong:

Because of its wide range and the immediacy of its attack, the piano was the only instrument capable of speaking at the great speed and in the very high registers

[7] PH/NS, pp. 179–184.

called for by some of the more virtuoso birds, such as the woodlark, the skylark, the garden warbler, the blackcap, the nightingale, the sedge warbler and the reed warbler. The piano was also the only instrument that could imitate the raucous, grinding, percussive calls of the raven and the great reed warbler, the rattling of the corncrake, the screeches of the water rail, the barking of the herring gull, the dry imperious sound, like tapping on a stone, of the black-eared wheatear, and the sunny charm of the rock thrush or the black wheatear.[8]

However, as Messiaen was to discover, it was one thing to write for orchestra, as in *Réveil* and *Oiseaux exotiques*, where the birdsong could be combined in medleys, each song coloured and differentiated by its instrumentation, and quite another to write for piano, where there was a limit to how many birdsongs could be combined by two hands on the keyboard, even with fingers as agile and intelligent as Loriod's. There was the danger that the music would become simply a succession of individual birdsongs, all too like a 'catalogue' indeed. Messiaen must have been aware of this: although by the summer of 1956, after more than three years' research, he had more than enough material, there was no sign that he had yet found a way to shape his birdsong material into music.

An important part of Messiaen's solution, which took several years to develop, came by chance when, from 1955, he started to use the *cahiers* not only for notations but as a sort of travel diary. Loriod had recently bought a car, and with her as driver Messiaen was able to range into some of the most remote areas of France. Armed not with a camera but with pencil and manuscript paper Messiaen recorded his vivid, spontaneous response to the scene before him. With typical attention to detail, he would describe the minutiae of trees, flowers and colours under the effect of changing light. At other times, his imagination took wing and his descriptions express a sense of the sublime in a way that recalls the paintings of Turner – especially with the grander sights of nature: the sun setting in the high Alps, a storm over the highest peaks of the Cévennes, or rocks lashed by Atlantic gales. Messiaen was anxious to deny that his depictions of landscape were impressionism.[9] His approach, instead, was to search for a musical process or structure that was analogous – trees reflected in a river conveyed by a two-voice canon, to give a simple example. Many of Messiaen's 'metaphors' involve variants of the quasi-serial writing he had developed in the late 1940s, with serial permutations standing variously for the orbits of a buzzard's flight, cliffs or mountains, and even something as intangible as the fear-filled darkness surveyed by the hunting tawny owl.

[8] Messiaen, 'La Nature, les chants d'oiseaux'.
[9] 'I am a French composer, but not a French Impressionist' – in conversation with Peter Hill.

A particular marvel of the *Catalogue* is Messiaen's achievement in finding musical means to integrate birds and their surroundings, with the structure of a piece acting as a metaphor for the spirit of the place. A simple example is the shortest piece in the *Catalogue*, 'L'Alouette calandrelle' (short-toed lark), which makes the point with extreme economy. Here the songs of three species of lark are linked to form a set of variations, an evolving musical structure that is held within the frame of a static symmetry – a form that expresses Messiaen's perception of the place, the arid, heat-stricken landscape of Provence, irrigated by the faint trickle of energy in the soloist's song.

The other side of Messiaen's solution was for the birds to take on musical functions. The more minimal calls – like the cluck of the quail or the 'boom' of a bittern – are used as punctuation points, while insistent calls (by Cetti's warbler or the black-eared wheatear, for example) act as refrains, articulating the phases of a rondo form, and often triggering an episode of varied birdsongs. Inventive songs, often from birds that are skilled mimics, are used for lengthy solos (the reed warbler), or divided into short phrases that recur like chains of variations (the spectacled warbler in 'Le Traquet stapazin'). Birdsongs that Messiaen perceives as gentle or lyrical are frequently employed as descants (the woodlark) or as codettas or afterthoughts (the blackbird, blackcap and robin in 'La Bouscarle'). Birds may also do double duty, used to evoke their surroundings. Thus in 'La Buse variable' the scale of the Alpine setting is established by the orbits of the buzzard's flight, as it glides in huge circles. Birds also act as time-keepers, their arrival signalling dawn or darkness, the heat of midday, or the onset of twilight when the skylark rockets upwards in a blur of beating wings and frenetic song.

Throughout the *Catalogue* there is a sense of freedom, of escape from restriction and convention, almost as if Messiaen were writing a musical diary for himself alone. A symptom of this is the way Messiaen reaches back into his musical past, so that the rich colours of his earlier music take their place alongside the very obviously modern style that had developed since 1949. At the same time they blend with Messiaen's musical memories from the early twentieth century and beyond, so that one finds in the *Catalogue* references to Debussy, Ravel, Berg and even Wagner.

Messiaen *felt* birdsong; he, so to speak, 'lived' it and experienced it rather than just observing it – just as he did with landscapes: '[The birdsongs] remained engraved on my memory with such poetic force that I was unable to turn them into music without emotion.'[10] Messiaen's apology has to be

---

[10] Messiaen, 'La Nature, les chants d'oiseaux'.

understood as part of the image he wished to project at the time of the first performance in 1959, justifying his use of birdsong by stressing the depth of his research, and the rigorous methods that he used in making transcriptions. Granted that the response to nature and birdsong was subjectively Messiaen's, nonetheless the achievement of the *Catalogue* is that he created an imaginary response to nature that we can accept, within its conventions, as real. The point is important because by believing in Messiaen's birds one can recognise when the music steps from realism into an interior world. Sometimes this may be through an exaggeration, like the huge cry of the tawny owl at the end of 'La Chouette hulotte', which Messiaen describes as 'like the shriek of a murdered child'. More usually the unreal occurs in a meditation, or *souvenir*: a birdsong receding into the distance, or heard in slow motion, lingering on the memory. One of the fascinations of performing the *Catalogue* – that can be exploited in different interpretations – is the ambiguity between real and unreal. An example is the return of the curlew's whooping cries at the end of 'Le Courlis cendré', which some pianists may suggest, through nuance and timing, as a 'memory' (not a literal recurrence) of the earlier solo; the notes are the same, but the meaning different, as the music fades into the darkness.

2 | Birdsong and the Genesis of *Catalogue d'oiseaux*

Birdsongs start to appear in Messiaen's music from the second movement of *L'Ascension* (1932–1933).[1] Even earlier there are hints of birdsong in 'Chant d'extase dans un paysage triste' from the piano *Préludes* (1928–1929). Another *Prélude*, 'La Colombe' (the dove) is unmistakably characteristic in the way Messiaen blends mode and tonality. At the opening (Ex. 2.1) the left hand is in E major; the upper descant is in mode 2^2 but with E as 'tonic' (the compass of this figure is E to E), while the melody itself – gently floated from the initial tritone (another Messiaen trait) – mediates between the two: although in E major, it leans expressively on pitches foreign to the key (F♮, A♯, D♮) but found in the mode. This sort of triple-layered texture is frequent in the *Catalogue*, as is the concern with integrating disparate strands through means of harmony and mode – in the opening page of 'Le Traquet stapazin', for instance.

As an approach to nature, however, 'La Colombe' and the *Catalogue* are worlds apart. The bird-like aspects of 'La Colombe' – the fluttering descant, the spiralling descent of the melody – make no claims to be realistic; they could, after all, depict any bird. Rather, the dove plays the traditional role of nature in music, as a mirror to human feelings, and perhaps as religious symbol (though the score is silent on this), with a particular beauty, tender and a little precious, found in Messiaen's earliest music, the *Préludes* in particular. Nearly three decades later, in the *Catalogue*, Messiaen observes nature through the sharp focus of a telephoto lens, so that the birdsongs have immediacy, definition and at times a disconcerting aggression that make us feel as though we are part of their world – although occasionally stepping back, so that what we hear is not the song itself but the song recollected in tranquillity, in the mind and memory of the spectator.

---

[1] The version of *L'Ascension* for organ dates from 1933 to 1934.

[2] Messiaen's mode 2 is the eight-note (octatonic) scale of alternating semitones and tones. A factor common to all Messiaen's modes is that they are of 'limited transposition', in the composer's words. Mode 2 can be heard in three different versions – starting on C♮, C♯ and D♮ – but the next transposition (starting on E♭) returns to the same notes as the first. For a full discussion see Anthony Pople, 'Messiaen's Musical Language: An Introduction' in Peter Hill (ed.), *The Messiaen Companion* (London: Faber and Faber, 1995), pp. 17–31.

Example 2.1 'La Colombe'

1940–1952

The first reports of Messiaen's notating birdsong come from the time of his military service at the beginning of the war. One witness remembered Messiaen filling 'any number of notebooks with the astonishing rhythmic and melodic virtuosity of birdsong'.[3] Others tell of Messiaen volunteering for the least popular hours for sentry duty in order to be out of doors for the dawn chorus.[4] The first signs of a new realism appeared just after this, in *Quatuor pour la fin du Temps* (1940–1941). In the opening movement, 'Liturgie de cristal', Messiaen's birds are still symbols, here used to evoke the 'harmonious silence of heaven', but for the first time Messiaen names the birds, a nightingale and blackbird, the birds of darkness and dawn.[5] The nightingale is recognisable in the violin's chirrups and oscillations; the clarinet seems to mingle blackbird and nightingale in a slow-motion melody that sleepwalks through the darkness before dawn.

Equally significant is the context engineered for the birdsongs, consisting of circling isorhythms on piano and cello, the piano repeating rotations of seventeen rhythmic values against twenty-nine harmonies that would take some hours to return to their starting-point, but of which we hear only a fragment, perhaps an image of time within eternity. The idea of framing

---

[3] PH/NS, pp. 94–96. The eyewitness was Guy Bernard-Delapierre, who was taken prisoner-of-war in June 1940 at the same time as Messiaen. From November 1943 Messiaen held classes in musical analysis at Bernard-Delapierre's home in Paris, 24 rue Visconti. Bernard-Delapierre's article 'Souvenirs sur Olivier Messiaen' was published in the Lausanne art periodical *Formes et couleurs* in 1945.

[4] This anecdote comes in a private communication from Alex Murray, who heard it from Gaston Crunelle, Murray's flute teacher at the Paris Conservatoire. Murray met the composer when competing in the flute competition in 1952, for which Messiaen composed *Le Merle noir* as a *morceau de concours*.

[5] Preface to the score of *Quatuor pour la fin du Temps*.

birdsong with rigorous process would be a feature of Messiaen's later work and a cornerstone of the *Catalogue*. In the *Quatuor* a recurring image is of birds as symbols of freedom, the one aspect of the work that reflects Messiaen's confinement in a prisoner-of-war camp. In the clarinet solo, 'Abîme des oiseaux', the 'abyss' stands for the prison of time from which birdsong offers escape; and one can imagine something similar in the final 'Louange à l'Immortalité de Jésus', with its implacable iambic short–long rhythm on the piano, above which the violin circles and soars as it reaches for the heights.

Visions de l'Amen (1942–1943) was the first work composed for Yvonne Loriod, and the part for the first piano, written with her particular kind of virtuosity in mind, has the bells and birdsongs that embellish the themes and harmonies given to the second piano, played by Messiaen. But at one point Loriod's part takes the lead, in the 'Amen des Anges, des Saints, du chant des oiseaux', with a medley of birdsongs. If this is stylised birdsong, in *Vingt Regards sur l'Enfant-Jésus* (1944) there are signs of growing realism. In 'Regard des hauteurs' (no. 8) a lark rockets skywards and beats against an upper note in the manner of later skylarks. Contrasted birdsongs are deployed in duets, in a way that foreshadows *Réveil des oiseaux* (from almost a decade later), as does the piano writing of the jubilant cadenza, with the hands an octave apart.

In *Harawi* (1945) Messiaen counterpoints stylised birdsong with the more realistic style found in the 'Regard des hauteurs'. Throughout the song cycle the 'green dove', an image influenced by Peruvian mythology, is identified with the beloved. 'Bonjour toi, colombe verte' is a love song in which three verses are marked off by piano cadenzas ('comme un oiseau') that suggest a blend of blackbird and skylark. At the start of the song the birdsong is imaginary, a descant designed to shadow the shape of the cyclic 'theme of love'. In the third verse these contrasting styles combine, with 'imaginary' elements taken from the first verse merging with more authentic birdsong from the cadenzas.

In *Turangalîla* (1946–1948) the most extensive use of birdsong comes in the sixth movement, 'Jardin du sommeil d'amour', originally the slow movement in Messiaen's initial four-movement conception.[6] The solo piano is given the nightingale, its motifs recalling the nightingale from 'Liturgie de cristal' (from which Messiaen quotes at one point), the song in slow motion, wrapped in a sort of Pre-Raphaelite dream, with languorous meanderings on the woodwind and the 'theme of love' given by muted strings. The most

[6] PH/NS, p. 171.

realistic-sounding birdsong comes in 'Turangalîla 2' (fig. 3), a heterophony that anticipates the medleys in *Réveil des oiseaux* and *Oiseaux exotiques*, with lines existing independently, 'entirely free from harmonic concerns'.[7]

Then in March 1948 came the interview with *France-Soir*, in which for the first time Messiaen spoke publicly about his studies of birdsong. The planned opera had to be shelved, however, when the following January the condition of Messiaen's wife Claire worsened; she had been giving concern since the early 1940s, and her forgetfulness and her vacant expression (seen in photographs) proved to be signs of incipient dementia. Limited to composing in short bursts whenever the opportunity arose spurred Messiaen to develop the theoretical ideas he had been noting in his diary. As early as 1945 a diary entry speculates on applying serial organisation to tempo. Later he planned a ballet on Time, in which all the musical parameters would be derived from a single 'serial theme'. The drive to renew his musical language was conscious: 'Look for melodic motifs, chords, rhythmic figures from beyond my language, make myself a little dictionary'.

Messiaen now embarked on a series of short pieces for the instruments he himself played, the piano and organ. The first piece to put his ideas into practice was *Mode de valeurs et d'intensités*, sketched in June 1949 when Messiaen was at the Darmstadt Ferienkursen summer course, and the first to be composed of a set of studies, the *Quatre études de rythme*. *Mode de valeurs* is constructed from a mode made up from four elements – pitch, duration, dynamics and attacks – meshed together in such a way that each sound has its unique 'envelope'. Later that summer, when teaching at Tanglewood, Messiaen incorporated a version of the 'mode de valeurs' technique into *Cantéyodjayâ*. This twelve-minute piano piece is unique in Messiaen's output, a work that can truly be described as experimental, and all the more exciting for that: music of extremes, which commutes between passages of rigorous control and cascades of virtuosity. Apart from the 'mode de valeurs' episode (score, pp. 8–10) almost all the ideas are quarried from the 'Tristan' trilogy (1945–1949) – *Harawi*, *Turangalîla* and *Cinq Rechants* – but transformed in shape, rhythm and character into a diamond-sharp sound-world that is quite new in Messiaen's music. Example 2.2 shows one of these ideas, a melody originating in the sixth movement of *Turangalîla* ('Jardin du sommeil d'amour') and passed on through *Cantéyodjayâ* and *Le Merle noir* to *Catalogue d'oiseaux*, where it represents the flowers at the lake's margin in 'La Rousserolle effarvatte'.

---

[7] Olivier Messiaen, *Traité de rythme, de couleur et d'ornithologie: en sept tomes* (Paris: Alphonse Leduc, 1994–2002), Vol. II, p. 293.

Example 2.2 (a) *Turangalîla*: 'Jardin du sommeil d'amour'; (b) *Cantéyodjayâ*; (c) *Le Merle noir*; (d) 'La Rousserolle effarvatte'

Above all, it is the structures of *Cantéyodjayâ* that are so original. The piece starts as a free-wheeling alternation of refrains and episodes, gathering momentum into a collage of brilliantly coloured and characterised fragments, striking sparks off one another in a blistering turnover of events. The music's energy comes from the sense that layers of timbre and register counterpoint one another, in opposition or dialogue, in ways that would come to fruition in the kaleidoscopic forms of the *Catalogue*.

The one thing missing from *Cantéyodjayâ* or the *Quatre études* was birdsong, apart from a single short phrase in *Ile de feu 1*.[8] This melody would reappear in *Messe de la Pentecôte* (1949–1950), in 'Communion', subtitled 'Les oiseaux et les sources'. Here the phrase from *Ile de feu 1* is identified as a blackbird (score, p. 18) within a passage of stylised birdsong marked simply 'oiseaux'. Earlier in the same movement a nightingale has the repeated notes, rapid gestures and a tremolo, that are all characteristic of the nightingales in *Catalogue d'oiseaux*. Throughout *Messe de la Pentecôte* birdsong seems ever-present – in the melodic garlands of 'Offertoire', for example, or the 'choeur des alouettes' of the final 'Sortie', whose climactic passage features brilliant unison writing in the manner of *Réveil des oiseaux*.

Oddly, it was in the *Livre d'orgue* (1951–1952), with Messiaen's music immersed in labyrinthine numerical processes, that birdsong writing took a determined step forward. The preface to *Livre d'orgue* tells of the inspiration of sites near Messiaen's summer retreat in the French Alps: the valley of the Romanche River; the glaciers of Râteau, Meije and Tabuchet; and the meadows around his home at Petichet. For the first time Messiaen identifies the places where the birdsong was collected: Fuligny (near Troyes, in eastern France), which was the home of Messiaen's two aunts; the forests near St-Germain-en-Laye to the west of Paris; and Gardépée in the Charente in south-west France.[9]

The final movement, 'Soixante-Quatre durées', seems to sum up the role of birdsong in Messiaen's music over the previous decade. As with the 'Liturgie de cristal' from the *Quatuor* the birdsong inhabits a rigorous process, as the music works its way through two 'scales of durations', from one demisemiquaver to sixty-four (a breve). The birdsong is experienced at first as improvisatory, but as the movement proceeds gradually gains in definition and character as the score starts to name the birds: blackbird, great tit, song thrush, blackcap. An even more advanced birdsong comes in the central movement, 'Chants d'oiseaux', where solos for blackbird, nightingale, song thrush and robin are all identified and sharply characterised, with the long passage for the blackbird particularly impressive. The order of the birdsongs hints at a cycle from daybreak to nightfall, with the blackbird and

---

[8] *Ile de feu 1*, p. 1, lines 3–4, where the marking is 'comme un oiseau'.
[9] The mention of Gardépée shows that Messiaen's dating of *Livre d'orgue* to 1951 is incorrect: the central movement, 'Chants d'oiseaux', must have been completed after Messiaen's visit to Gardépée in April 1952, described later in this chapter.

song thrush prominent in the early stages, while the piece ends with a solo for the nightingale, fading at the end into silence.

One can sense that by 1952 Messiaen felt himself pulled in opposite directions. Matters came to a head in two works composed in March 1952. *Timbres-durées*, Messiaen's only foray into studio-composed tape music, represents the side of his work since 1949 that had come to be admired by the younger generation of avant-garde composers. The piece is constructed from sounds selected by Messiaen that were spliced together by Pierre Henry (a student of Messiaen from the 1940s) according to a rhythmic blueprint.[10] From the viewpoint of *Catalogue d'oiseaux* the interest of *Timbres-durées* is that it opened up a possibility that Messiaen chose not to follow – that of developing his *style oiseau* as a collage composed using sampled recordings of birdsong.

Instead, he resumed writing birdsong for instruments, with *Le Merle noir* for flute and piano, answering a request from the Conservatoire for a test piece for a competition. Messiaen revels in the agility of the flute to create, in its cadenzas, a more brilliant and life-like birdsong than any to this date. The piano is the foil, including a backward glance to the enchanted garden of *Turangalîla* (as seen earlier, in Ex. 2.2(a)), possibly as a way of describing the bird's habitat, or as a forerunner of those moments of stillness, so riveting in *Catalogue d'oiseaux*, that step from the active 'real' world into the quietness of inner contemplation. The interest in process is still there: in the coda the piano accompanies the blackbird's song with serial writing combined with permutations of rhythmic cells. Again, the image is one of freedom and confinement. Fittingly, it is the birdsong that comes to the fore, as the patterns on the piano, played at speed with continuous pedal, form a blurred texture of high-pitched points of sound.

Delamain, the *Cahiers* and Birdsong Research, 1952–1953

Le Merle noir proved to be a catalyst for another change of direction and a new phase of experiment. The first step came in April 1952 with a visit Messiaen paid to Jacques Delamain, one of France's best-known ornithologists. Delamain was by profession a producer of cognac but was also a prolific author of popular books on birds. His business premises were in Jarnac, and he lived in the country between there and Cognac. The house has a large garden, densely planted with trees and shrubs as a sanctuary for birds,

---

[10] PH/NS, pp. 198–199.

Figure 2.1 Jacques Delamain's house

sloping down through the woods to the Romanesque church of La Châtre, all that remains of a medieval abbey (Fig. 2.1).

Messiaen later supplied a preface to Delamain's *Pourquoi les oiseaux chantent*, in which he recalled his first visit:

> How I met Jacques Delamain is very simple. My publisher, Alphonse Leduc, who owned a property in Charente not far from Delamain, talked to him about my endeavours. Some time later, Jacques Delamain wrote to me: 'Come, I'm expecting you.' His home, at Branderaie de Gardépée, was, I seem to remember, a large two-storeyed house. I had a bedroom on the first floor with a vast balcony on which I could settle down with my music paper from four in the morning, and take down birdsong from the break of day without disturbing anyone.[11]

Reading *Pourquoi les oiseaux chantent* makes it clear that Delamain and Messiaen viewed birds as having human personalities. The difference is

---

[11] From the preface by Messiaen to the 1960 edition of Jacques Delamain's *Pourquoi les oiseaux chantent* (trans. Roger Nichols). See also PH/NS, pp. 200–201. Messiaen's recollection was confirmed (in conversation with Peter Hill) by Delamain's granddaughter, who was at Gardépée at the time of Messiaen's first visit.

that where Delamain is whimsical Messiaen's birds are red in tooth and claw: the 'human cry' of Delamain's tawny owl becomes with Messiaen 'the shriek of a murdered child'. Here Delamain describes birds in winter:

> From the clump of blossoming, snow-sprinkled furze, the Wren's precipitated trill gushes out, so strong and vibrant that it is astonishing to see a tiny brown bird rise up, fleeing at the level of the frozen soil on little round wings. The bare hedge has its winter song, sweet and a little sad, that of the Hedge-Sparrow. The Lark drops from on high onto the field, still all white, the joyous torrent of his song, and like an inevitable and charming accompaniment, the voice of the Robin Redbreast modulates, tireless and clear. Even the icy January night has its song: the primitive, savage refrain of the great Tawny Owl, articulated now and then like a sorrowful human cry.[12]

Delamain may have been unscientific, but there was no doubting his expertise, as Messiaen recalled:

> I had already, for a long time, devoted myself to noting more or less accurately the songs of birds, without knowing which of them I was writing down ... It is [Delamain] who taught me to recognise a bird from its song, without having to see its plumage or the shape of its beak. Or its flight, so that I no longer mistook a blackcap for a chaffinch or a garden warbler![13]

Under Delamain's guidance Messiaen took a more systematic approach to notating birdsong. The *cahiers* enable us to follow Messiaen's movements, in spring and early summer in Paris and in the forests around St-Germain-en-Laye and Orgeval, in late summer at his retreat at Petichet in the Alps, his journeys throughout France, and in later years (from the trip to Japan in 1962) his travels abroad. They also contain a huge quantity of notations that went far beyond what Messiaen could possibly have needed for his music. Inspired by the natural world his mind and imagination were in a heightened state when out of doors, so that besides birdsong the *cahiers* are filled with musical sketches, plans for future works, descriptions of scenery and architecture, and jottings of every kind.

Despite Messiaen's claim to accuracy in his reminiscence of Delamain, the early notations are surprisingly elementary. The very first notation, made on 14 May 1952, recycles the motifs of the nightingale in the first movement of the *Quatuor pour la fin du Temps*, lacking the weird sonorities

---

[12] Jacques Delamain, *Why Birds Sing*, trans. Ruth Sarason and Anna Sarason (London: Victor Gollancz, 1932), pp. 47–48.

[13] Messiaen, preface to Delamain, *Pourquoi les oiseaux chantent* (1960 [1928]), trans. Roger Nichols.

Example 2.3 (a) Nightingale, 14 May 1952; (b) Nightingale, 27 April 1953

and explosive tremolos of the nightingales in the *Catalogue*.[14] Messiaen made rapid progress, however. A year later another nightingale has a richer and more coherent detail, and indeed leaps from the page as music: this point is crucial, for as Messiaen's knowledge grew, so his search for truthful ways to translate every facet of birdsong started to make his notations more imaginative, richer in musical possibilities.[15] This nightingale was to become the opening of the piano solo that begins *Réveil des oiseaux*, the first major work based on birdsong (Ex. 2.3).

In the month after the visit to Delamain Messiaen is frequently hesitant in identifying even relatively common species (like the blackcap), and some of these early notations (such as one of the ortolan bunting that would figure so lyrically in 'Le Traquet stapazin') are little more than a primitive premonition of the birds in the *Catalogue*. With more familiar birds the notations are more assured: a blackbird 'dans mon jardin' (31 May) continues in the vein of *Le Merle noir* and forms a chain of tiny variations,

---

[14] 23077, p. 1. The manuscripts of Messiaen *cahiers* are in the Bibliothèque nationale de France, Département de la Musique, each *cahier* being catalogued with its own manuscript number.
[15] 23081, p. 10.

bearing out Messiaen's description of the blackbird to *France-Soir*.[16] Almost all the birdsongs in the early *cahiers* are fair copies, in a rather stilted script. Occasional examples of rough working show Messiaen employing a shorthand of rapid dots (for the pitches) with hints here and there of articulation and rhythm.

A return visit to Gardépée in June 1952 shows a growing assurance. Several of the notations would be used in *Réveil*. Among them is the blackcap (*fauvette à tête noire*) for the piano cadenza at fig. 28, unconsciously echoing the main theme of the 'Séquence du Verbe' from *Trois petites Liturgies*. The songs of a blackbird, golden oriole and robin are combined in a medley that would become the *grand tutti* (*Réveil* after fig. 18) where they join a robin (played by the piano) transcribed at St-Germain-en-Laye (2 June 1952).

Réveil des oiseaux

During the summer of 1952 Messiaen turned his thoughts to a commission from Heinrich Strobel for the 1953 Donaueschingen Festival. He had been toying with ideas for a concerto for two pianos based on an all-encompassing mode of durations involving every note on the piano. By August 1952 this had become a 'Piano Concerto (birdsongs)', with Peruvian melodies (as in *Harawi*), rhythms and timbres from *Timbre-durées* and a twelve-note 'mode de valeurs'.[17] A single-page sketch of this hybrid work survives, with springing rhythms on the brass, high jangling tremolos for piano, woodwind and glockenspiel, and a twelve-note chord (*fff*) to finish: a note in the margin reminds Messiaen to look again at Ravel's *Gaspard de la nuit* and *Miroirs*, as well as Hindu, Greek and plainchant sources, and the harmonies and rhythms of *Quatuor*.

Why, then, did Messiaen now go to the opposite extreme, with the cool precision of *Réveil*? The abandoned sketch forms the one solid piece of evidence as to his thinking. It is not difficult to imagine him rejecting this extravagant conception as a return to the old pre-1949 uses of birdsong. Better, instead, to use his new-found expertise to compose a work in which birdsong is not a decorative feature but actually *is* the music, a work entirely of birdsong, and birdsong as truthful as Messiaen could make it. He may well also have viewed birdsong as part of the project to renew his language

---

[16] 23077, p. 15.
[17] PH/NS, pp. 203–204.

that had occupied him since 1949. In particular birdsong was a source of melody of a new kind, compatible with contemporary sound-worlds, which Messiaen found lacking in the avant-garde music of the early 1950s.

What makes *Réveil* so fascinating is that it was evidently composed in the same spirit of experiment as *Cantéyodjayâ* and the *Quatre études de rythme*. In *Réveil* the aim of the experiment was to translate birdsong into music with the minimum of intervention. The limiting factor, of course, was that Messiaen's material – the notations he made of the dawn chorus in Delamain's garden or in the forests of St-Germain-en-Laye – was birdsong as he himself apprehended it, filtered through his own musical sensibility. That said, the notations were as true to nature as Messiaen could make them, and were transferred to the score with minimal alteration, as is shown by a comparison between the birdsong in the *cahiers* and the finished score. Even the form of the work was dictated by the dawn chorus, with Messiaen deploying the birdsongs in the order they occur in nature (although he did introduce an element of cheating, by mingling birdsongs collected in different places). For Messiaen, indeed, the birds were the true composers, as he made clear in a letter to Heinrich Strobel enclosing his programme note for the premiere: 'Don't include any biography, or any personal or musical information with my analytical note: I'm anxious to disappear behind the birds.'[18]

Messiaen's new direction in *Réveil* puzzled the pianist as well as the audience. Loriod remembered her first rehearsal with Messiaen, at which she played the demanding solo piano part (which she had learnt in a week) from memory. But though 'almost without fault' it was not at all what Messiaen had imagined, and it was only after doing her own research, experiencing a dawn chorus at Orgeval, that she felt she understood his intentions. The premiere took place on 11 October 1953. The audience seemed indifferent, uninterested in the birdsong, as Loriod recalled:

The musical world at the Festival had ears only for *musique concrète* and the rivalry between Pierre Schaeffer and the experimental group from Cologne. *Réveil* was not understood, not only because of its new aesthetic, but because human arrogance was doubtless unable to admit that birds are of interest. It was already the era of scientific research and machines. Anything poetic was trampled underfoot.[19]

It is while Messiaen was completing *Réveil*, in July 1953, that we find the first mention of a new birdsong work: 'For the piano pieces on birds,

---

[18] *Ibid.*, p. 208.
[19] From OMR, Yvonne Loriod-Messiaen's unpublished document with excerpts from Messiaen's diary annotated by herself. The charming anecdote about the rehearsal for *Réveil* came in conversation with Peter Hill, with further details from OMR, pp. 64–65.

notate the rhythms and silences within the sounds of the forest, which make the environment within which the bird sings.'[20] The idea of attending to the sounds of nature other than birdsong may have been at this stage only a passing thought, but it was a change from *Réveil*, which had consisted exclusively of birdsong, that was to have a huge significance for the *Catalogue*.

Apart from this there are few birdsong notations from the late summer of 1953, probably because Messiaen was fully occupied completing *Réveil* to a deadline. But when research resumed in October he returned to the 'pièces piano', now enlarged into a project of encyclopedic ambition. Messiaen was in Donaueschingen for the rehearsals and premiere of *Réveil*. On the evening of 6 October, in the Black Forest, he heard the calls of a tawny owl, a 'vocifération douloureuse et lugubre' (Ex. 2.4). For almost the first time in the *cahiers* a birdcall is harmonised, probably as a way of capturing changes in its timbre; at the same time the owl's motif is developed rhythmically as well as varied in dynamic, suggesting the cry approaching and receding in the darkness. Messiaen must have recognised these patterns of development as something new, and with an enormous potential that would take him far beyond the literalism of *Réveil*. It seems to have been a defining moment: for immediately below the tawny owl is a sketch for a birdsong project so vast and all-encompassing that it might have occupied Messiaen for the rest of his life.

The list of birds is drawn up according to habitat, among them twelve species that were to be in included in *Catalogue d'oiseaux*, of which four would give their names to the titles of pieces:[21]

Birds of the high mountain: chough
Birds of the vineyards: linnets, ortolan bunting
Night birds: tawny owl
Tropical birds: shama, Indian minah, white-throated laughing thrush
Seabirds: curlew
Birds of the reeds and ponds: great reed warbler
Birds of the pine woods: willow warbler, great tit
Birds of the cornfields and open sky: lark
Birds of orchards and woods: blackbird, robin
Birds of the oak trees: golden oriole
Birds of gardens and parks: blackcap, garden warbler, starling, chiffchaff
Birds of the copses: robin
Birds of the woods: green woodpecker, great spotted woodpecker

---

[20] 23086, p. 7.
[21] 23001, p. 9.

Example 2.4 Tawny owl, 6 October 1953

The disappointing reception of *Réveil* was the start of a difficult time. Claire's condition had worsened, and in December she was placed in a nursing home. To add to Messiaen's distress, in 1954 came the death of two of his colleagues, Claude Delvincourt, director of the Conservatoire, and Line Zilgien, Messiaen's deputy at the Trinité. Messiaen visited Claire weekly at La Varenne, confining his researches that summer to the forests on the western fringe of Paris.

Oiseaux exotiques

As far as Messiaen was concerned, 1954 was to be devoted to research for the great project outlined in the Black Forest. But amidst the notations Messiaen made at St-Germain or Orgeval he recorded two visits (18 and 25 May) to a private aviary at St-Cloud, which belonged to a Mme Billot. Her collection seems to have been mainly of tropical birds, but among them was a Virginia Cardinal, whose song, prefaced by descriptions of plumage, colouring, timbre and character, takes pride of place in Messiaen's notations; there are extensive rough notes and a fair copy running to six pages.[22]

[22] 23036, p. 49; and 23088, pp. 15–20.

Otherwise, perhaps because of the unfamiliarity of the songs, or because the cages were crowded, the notations of the tropical birds are sketchy, although two of them – the red-billed mesia and Indian shama – would feature in *Oiseaux exotiques*. These were the first notations in the *cahiers* of birds from outside France.

Mme Billot's Virginia Cardinal seems to have prompted Messiaen to explore further from a recording of North American birds – *American Bird Songs* – a comprehensive anthology that crams seventy-two American birds on to six 78 rpm discs. This may have been in Messiaen's possession since his visits to the United States in 1949, but a more likely explanation is that it was among a gift of birdsong recordings from Darius Milhaud, which Messiaen noted in his diary in January 1954.[23] It seems odd that Messiaen was so slow to take advantage of commercial recordings of birdsong, which had been available since the 1930s. But from now on he became an avid collector, spending winter evenings notating birdsong from the gramophone in Loriod's apartment in the rue Marcadet.

Recorded birdsong became the cornerstone of Messiaen's researches in the 1950s: no fewer than thirteen *cahiers* are devoted wholly or in part to notations from gramophone records. Despite this Messiaen was reticent about recordings, and his public comments tend to be disparaging: 'To know the song of the meadowlark, one has to have heard thousands of meadowlarks for hours, days, months, and years; so, you see, a phonograph recording is an incomplete tool in as much as it only gives a portion of song, just as a photograph conveys a snapshot.'[24] The fact is, however, that it was recordings that gave Messiaen the majority of the birdsongs for the *Catalogue* during the first three years of research (1954–1956).[25] This became one of the main differences between the two waves of composition; with the later pieces, those composed after April 1957, the balance swings back to notations from nature. That said, however, Messiaen's live notations, for example of the Mediterranean birds he found for the first time in the summer of 1957, owe much to his prior study of their songs from recordings.

Recordings enable us to take an informed view on Messiaen's claims for the accuracy of the birdsong in his music. Far more important,

---

[23] OMR, p. 69.

[24] Quoted in Claude Samuel, *Music and Color: Conversations with Claude Samuel*, trans. E. Thomas Glasow (Portland: Amadeus, 1994), p. 89; see also Messiaen, *Traité*, Vol. V, Part I, pp. 19–20; and Vol. V, Part II, pp. xiii–xxiv.

[25] Allowance needs to be made for the fact that notations for 'La Rousserolle effarvatte' from a trip to the Sologne region in 1955 are missing.

however, is that they offer priceless insights into Messiaen's imaginative musical response to birdsong by allowing us to trace his ideas to their source. In order to do this, however, we have to be confident of tracking down the recordings Messiaen actually used – no easy task because in the *cahiers* gramophone records are identified only vaguely, if at all: 'Disques Angleterre', 'Disques suédois', 'Suisse' etc. An obvious sign that a recording has been used is when a notation lacks details of place, time etc., invariably found with live notations. Establishing a date for the notation can therefore be tricky. Fortunately, there are clues in Messiaen's fair-copy script, which changes markedly over quite short periods of time, and also in the types of manuscript paper used at different times in his life. With Messiaen's work on *American Bird Songs* a dating to 1954 seems highly likely because preliminary rough work appears in the same *cahier* as the notations made at Mme Billot's aviary.

It seems unlikely that at this stage Messiaen had a composition in view. He began by making entries for all the birds in the order they appear on the recording, with a musical précis, rather than a full transcription, that gives a summary of the characteristics of each song. The birds are grouped according to the categories on the discs: birds of the North Woods, Birds of Southern Woods and Gardens etc., each carefully copied along with the names of the birds in English (a few are translated into French). As well as notations there are notes on timbre and character: 'strident', 'ironic', 'screeching' for the mockingbird; 'mewing', 'screeching' (catbird); 'very low, muffled, exactly like the noise of a motor starting' (ruffled grouse); 'a lugubrious call, a train's whistle, or the siren of a boat' (burrowing owl). Very likely this was done during the autumn of 1954. But by early 1955 a request had come from Boulez for a work for the Domaine musical concerts.[26] The idea of answering Boulez's commission with a work based on American rather than French birdsongs must have appealed to Messiaen as a way of avoiding upstaging the *Catalogue*.

Working from recordings was a new departure that would revolutionise Messiaen's approach to composing with birdsong. His first problem was that where *Réveil* had unfolded from lengthy live notations, in *American Bird Songs* each excerpt was brief, under half a minute. The compensation was that Messiaen could check, revise, refine and re-notate as often as he liked, each time finding something new in the song. A number of the American birds received multiple notations. Sometimes Messiaen was unable to decide which was best, and so used two: this accounts for the

---

[26] PH/NS, p. 211.

frequency of binary forms in *Oiseaux exotiques*. The long piano cadenza (fig. 24, pp. 62–65), for example, uses one version of the bobolink in its first half, another of the same song in the second.[27]

The *cahiers* for *Oiseaux exotiques* show Messiaen taking a much more creative approach to notating birdsong and to its use in composition. The point is made by comparing the ways he used the Virginia Cardinal from *American Bird Songs* with the Cardinal notated live in the St-Cloud aviary. Messiaen's first notation from the recording already has an element of composer's licence, introducing a repeat not apparent on the recording. This creates a suggestion of a binary form, which is then amplified in two later transcriptions.[28] The second of these was conceived with an ensemble of glockenspiel, xylophone, piano, temple block, 'and perhaps piccolo and E flat clarinet'. When playing through the passage Messiaen must have been struck by its pianistic qualities, because he started to add fingerings; indeed, this may be the moment when he decided to give the piano a solo role. The final version of the passage is a cadenza for piano alone. However, with the Cardinal from the aviary Messiaen took the opposite approach. Instead of using the notation in full, he omitted the opening flourishes, presumably because this aspect of the song had been already covered by the Cardinal from *American Bird Songs*. Instead, he used the song selectively, choosing only certain promising motifs for development.

The final break with the ideology of *Réveil* came during composition itself, which began in October 1955.[29] At this stage the work was entirely based on American birds. But in mid November Messiaen visited a bird exhibition in the centre of Paris where the tropical birds made such an impression on him that he decided to remodel the work drastically so as to include them. The juxtaposition of oriental with American birds created an impossibility that could never occur except in the artificial surroundings of a zoo or aviary. Messiaen would later excuse *Oiseaux exotiques* as a special case, in which he had departed from strict authenticity because he had combined birds from different parts of the world in an imaginary musical aviary: '[There's] a certain element of composition in the "birdsong material", since I've randomly placed side by side birds of China, India, Malaysia,

---

[27] Peter Hill and Nigel Simeone, *Olivier Messiaen: Oiseaux exotiques* (Farnham: Ashgate, 2007), pp. 67–8.

[28] Ibid., p. 39.

[29] Messiaen's note in the printed score dates the beginning of the composition of *Oiseaux exotiques* to 5 October 1955.

and North and South America, which is to say, birds that never encounter each other.'[30]

Messiaen's explanation is valid for the form of the work, with the birdsongs divorced from their natural surroundings, unlike *Réveil*, in which the music follows the order of birdsongs in a dawn chorus. But it cannot explain the new freedom with which he handles birdsong. Example 2.5 shows the sketches for the American wood thrush as they move through four distinct phases. The first is the initial précis. After this Messiaen returned to the recording in order to create a second, much more detailed, version, taking great trouble to get the events of the song in the correct order (his rough notes are a tangle of inserts and crossings-out). Accuracy was still important to Messiaen, but there are already signs that the song is being developed creatively: the high repeated notes are transferred to the bass, for example, but more significant is the first phrase, with the leap of a seventh (A to G♯) transformed into the opposition of D♭ with an arpeggio of C major. The third sketch goes further, with simultaneous broken chords of D♭ major and C major. The repeated notes are now in both bass and treble, the latter with a harmony of E major (plus added notes). The final version is the most radical step. Instead of using an ensemble, with the piano just one among a number of instruments, Messiaen now gives the passage to the piano alone, at a slower tempo, with *rubato*, while the D♭/C and the E major harmonies reverberate in the pedal – in context the effect is thrilling, the climax of the piano's first cadenza, and a rhetorical flashback just before the end of the work. The paradox is that the more the music becomes the product of Messiaen's imagination, the more the birdsong sounds authentic.

Oiseaux exotiques is equally inventive in its structures with a plethora of devices at local level – binary forms, variations, cadenzas, and the sorts of refrains and flashbacks found earlier in *Cantéyodjayâ* and the *Quatre études* – combining to create a dramatically vivid argument. *Oiseaux exotiques* proved that the lessons of the years of experiment – which had included *Réveil* – had been absorbed:

By the time of *Oiseaux exotiques* the changes in language brought about by experiment had taken root. Messiaen's music had become recognizably more modern in sound and spirit, stripped of excess emotional baggage (a world away from *Turangalîla*), with sharply sculpted ideas and concentrated structures. Most of all, *Oiseaux exotiques* was the work in which birdsong ceased to be an end in itself and became the starting point that challenged Messiaen's creative imagination.[31]

[30] Samuel, *Music and Color*, p. 131.
[31] Hill and Simeone, *Oiseaux exotiques*, p. 112.

Example 2.5 Wood thrush, from *Oiseaux exotiques*

(a)

(b)

(c)
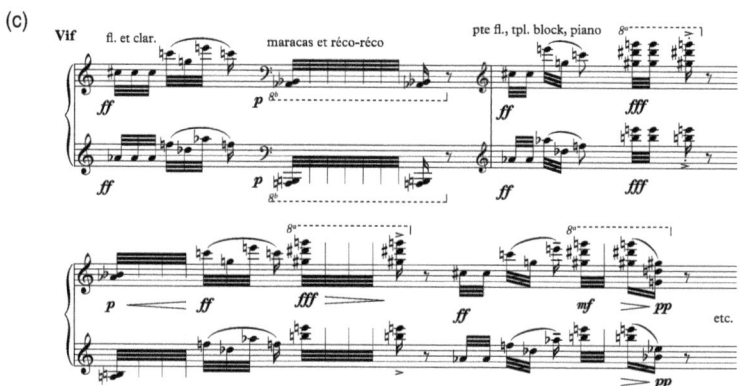

(d)
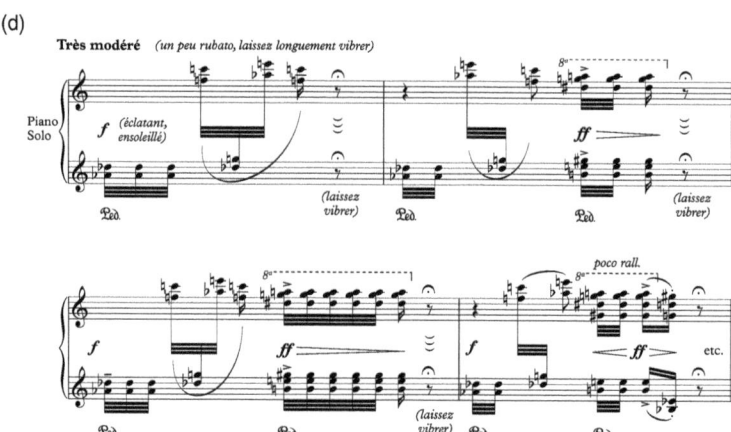

The English Recordings

The first recordings relevant to the *Catalogue* were by Ludwig Koch, a pioneer in the field. These were what Messiaen called the 'English discs', *Songs of British Birds* and *More Songs of Wild Birds*, which he may have acquired on a trip to England in April 1954, if they were not part of the gift from Milhaud.[32] Whereas with the American discs Messiaen's approach was experimental, each notation being a fresh exploration, with the English discs he seemed intent on reaching a definitive version that captures all aspects of the song. Indeed, the handwriting is so elegant and the notations so meticulous that one wonders whether Messiaen intended this *cahier* for publication, perhaps as a facsimile.

For the first time Messiaen was in a position to study in microscopic detail birds commonly found in France. By this time he must have notated dozens of blackbirds, but never before observed one so minutely. Under Messiaen's scrutiny the blackbird's song reveals a structure, with refrains, variations and afterthoughts, each phrase numbered in his notation. The song is punctuated by 'whispered' echoes, audible only when close to the bird. The character, as evinced by its timbre, is equally rich: 'Whistling, somewhat raucous, with a mocking character, a disillusioned cheerfulness, sneering – but also with a real joyfulness'.[33]

The most detailed of Messiaen's notations from the English discs is of a nightingale (Ex. 2.6). Messiaen likens its timbre to a 'damp harpsichord' while the different phrases are variously 'strange, tender, mysterious, passionate, victorious, imploring, quick-tempered, plaintive, mocking, despairing'. A number of motifs are new (the descending chromatic motif on line 2, for example) and the complexity and explosive intensity far outstrip the notations used for *Réveil*.

Koch's recordings enabled Messiaen to extend his researches to include birds he had not previously encountered, notably the water birds such as the reed warbler, sedge warbler and marsh warbler. These show a new imaginative resourcefulness in the way Messiaen finds equivalents to unpitched noise. The notation of the reed warbler is close in style and content to the opening solo of the reed warbler in 'La Rousserolle effarvatte' (Ex. 2.7).

---

[32] It is impossible to date with certainty Messiaen's work on the English discs, but there are signs in the spring and summer of 1954 that the Ludwig Koch recordings were influencing Messiaen's live notations. It seems likely, therefore, that Messiaen worked on the English discs in the early months of 1954. His notations are found in 23037.

[33] 23037, p. 21.

Example 2.6 Nightingale, from *More Songs of Wild Birds*

Example 2.7 Reed warbler, from *Songs of British Birds*

At the other extreme the most songful of these English birds is the woodlark, which appears in both sets, and thus receives two notations.[34] Already Messiaen has begun to edit the song, omitting occasional phrases that he may have found uninteresting or repetitive. The song forms a chain of variations. Each phrase has preliminary upbeats, like hesitations, hovering on a point of balance from which the phrase tips forward into a chromatic scale that, as it descends, pivots against an upper note. The resemblance to the woodlark in 'L'Alouette lulu' is unmistakable. Indeed, these notations became the most significant source for the piece: excerpts from the first woodlark (from *Songs of British Birds*) were used for the middle section, while the second notation (from *More Songs of Wild Birds*) is used almost in its entirety, beginning with the music of the transition that links the exposition with the entry of the nightingale ('L'Alouette lulu', score, pp. 2–3) (Ex. 2.8).[35]

The advantages of recordings for Messiaen's research are so obvious that we need to consider why he continued to collect live birdsong so assiduously. One answer is that while a recording could represent the characteristics of a blackbird (for example), no two blackbirds are exactly alike. Messiaen correctly took the view that birds are individuals, and when he heard a particularly interesting song he was eager to preserve it, no matter how many notations he already had of that species. Frequently the *cahiers* show him tumbling down to the street in the early hours of the morning to capture the song of a blackbird 'on my rooftop'.

Live Research, 1954–1955

Another disadvantage is that recordings cannot show the timing of birdsongs as the day unfolds, nor for the most part their interaction with other songs. Both were prominent features of the live notations Messiaen made in the spring and summer of 1954:

It is night – at 5 a.m. the first glimmers of dawn – the first robin strikes up, alone in the half-shadows, with an inexpressible expression of the tenderness of life and

---

[34] Ibid., pp. 2 and 12.
[35] In both *cahiers* and scores Messiaen writes '16' for music that is played/heard two octaves above the written pitch. This may seem like an error on the composer's part, but in the *cahiers* he also uses '32' and '64' – the latter surely denoting four rather than eight octaves above the written pitch. So it seems that a more personal, organ-pipe-related system is at work, rather than a miscalculation of the interval spanning two octaves (a fifteenth). We have followed his notation in all cases. It is also something of a French music convention; for example, Jobert's edition of Maurice Ohana's *Douze études d'interprétation* (Paris: Jobert, 1983), Vol. I, p. 25.

Example 2.8 Woodlark, from *More Songs of Wild Birds*

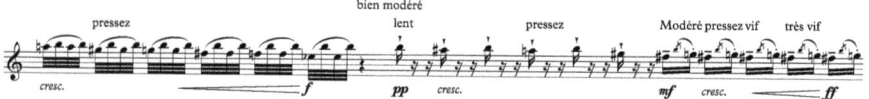

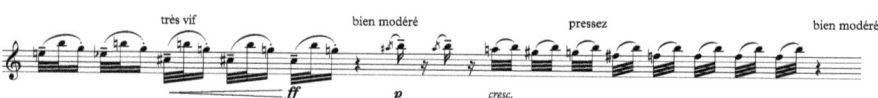

of poetry – a second robin makes a counterpoint, for six or seven minutes – by the end of quarter of an hour a complete *chorus* of robins, over which come to be superimposed (in this order): the song thrush (long solo), great tit, wren (at 5.30 a.m.), chiffchaff (six o'clock), chaffinch and woodpecker.[36]

With his growing experience and skill, birdsong started to become more individual, sharper and more distinctive in profile and character. With the song thrush (*grive musicienne*) he set out to capture, in a long solo, what he called the 'fantasy' and 'unexpected rhythms' of the song along with its incantatory quality, all with a huge variety of timbre: 'flute-like, screeching, mewing, bright and very dry, like "snatched" pizzicati or droplets of water'.[37] The robin loses the busy style of *Réveil* and becomes lyrical, almost a series of caressing gestures – 'friendly, tender, trusting, the timbre moist and soft' – and always legato, Messiaen emphasises.[38] A description of a nightingale suggests that Messiaen had by now studied the English discs, the timbre now analysed in musical terms – 'somewhat pinched and loud like a harpsichord or guitar; rounded like an alto flute; moist and quiet, like droplets of water; dry and disquieting like dead wood crackling underfoot beneath pine trees'.[39] In April came the first live notation to be used in the *Catalogue*, a long solo for the redstart (*rouge-queue*) that merited an exceptionally detailed fair copy. Eventually, in 'Le Loriot', Messiaen made selective use of the song, shadowing the melody from the *cahier* with a descant at a quieter dynamic.[40]

Loriod frequently accompanied Messiaen on his birdsong trips. Photographs show her shadowing him with a cumbersome portable tape recorder. It is possible that Messiaen made use of her recordings when reviewing his field notes, but there is no evidence for this in the *cahiers*, and no tapes have yet come to light. Indeed, from now on Messiaen largely confined fair copies to his work from birdsong recordings. His live notations are spontaneous field notes, reflecting the way recordings had enriched his birdsong language and contributed to the speed and virtuosity with which he now translated birdsong into music. The boundary between research and composition was becoming indistinct, and increasingly in the *cahiers* notations are interspersed with sketches for the *Catalogue*.

Loriod's Renault 4CV was a godsend to Messiaen. He even used it as a birdwatcher's hide, camping out in the car overnight in order to catch the

---

[36] 23003, p. 5.
[37] 23002, p. 8.
[38] *Ibid.*, p. 10.
[39] 23086, p. 15.
[40] 23085, pp. 25–27.

dawn chorus, or the nocturnal songs of reed warblers, as happened in the summer of 1955 in the Sologne region, south of Orléans, an area noted for its lakes and ponds, and the setting for 'La Rousserolle effarvatte' (reed warbler), the central piece of the *Catalogue*.[41]

In June Messiaen and Loriod travelled to Petichet. This was Loriod's first visit to Messiaen's summer retreat, the modest house that he and Claire had had built in the 1930s. Loriod recalled her enchantment at the situation of the house, in a meadow just below the Route Napoléon (between Grenoble and Gap), looking down to the lake of Laffrey and across to the mountain of the Grand Serre.[42] The weather in the mountains was unseasonably cold, and with few birds to be seen or heard Messiaen turned his attention to the scenery. For the first time we start to find the *cahiers* filled with descriptions. As with birds, these blend attention to detail with flights of imagination.

At La Grave, deep in the mountains, Messiaen descended to the Romanche River, fed by melting snow from the Meije massif, which rises opposite the village to a height of 3,983 metres:

The meadows are full of mountain flowers: yellow, sky blue, pink, violet – all the colours of the rainbow. A forest of fir trees, close to the Meije. Full sun, the Meije glacier, with its peaks and tormented rocks. The Tabuchet glacier, to the left of the Meije: more snow completely white, wearing a huge cloud. Between two peaks an immense path of snow climbs towards the sky like a giant's highway. The firs – like large dark green hoods – press together to see the giants who scale the highest snows towards a terrible immortality.[43]

A pair of Alpine choughs flew over an abyss, twisting in the wind and emitting their 'cri typique':

A high-pitched, strident rumbling, very intense at the outset, then *diminuendo*. The sharp, cold wind, whistling in the ears, falls silent: a great silence, terrible silence. Each massif is an ensemble of waves of rocks, in which the snow picks out fantastic shapes: dragons, furious wolves, mountain spirits, giant birds with wings outstretched.[44]

Later that summer Messiaen returned, describing the view as the sun began to sink, on 4 July 1955, at six in the evening:

Clouds mass in the valley behind me like an army of white griffons. The sun passes above the mountains tops, gilding the eternal snows. Slanting rays fall. The

---

[41] OMR, p. 79.
[42] *Ibid.*, pp. 79–80.
[43] 23065, p. 2, dated 3 June 1955.
[44] *Ibid.*, pp. 17 and 18.

Example 2.9 Waves off the Brittany coast

river Romanche glimmers like gold at the foot of the valley. Mont Aiguille and Lake Laffrey have disappeared in the mist. Huge clouds hang on the sides of the mountains.[45]

The first musical descriptions of nature found in the *cahiers* came in September in Brittany. This was a less happy trip for Loriod, who became prostrate with seasickness.[46] Messiaen was indefatigable, fascinated by the undulations of the waves and the changing colours on the crossing from Brest to the island of Ouessant:

Blue sea, marine blue, Prussian blue, with reflections of silver and gold. The wake behind the boat glistens with white foam … Huge waves: hills becoming valleys, valleys transformed into hills, in ceaseless exchange. Within the blue of the sea the sun traces figures-of-eight, grey-orange, and at the centre a murky pale green.[47]

Finding musical translations for his visual impressions, the sights as well as sounds of nature, was to be an important step forward. Example 2.9 shows Messiaen's depictions of waves, harmonised with 'two or three sounds for each note'.[48]

The Swiss and Swedish Recordings

Over the winter of 1955–1956 Messiaen returned to the gramophone in Loriod's apartment in the rue Marcadet to study two further anthologies of recordings. These were the 'Swiss discs' (Hans Traber's *So singen unsere Vögel*) and the Swedish radio recordings by Gunnar Lekander and Sture Palmèr, *Radions fågelskivor*. Messiaen began work on the Swiss recordings

---

[45] *Ibid.*, p. 19.
[46] OMR, p. 81.
[47] 23040, p. 2.
[48] *Ibid.*

shortly after his return from Brittany.[49] One of the first birdsongs notated was a woodlark, familiar from the English discs, but here surprisingly different, without a fixed upper note to anchor the chromatic descents, and with a much greater range of motifs – echoes of this can be heard in a woodlark that post-dates the *Catalogue*, found in *La Fauvette Passerinette* (1961).

The notebooks devoted to the Swiss and Swedish discs are among the most exciting of all Messiaen's *cahiers*, the notations on a new level of ornithological detail as well as musical imagination.[50] In contrast to his work on the English discs, Messiaen's purpose throughout these *cahiers* was musical, finding ways of transforming his notations into composition. An example of how this was done is the call of the red-backed shrike (*pie-grièche écorcheur*) from the Swiss discs, used for 'La Buse variable', and, incidentally, the very first surviving sketch for the *Catalogue*. The shrike's brief motifs were meticulously characterised – 'raucous, cutting [*piqué*], quasi-*glissando*, snatched, creaky twitterings' – and its call of alarm received repeated notations, finally elaborated into a version for piano exactly as it will appear in the score (p. 7), apart from being an octave or two octaves too high (Ex. 2.10). Two of the Swiss notations would be used in 'La Bouscarle'. One is the sandmartin (*hirondelle de rivage*) in a version for piano, again as in the score.[51] The exquisite solos for the blackcap from the middle part of 'La Bouscarle', where they act as descants to the cadences of the chorale that depicts the river, follow the structure that Messiaen discerned in the song, with a pattern of preludes and refrains. In the score the slight modifications of the original pitches tend towards a simpler patterning. The not-quite-parallel upper line in the refrains, colouring the principal line, became a typical feature of Messiaen's realisations of the more lyrical songs (Ex. 2.11).

The Swedish discs were to be the most important single source for the *Catalogue*. Again, the focus is very much on composing with birdsong, so that sketches outnumber notations. Given the emphasis on water birds it seems likely that Messiaen was already planning the piece that would become 'La Rousserolle effarvatte'. At this stage the soloist he had in mind may well not have been the reed warbler but the water rail (*râle d'eau*), which received a lengthy notation and a series of sketches, from which Messiaen selected the passage in which the bird screams like a 'piglet with its throat cut'.[52] Another candidate for soloist may have

---

[49] The Swiss notations appear in the same *cahier* as the trip to Brittany: 23040.
[50] *Ibid.*, and 23045–23048.
[51] 23040, p. 11; score, pp. 18–19.
[52] See 'La Rousserolle effarvatte', p. 37. The possibility that the *râle d'eau* was to be the main soloist in the piece that became 'La Rousserolle effarvatte' is found in a note in Messiaen's diary for 1956: 'Calandrelle avec de beaux accords genre Harawi … Râle d'eau, avec Effarvatte et Foulque … hulotte avec modes de valeurs et intensités dans le grave – sur 4 octaves, 48 durées chromatiques'.

Example 2.10 (a) Red-backed shrike; (b) Red-backed shrike harmonised

Example 2.11 (a) Blackcap; (b) its realisation in 'La Bouscarle'

been the great reed warbler (*rousserolle turdoïde*), represented by several pages of a fair-copy sketch for piano: this sets the style for the solo in 'La Rousserolle effarvatte' (p. 22), though there are no exact correspondences between sketch and score. A bird whose song has a resemblance to that of the reed warbler is the marsh warbler (*rousserolle verderolle*), from which Messiaen may have borrowed the sweeping demisemiquaver gestures found in the central section of 'La Rousserolle effarvatte' (score, p. 30).[53]

The reed warbler's opening solo in 'La Rousserolle effarvatte' is found here in its entirety. A preliminary note gives details of the bird's habitat and a musical précis of the song's essential characteristics along with a description: 'The song is wild, chanted, practically in equal values, made up of notes repeated two or three times. The timbre is metallic, low and murmuring.' The finished score adheres so closely to the notation that one can follow the music from the *cahier*, so that with this particular bird, at least, Messiaen worked as he had done in *Réveil*.[54] The difference is that in *Réveil* the piano played in octaves (except when a duet for two birdsongs), whereas here the writing is constantly imaginative, probing the timbre of the song just as much as its melodic contour. Example 2.12 compares the *cahier* with score, first with the opening bars, then with a short excerpt from later in the solo where the piano writing with its abrupt switching of register heightens the contrasts. The articulation of the grace notes, along with the wide spacing of the hands (designed, perhaps, to capture both the depth of the song and also its metallic edge), make this one of the most awkward passages in the *Catalogue* to play, especially as Messiaen insisted the leaps must be attacked fearlessly, without hesitation.[55]

Many other songs in the *cahier* either appear exactly as they will in the *Catalogue* or are recognisably similar. A powerful example is the eagle owl (*hibou grand-duc*) found in the opening and closing pages of 'Le Merle de roche'. The Swedish recording features a dialogue between male and female, the latter interpreted by Messiaen as being like 'ample, percussive laughter'; the hooting of the male owl comes with massive and ominous chords (score, pp. 1–2). All this is fully worked out in the *cahier*, complete with accentuations, pedalling and fingering.

---

[53] For *la rousserolle verderolle* see 23045, p. 16, line 7.
[54] The only difficulty comes towards the end, which is somewhat varied. The *cahier* source for the reed warbler is 23045, pp. 22–23.
[55] To Peter Hill.

Example 2.12 Reed warbler notated from the Swedish discs and as realised in 'La Rousserolle effarvatte'

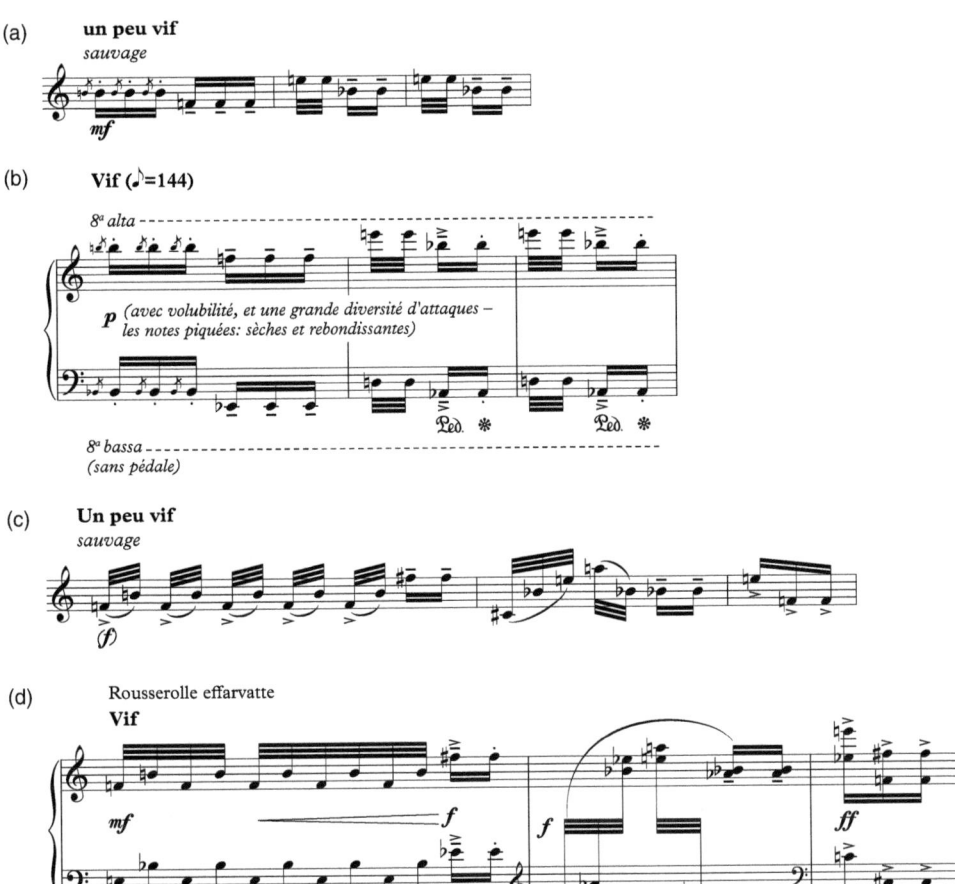

Throughout one is struck by the quirkiness of Messiaen's imagination, especially (as with the female eagle owl) when he invents pianistic equivalents for the less lyrical songs or cries. The timbre of the song is as important as its contour: the black redstart (*rouge-queue tythis*) from 'Le Merle de roche' (p. 7) – 'crackling, like paper rustling', or the bittern (*héron butor*) from 'La Rousserolle effarvatte' (pp. 3 and 51): 'Bellowing, mooing, sucking in air – the timbre is fat, huge, rather cavernous, a mixture of bass clarinet and tuba, above all *tuba*!' The musical sketches may be based on the closest observation, but Messiaen has by now freed his imagination, even taking liberties: with the long-eared owl (*hibou moyen-duc*) the 'yapping' cries are interspersed with the flapping of the owl's wings, represented by low Cs on the piano; in the score for 'La Chouette hulotte' these become a stuttering pulse, 'fear'.

Prominent among the birds not yet encountered in Messiaen's live notations are the seabirds for 'Le Courlis cendré'. Three of these – the guillemot (*guillemot de troïl*), redshank (*chevalier gambette*) and oystercatcher (*huîtrier pie*) – receive particular attention, with a long solo for the guillemot forming the basis for much of the central section of 'Le Courlis cendré'; the redshank's cadenzas mediate between the driving rhythms of the guillemot and the haunting refrains of the oystercatcher ('doux et flûté'). The foghorn faintly audible on the Swedish recording may have sown the seed for the climax to 'Le Courlis cendré': the huge cluster of sound, the siren of the lighthouse.

1956: Camargue and Brittany, First Sketches

In July 1956 Messiaen and Loriod embarked on their longest trip to date, to Provence and the Camargue, the delta of the Rhône with its salt flats, marshes and lakes teeming with bird life. The *cahier* and Messiaen's diary record the journey down through France, filled with descriptions of scenery and architecture – the Palais des Papes at Avignon, the sculpture of the west portal of St-Trophime at Arles, Aigues-Mortes with its medieval walls and battlements. Near the Abbey of Montmajour, east of Arles, Messiaen found a harsh landscape, inspiration for the shortest piece in the *Catalogue*, 'L'Alouette calandrelle'. There he worked throughout the oppressive afternoon heat, noting the fragile song of the short-toed lark, along with the cries of the kestrel and the whirlwind song of the skylark. In the Camargue Messiaen based himself around the nature reserve at Salin de Badon, working day and night, his imagination caught by the incendiary sunsets over the vast lake, the Etang de Vaccarès, and the incessant nocturnal songs of the reed warblers. At times the mistral scoured the marshes, banging the shutters of the old farmhouse (*mas*) and threatening to snatch Messiaen's linen jacket from his shoulders, as birds with bedraggled feathers struggled against the gale.

On the journey back to Paris Messiaen and Loriod spent two nights in the Forez, a mountainous region between Clermont-Ferrand and St-Etienne. A woodlark (*alouette lulu*) singing at seven o'clock in the evening gave rise to a lengthy solo in the *cahier*.[56] Messiaen noted the 'magnificent forest of fir

---

[56] 23042, p. 10.

trees – the silence, coolness', and as night fell a 'sublime calm' mingled with a sense of terror as the trees loomed in the darkness like 'ghostly giants'.[57] It was here, perhaps, that Messiaen started to imagine the complementary pair of nocturnes that make up Book 3 of the *Catalogue*, 'La Chouette hulotte' (tawny owl) and 'L'Alouette lulu' (woodlark).

At this point, after three years of research, and with a vast reservoir of birdsong notations, one would expect Messiaen to begin composing the *Catalogue*. Instead, during the summer break of 1956, Messiaen was occupied with other matters. He supervised the editing of his recording of the organ works (for Ducretet-Thomson), fretted about *Oiseaux exotiques* and whether Durand would agree to publish it, and organised his ideas and material for the *Traité*, drawing up a detailed plan in seven volumes.[58] The real reason for the delay may well have been that Messiaen had yet to find a solution to the problems of composing birdsong-inspired music for piano solo.

The solution came in the trip Messiaen made to Brittany (10–16 September). Arriving by boat from Brest on the island of Ouessant Messiaen at once started to cram down in the *cahier* his impressions of the scene. In the distance was the silvery-white horizon, 'shining, luminous, separating sea from sky'. In the foreground the sea 'perpetually at work, agitated, furious' was repelled by the 'immobile rage' of the rocks. Seen in silhouette these took on fantastic forms: 'lion's teeth, the tongues of dragons, the snouts of hippos, the jaws of crocodiles, geometric figures … ghosts, iguanodons …'.[59] Throughout the *cahier* snatches of song from the seabirds are interspersed with notations of the sounds of the environment: the eddying water; the crash of waves; and the boom of the siren emitted by the Créac'h lighthouse, as darkness and fog descended over the sea. The lighthouse keeper must have been startled to receive a visit from Messiaen at 11.30 at night; his answers to Messiaen's interrogation on the movement of tides and the formation of waves are noted verbatim in the *cahier*, along with a description of the lighthouse ('higher than the tower of a medieval castle').[60]

Altogether the sights and sounds of the environment take precedence over the songs and cries of the seabirds, captured in fragmented notations

---

[57] Ibid., p. 7.
[58] See OMR, pp. 88–89. Messiaen's plan reads: Traité de composition musicale: 1) les modes; 2) les mélodies humaines (pl. chant, folklore); 3) les mélodies naturelles (chants d'oiseaux); 4) philosophie de la durée et sources du rythme; 5) les rythmes antiques (Grèce, Inde); 6) styles rythmiques (Mozart, Debussy, Stravinsky, Boulez; 7) auto-analyse (mes oeuvres), avec une préface et un catalogue de mes oeuvres avec principales exécutions.
[59] 23044, p. 5.
[60] Ibid., p. 16.

as they were snatched away by the wind and drowned by the crash of the waves. The piece based on Messiaen's time on Ouessant, 'Le Courlis cendré' (curlew), accurately reflects his experience. Only the solos for the curlew itself are unaccompanied. The remaining songs and cries are heard mingled with the sounds of the Atlantic, while the development at the heart of the piece depicts the fog creeping over the sea as darkness falls.

The importance of this is that Ouessant provided Messiaen with the solution to his problem of continuity. The answer was to incorporate the environment as the frame to the birdsongs – a departure from *Réveil* and *Oiseaux exotiques*, which had consisted of birdsong pure and simple. It was against this background that Messiaen started to compose.[61] It seems that he had only one *cahier* with him, which now had to serve a dual purpose: he notated the sights and sounds of Ouessant working forwards from the beginning of the *cahier*, while using the pages at the back for musical sketches.[62]

The first page of sketches shows Messiaen developing his ideas for 'L'Alouette lulu'. He begins with a realisation for piano of a notation of a nightingale, exactly as it will appear in the middle section of the piece. Below this the woodlark itself is developed, first using the long notation from the Forez – which would be for the music that begins and ends 'L'Alouette lulu' – and then from Ludwig Koch's *More Songs of Wild Birds*,[63] Messiaen reminding himself to 'use the modulating chords and the English woodlark [i.e. from Ludwig Koch] after leaving the key of B♭ major'.

In notes squeezed sideways into the margin of the page are speculations on the structure of the *Catalogue*: Messiaen envisaged the use of rhythmic pedals on Hindu and Greek rhythms, 'with a thousand variations'. Particularly striking is a serial plan for the *Catalogue* – 'create a piece with a series of rhythms – another with a series of dynamics and attacks, etc., etc., – see Boulez, Stockhausen'. Though the serial idea was abandoned, serial writing remained an important aspect of the *Catalogue*, with the majority of pieces having serial passages. These have a descriptive role that avoids the sort of musical impressionism that Messiaen disliked, musical 'metaphors' for the natural setting – the darkness in 'La Chouette hulotte', the ice and snow of 'Le Chocard des Alpes', or the reflections of trees in water ('La Bouscarle').

The next page of the *cahier* contains ideas for individual pieces, tiny snapshots that prove remarkably prescient. What strikes one at once is the return

---

[61] The sketches occupy the last four pages of the *cahier* (23044). It seems probable that Messiaen was working backwards from the final page (p. 20), to end on p. 17.

[62] The compositional sketches for the woodlark at the back of 23044 suggest that Messiaen may have had with him the earlier *cahier* with notations made in the Forez (23042).

[63] See score, p. 4, line 3.

to major and minor triads, almost completely absent from Messiaen's music since 1949.[64] A sketch for 'Le Loriot' has cadences in E major, and a phrase that steps down in whole tones in a glowing sequence of dominant ninths, used in the finished piece to introduce the song of the blackbird.[65] For the end of 'Le Courlis cendré' Messiaen has two massive chords of C minor ('lent, funèbre') above which is the curlew's repeated cry, *quasi glissando*. Just possibly the chords represented the rocks, 'pointed like organ pipes', described in a note nearby. This ending was discarded, but the minor colouring lingers on in the harmonies (of E♭ minor and D minor) that underpin the curlew's solos at the beginning and towards the end of the piece. At the other extreme of harmony are dissonant bass clusters for the introductory music to 'La Chouette hulotte', standing for darkness and terror ('avant la Hulotte, pour la nuit – peur').

There remains what was probably the last sheet of the *cahier* to be filled (23044, p. 17), the writing becoming smaller and smaller as Messiaen squeezes his thoughts on to his remaining sheet of manuscript paper, and so hard to decipher that one wonders if he may have been working on the train back to Paris. At the top of this page is the final notation made on the beach at Ouessant: the roar and crash of the surf that would become the closing gesture of 'Le Courlis cendré', though reduced from *fff* to a fragmented whisper. Messiaen then used the remainder of the page for sketching. He begins with the song of the loriot (golden oriole), adding a descant of harmonies. In the margin is a pair of dominant sevenths (on F♯ and G♯) and a note reminding himself where to look in the *cahiers* for the birdsong.[66]

'L'Alouette lulu' (Woodlark)

Messiaen then turned his attention to 'L'Alouette lulu', searching for harmonies to represent the darkness. He began with three dissonant chords, moving outwards chromatically. These were discarded, but the chromatic movement remains in a series of cadences that gravitate towards the harmony of B♭ major. The key of B♭ has already been mentioned, as we have

---

[64] The exception is the use of E major in *Oiseaux exotiques* (along with harmonies of C and D♭), particularly in the song of the American wood thrush. See Hill and Simeone, *Oiseaux exotiques*.

[65] Score, p. 2, line 2.

[66] The places specified are Orgeval (in the forests to the west of Paris), Delamain's old home at Gardépée in the Charente, and Les Maremberts (Loir et Cher) in the Sologne region between Bourges and Orléans.

seen, at the back of the *cahier*, and very possibly was chosen as the key furthest removed from E major, which had symbolised for Messiaen all that is light and luminous since the first *Prélude*, 'La Colombe'.

The chains of chords form a chorale, while between each phrase one can just discern in Messiaen's spidery script the sources for the birdsong – 'Anglais … Suédois … Forez'. The passage as a whole makes an extraordinarily precise and comprehensive blueprint for 'L'Alouette lulu'. The phrases of the chorale are as yet in the wrong order, but already a shape to the piece is emerging, with the opening (in B♭) followed by a modulation via a sequence of rising chords, then a descent and a return to B♭ (Ex. 2.13).

In the finished version the curve of the harmony moves from 'contemplative' to 'active' and back again. The first modulation triggers a more animated version of the woodlark's song, with the rising and descending harmonic sequences corresponding to the central development of the piece, featuring the nightingale. The return to the music of the opening is achieved by means of a transition, with a hugely extended chromatic scale that flows from an unstable major–minor harmony (a harmony of B♭ with D♮ in the treble and D♭ in the bass), with the scale descending to the depths of the keyboard before resolving in B♭ major, summarised as follows:

Exposition – Transition: modulation and development of the woodlark – Development: solos for nightingale, woodlark and nightingale, followed by a dialogue between woodlark and nightingale – Transition: chromatic descent – Coda: B♭ major regained, the woodlark fades into the darkness.

All that remained for Messiaen to do was to finalise the shape of the piece by determining the order of the phrases of the chorale, and then to combine these with the birdsong, most of which (as we have seen) had already been composed in the pages at the back of the *cahier*. The whole conception was then rationalised in Messiaen's preface:

The Col of the Grand Bois at Saint-Sauveur en Rue, in the Forez. Pinewoods to the right of the road, meadows of pasture to the left. High in the sky, in the darkness, the Woodlark picks out its two-by-twos: a chromatic, fluid descent. Hidden in a thicket, in a clearing in the wood, a Nightingale responds, its biting tremolos set in contrast with the mysterious voice from on high. A Woodlark, invisible, draws near, fades. The trees and fields are dark and still. It is midnight.

The preface is clearly based on the episode in the Forez when Messiaen and Loriod were returning to Paris from the Camargue in July 1956, but with reality turned into an idealised fiction to suit Messiaen's musical purpose: a summer evening became deepest night, and at the same time

Example 2.13 Sketch for 'L'Alouette lulu': the numbers in brackets indicate the order of phrases in the finished score

Messiaen created an opportunity for contrast and dialogue by importing a nightingale from the Camargue. Meanwhile, the live notation of the woodlark from the Forez was not long enough, and so was divided in two, being used for the outer frame of the piece, while the woodlark in the central development comes from three recorded sources: the two collections by Ludwig Koch and the Swedish discs.

The general conception must already have been clear in Messiaen's mind when he came to sketch the chorale on p. 17 of the Brittany *cahier* (Ex. 2.14). The harmonies he devised create the nocturnal setting and articulate the shape of the piece; but they also complement the song of the woodlark, sharing its tonality (the woodlark's 'tonic' is B♭) and its chromatic movement. The 'liquid, chromatic descent' (in Messiaen's words) of the woodlark is mirrored in a four-chord sequence that begins chromatically (G♭, F, E♮), then falls in a typical Messiaen cadence by a tritone to the tonic of B♭. Meanwhile, in the right-hand chords the upper and lower lines move in semitones (Ex. 2.15). The exception is the 'alto', which moves from the tonic up a minor third (B♭ to D♭) and back – anticipating the harmonic move towards the end of the piece (just after the nightingale has fallen silent) to the major/minor dissonance, a 'suspension' resolved by the long descent to the tonic.

The effect of this opening page is subtle and difficult for the pianist to catch. First, the chords in the right hand have to be balanced very precisely with the bass octaves, 'on the edge of silence' (as Messiaen asks) but still audible and not entirely submerged.[67] Next the pianist has to establish the relationship between the chords of 'la nuit' and the woodlark's song – 'like a voice which falls from the stars'.

This is one of only two occasions in the *Catalogue* where Messiaen 'harmonises' the tempi of two ideas: in this instance demisemiquavers counted through 'la nuit' become quavers with the woodlark. (The other instance comes with the equally still and trance-like opening of 'L'Alouette calandrelle'.) In the early stages the pianist needs to establish this by carefully calculating a common pulse, at the same time recognising that the effect should be for the woodlark to float free as it articulates a 'triplet' rhythm. Meanwhile, the phrasing of the woodlark counterbalances the tendency of the ear to hear the descending chromatic line as the pulse.

Another kind of ambiguity arises as the music proceeds. The tritone E♮–B♭ in the left hand is mirrored by the woodlark, in its first phrase, and again in its fifth and sixth phrases, just as the chords return to the cadences of the

---

[67] Messiaen made this point when working with Peter Hill.

'L'Alouette lulu' (Woodlark) 53

Example 2.14 Woodlark from the Forez, 14 July 1956 (facsimile)

(a)

Example 2.14 (cont.)

(b) Alouette lulu

opening. At the same time the birdsong starts to establish an independent trajectory as the dynamics start to increase. Thus although the birdsong echoes the ternary shape of this opening paragraph of 'la nuit' by returning to the E♮–B♭, in other ways it intensifies as the chords sink back.

As so often in the *Catalogue* the ideas contained in the opening provide the key to the structure as a whole. On paper the shape of 'L'Alouette lulu' is a simple ABA, simple because of the contrast between the serene outer sections and the rasping brilliance of the nightingale. The reality, however, is that Messiaen goes to great lengths to blur the edges of the ABA design by bringing nightingale and woodlark closer together – a counterpart to the opening where he does the opposite, gradually dissolving the partnership between night and woodlark.

On the surface the woodlark and nightingale are in opposition in every way. The nightingale ('brilliant, biting') is dissonant, abrupt, fragmented, contrasting rapid repeated notes or tremolos that end with explosive gestures, and mysterious harmonies 'like a harpsichord blended with a gong', or in its second solo 'distant, lunar'. One point of contact, however, is the tritone. As we have seen, the interval E♮–B♭ has been emphasised towards the end of the woodlark's first solo. After the 'modulating chords' (p. 2) the tonic shifts up a semitone, to B♮. The new tritone is F♮–B♮, heard insistently (at the top of p. 3), echoed twice by the nightingale towards the end of its first solo, and more subtly elsewhere – in the chords using F♮–E♮–B♮, for example.

Example 2.15 Opening of 'L'Alouette lulu'

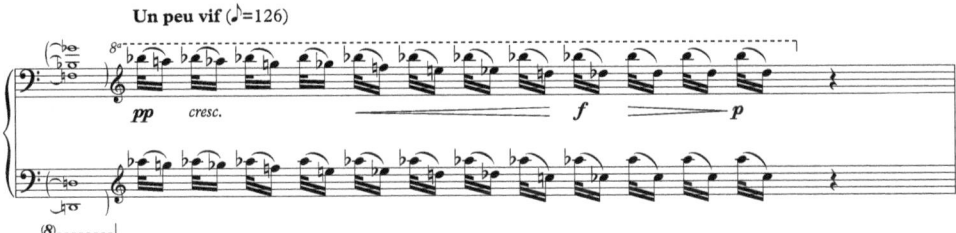

In the third and final phase of the middle section (pp. 6–7) the woodlark moves briefly up to a tonic C♯, before returning to B♮, again emphasised by the F♮–B♮ tritone, and again echoed very noticeably by the nightingale (p. 7, line 2). A last twist in this section is given by transposing the woodlark to a new tonic on F♯, down a fourth from the notation in the *cahier* (p. 7, line 3), so that it now follows the downward curve of the chordal interjections. At the same time the contrast between the birdsongs has been lessened – a merging of characteristics that sees the woodlark borrow the nightingale's tremolo (p. 7, line 4) – with the joins smoothed by more instances of voice leading. The nightingale ends with the same three-note chord as before, transposed from F♮–E♮–B♮ (p. 4, b. 2) to D♮–C♯–G♯ – a sonority that anticipates the chord (with its D♮/D♭) at the end of the next phrase of 'la nuit'.

This major–minor harmony is a crucial point in the design, signalled as such by Messiaen with a *portato* sign, the only one in the chorale. The pianist can mark the moment by making the sound a little 'dry', as the hands move into a close position with parity of dynamics.

The way Messiaen interweaves his material establishes a structural principle for the remainder of the *Catalogue*. The woodlark, nightingale and the harmonies of the darkness have been kept distinct, not least by the colouristic use of different registers of the piano; each has its own independent curve of development, its own life cycle, though allowed to intersect and react to one another as the piece proceeds. The nightingale has fallen silent and the remaining layers exchange roles, background becoming foreground as the chords at last step centre stage. The major–minor harmony acts as a dissonance that needs resolution, and the left-hand octaves fall away from the D♭ (the minor third) with a slow pendulum swing downwards, a huge descending chromatic scale that when it reaches the extreme bass of the piano comes to rest on a harmony of B♭ major (the scale is the final and fullest development of the chromatic motif). Almost unnoticed the music has changed gear, with the 'emotion' Messiaen spoke of in his article for *Guide du concert*. In doing so 'L'Alouette lulu' ends in a quiet foretaste of later pieces in the *Catalogue*, as when the songs of the oriole ('Le Loriot'), blue rock thrush ('Le Merle bleu') or spectacled warbler ('Le Traquet stapazin') are suspended in slow motion in the memory.

3 | Beyond the Birdsong of *Catalogue d'oiseaux*

Time and Memory, Opera and Colour

We now broaden the focus to include the influences that Messiaen drew upon alongside the birds. Although events in the *Catalogue* happen largely in the present tense, it is also a work in which Messiaen comes to term with the past, both recent and distant, musical and personal. As well as a daring return to tonality in the midst of the avant garde, it is – as some commentators have already noted – distinctly autobiographical.[1] Messiaen was acutely aware of history, and the way he engages with it in the *Catalogue* adds depth to its depiction of the here and now.

Catalogue d'oiseaux also marks the beginning of Messiaen's tendency to identify colours within the score: the plumage of the birds, the timbre of their song, and the hues of the landscapes they inhabit. It is a sign of renewed confidence that he was able to do this, after the ridicule that his sound–colour associations attracted in some quarters of the French press in the 1940s.[2] For Messiaen colour and time were intrinsically linked, as seen in the title of *Chronochromie* (1960), and his notion of a form that 'depends entirely on the colours' in *Couleurs de la Cité céleste* (1963).[3] Questions naturally arise as to the nature of this link.

The *Catalogue* provides us with some answers. The passage of time governs much of the work's structure, as Messiaen explained to Claude Samuel:

> It's in my *Catalogue d'oiseaux* and in *La Fauvette des jardins* that you'll find my great formal innovation. There, instead of referring to an antique or classical mould, or even to some model I might have invented, I sought to reproduce in condensed form the vivid course of the hours of day and night.[4]

---

[1] See for example Christopher Dingle, *The Life of Messiaen* (Cambridge: Cambridge University Press, 2007), p. 152.

[2] For a full account of this controversy, known as 'Le Cas Messiaen', see PH/NS pp. 144–168.

[3] Preface ('Première note de l'auteur') to the orchestral score of Olivier Messiaen *Couleurs de la Cité céleste* (Paris: Alphonse Leduc, 1967).

[4] Claude Samuel, *Music and Color: Conversations with Claude Samuel*, trans. E. Thomas Glasow (Portland: Amadeus, 1994), p. 117.

Messiaen is by no means the only composer to have adopted such a strategy. Claude Debussy begins a work Messiaen treasured, *La Mer*, by depicting 'dawn to midday on the sea' ('De l'aube à midi sur la mer'). Richard Strauss's *Eine Alpensinfonie* is perhaps a closer model, anticipating the day-long arch form of 'La Rousserolle effarvatte'.[5] Post-1959, George Crumb's *Vox Balaenae*, with geological periods assigned to variations, bears Messiaen's imprint (if not necessarily that of the *Catalogue*); and Karlheinz Stockhausen's unfinished chamber cycle *Klang: Die 24 Stunden des Tages* (*Sound: The 24 Hours of the Day*) associates a colour with each hour of the day.

Messiaen's claim ignores his own prototype, *Réveil des oiseaux*, which follows the course of a morning from midnight to midday. The *Catalogue*, though less literal, seems more real (partly because it evokes place as well as time). Eleven of the thirteen pieces are set at certain times of the day, with the three that occupy a book of their own charting the passage of specific hours, as is explained either in Messiaen's prefaces or in annotations to the score. All thirteen are concerned with sounds and events that occur as time passes, slowing them down in the case of much of the birdsong, and speeding up other sequences of events.[6] The passage of time is often conveyed by the sun's motion (usually in the form of a richly harmonised chorale), or inferred by birdcalls – for example the static midday songs of the chiffchaff and grasshopper warbler in 'Le Loriot' and 'La Rousserolle effarvatte'. 'Le Merle de roche' – the third of the three pieces that last a full day – is more oblique; though set in the warmest region of France, Languedoc, the sun is not depicted in the music, and the sonorities that depict the rocky setting of the Cirque de Mourèze – an assortment of durations and harmonies, scattered about the keyboard, that eschew any sense of progression – seem to suspend time altogether.

Many of the pieces are also set at specific times of the year, so that more than one time-scale is in operation at once. It is clear from Messiaen's writings that he had a stratified view of time, resulting in part from the difference between experiencing and observing it. In the opening chapter of Volume I of the *Traité de rythme, de couleur et d'ornithologie*, in a passage entitled 'Temps superposés', he outlines how an array of western writers,

---

[5] Robin Freeman acknowledges the Debussian model in 'Courtesy towards the Things of Nature', *Tempo* 192 (April 1995), 9–14.

[6] Both Alain Louvier and Paul Griffiths have noted that, like other composers, Messiaen stretches time in both directions when simulating it. Alain Louvier, *Messiaen et le concert de la nature* (Paris: Cité de la musique – Les Editions, 2012), p. 92; and Paul Griffiths, *Olivier Messiaen and the Music of Time* (London: Faber and Faber, 1985), p. 16.

philosophers and scientists have influenced his thinking.[7] He draws most heavily on St Thomas Aquinas from a theological stand point, focusing on the distinction between time and eternity (which according to Aquinas is timelessness rather than endless time), and on Henri Bergson from a philosophical one (in particular Bergson's notion of 'durée vécue' – perceived duration – versus 'temps structuré' – structured, i.e. measured, time). The interpretations vary in their sophistication, but are compelling in that they point directly to temporal effects in his music.

The collage-like material of *Catalogue d'oiseaux* is a realisation of these notions, anticipated by pieces such as 'Regard du Temps' (from the *Vingt Regards*), which alternates strands that address time in different ways. The *Catalogue*'s title page reflects this outlook: 'The composer was able without difficulty to re-awaken old memories, whether from a few hours or several years ago.' The recent and the ancient were equally alive to Messiaen – and this is true of his whole compositional outlook, not just his attitude to birdsong.[8] The first musical contrast in 'Le Chocard des Alpes' pits the permanence of the mountains against the Alpine chough's 'tragic cries in the solitude'; it illustrates Messiaen's summary of 'temps superposés' in the *Traité*:

The ephemeral which lasts several hours, the man who lives for several years, the mountain which lasts for many centuries, the star which remains for countless centuries, each achieve their complete function by the time of their death or disappearance: their duration is therefore the same. These superimposed times are only different for a foreign observer; they are identical for those that live them, each in the totality of its function, in its durational force.[9]

The contrast between the frieze-like music of the mountains and the short, sharp cries of the chough suggests different planes of time. Messiaen finds a way of reconciling these by following up the bird's opening outbursts with a more sustained cry consisting of a powerful nine-note sonority – one of his most radical distortions of *cahier* material, at least in rhythmic terms (see Ex. 3.1).[10]

---

[7] Olivier Messiaen, *Traité de rythme, de couleur et d'ornithologie: en sept tomes* (Paris: Alphonse Leduc, 1994–2002), Vol. I, pp. 5–36.

[8] In *ibid.*, Vol. V, Part I, p. 17, Messiaen suggests another kind of temporal layering by contrasting the evolution of western music history with the unchanging music of the birds (a reflection of their exalted status in relation to humans).

[9] *Ibid.*, Vol. I, p. 36.

[10] This memorable moment closely resembles one of the first musical illustrations in *ibid.*, Vol. I, which features a rhythmic cell (very long/short) that must be 'perceived duration' at the moment of hearing, and 'measured duration' in retrospect, once the shorter rhythmic unit has been heard (pp. 32–33).

Example 3.1 The 'tragic cry' of the Alpine chough in the *cahier* (a) and in the score (b)

(a) cri typique du Chocard des Alpes: (**au vol**)

(b) Très lent (♪ = 40)

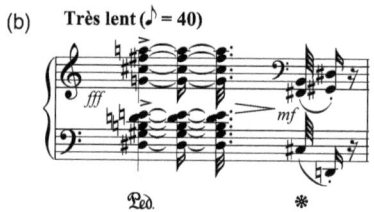

This outburst, magnified beyond its natural proportions, demonstrates that the literalism of *Réveil* is a thing of the past, and that musical argument in the *Catalogue* will not just be an endless series of contrasts: more a polyphonic treatment of temporality where several strands of time can be in play at once, providing the formal basis for each piece. One strand is indeed the whole cycle, for instance its progression from the intense heat and light of Book 2 ('Le Traquet stapazin') to the pair of nocturnes in Book 3 ('La Chouette hulotte' and 'L'Alouette lulu') and the full day–night cycle of Book 4 ('La Rousserolle effarvatte').

How, then, does Messiaen use colour to animate time, a rather more elusive notion? This approach developed during the *Catalogue*'s composition (colour indications are much more prevalent in the score during the second wave of composition). The evolution can be seen in the piece that begins the second wave, 'La Bouscarle', where the 'river' refrain that binds the form together and explores hues of blue in mode 3^3 and A major is closely related to (but subtly differentiated from) the sudden bursts of a 'blue-green arrow' representing the kingfisher's 'nuptial flight', which – at least at first – is in pure mode 3^3. The harmonic relationships (Messiaen would say the colours) ensure that beings and events both blend in with, and can be seen against, their surroundings. In this instance reflective music (the river) can be distinguished from immediate events (the flight), mimicking the way we might experience an outdoor scene, and generating an integrated musical form that does indeed simulate our sense of time passing at variable speeds.[11]

Messiaen sought to explain the correspondences he saw in his mind between sound and colour during his 1971 Erasmus Prize address in Amsterdam: 'This [sound–colour] relationship is entirely subjective. In my particular case, I'll not deny certain literary and artistic influences, certain emotional impressions made in childhood.' Here he opens the door to an otherwise closed realm of experience by providing a proxy for his synaesthetic experiences: specific associations or images that are a useful foil for the abstraction of sound–colour synaesthesia.[12] The more obviously 'coloured' music tends to be allusive in *Catalogue d'oiseaux* – the kingfisher passages, for example, sound in places like a Chopin *Etude*, and climax with Messiaen's own 'litanies' progression from the 1930s ('La Bouscarle' p. 16, bb. 6–12) – itself borrowed from Debussy's 'Hommage à Rameau'. These allusions simultaneously open a window onto the past and make the moment being depicted all the more vivid.

Amongst the crucial stimuli of Messiaen's youth are his mother Cécile Sauvage's poetry, Shakespeare, Perrault's fairy tales and numerous operatic vocal scores given to him before the family's move to Paris in 1919 – above all Debussy's *Pelléas et Mélisande*.[13] These scores exerted a powerful influence on the composer-to-be, and after the premiere of his only opera, *Saint François d'Assise*, Messiaen turned his Erasmus statement around by remarking to Almut Rößler that 'here we're dealing with a stage-play with a libretto, with spoken words in which the music follows and, at least in part, one can see the colours which I've inwardly seen'.[14] In the *Catalogue* the French landscape is Messiaen's stage.[15]

---

[11] Robert Macfarlane echoes Messiaen's multi-layered view of time in *The Wild Places* (London: Granta Books, 2008), pp. 60–61: 'The Basin kept many different kinds of time, and not all of them were slow. I had seen quickness there too: the sudden drop of a raven in flight, the veer of water round a rock, the darts of the damselflies, the midges who were born, danced and died in a single day. But it was the great chronologies of its making – the ice's intentless progress seawards, down the slope of time – which had worked upon my mind most powerfully.'

[12] Almut Rößler, *Contributions to the Spiritual World of Olivier Messiaen* (Duisberg: Gilles and Francke, 1986), p. 43.

[13] During Messiaen's childhood he would perform Shakespeare for his brother Alain, and experiment with coloured lighting in his own toy theatre; PH/NS, p. 13.

[14] Rößler, *Contributions*, p. 125. At another time Messiaen comically revealed his predilections: 'Pelléas wore a red costume, what a mistake!' (Samuel, *Music and Color*, p. 63).

[15] Messiaen had a particular interest in stage directions (Samuel, *Music and Color*, p. 19), and the prefaces in the *Catalogue* sometimes adopt the terse prose style typical of this genre (for example 'La Chouette hulotte': 'Silence. The hooting is more distant, like a bell tolling from another world …'; and 'L'Alouette lulu': 'Unseen, the lark approaches, then moves away. The trees and the fields are black and calm. It is midnight').

Example 3.2 'Le Courlis cendré', b. 1

These childhood discoveries stayed with Messiaen throughout his life, and a growing number of commentators are starting to detect their imprint in his music.[16] Given that the *Catalogue* marks a return to tonality after Messiaen's experimental years, and is a depiction of familiar landscapes, it is hardly surprising that plentiful quotations and references can be found. Most of the pieces in the cycle allude to earlier music in some way or other. Opera figures strongly – not just a set of fingerprints from, predominantly, Wagner and Debussy, but also in locations and scenarios: Brittany is the final destination for the *Catalogue*, just as it is for the opera that is overtly referenced in Messiaen's *oeuvre*, *Tristan und Isolde*. The closing piece ('Le Courlis cendré') begins with an E♭ minor chord that combines the opening tonality of *Götterdämmerung*, the spacing of the first chord of *Tristan* Act III, and a sonority from the final bars of Ravel's 'Oiseaux Tristes' – the last two perhaps acknowledged in the marking 'flûté, triste' in the score, not the only time that Messiaen hints at his sources on the page (Exx. 3.2–3.4).

If Messiaen had retained his original ending for 'Le Courlis cendré', marked 'lent et funèbre' (Ex. 3.5), the entire piece would have followed the tonal journey of *Götterdämmerung* from the E♭ minor Norns' scene to the C minor Funeral March. Perhaps he ultimately regarded the two climactic C minor chords as too obvious a reference; this more 'heroic' ending was eventually replaced by watery oblivion, the sound of the surf ('bruit du ressac').[17]

The subdued ending that Messiaen ultimately chose for the cycle is difficult to untangle from the circumstances that weighed him down throughout

---

[16] For example Julian Anderson, 'Olivier Messiaen and the Notion of Influence', *Tempo* 247 (January 2009), 2–18; and work by Yves Balmer, Thomas Lacôte and Christopher Brent Murray.

[17] Messiaen and Loriod attended performances of *Götterdämmerung* conducted by Hans Knappertsbusch at the Opéra Garnier during the *Catalogue*'s composition; OMR, p. 112.

Example 3.3 Richard Wagner, *Tristan und Isolde*, Act III, bb. 1–4

Example 3.4 Maurice Ravel 'Oiseaux tristes', b. 29

Example 3.5 The first planned ending of 'Le Courlis cendré (23044, p. 19)

the decade, and quite possibly earlier tragedies, such as the death of his mother in 1927. Messiaen told Rößler that the *Catalogue* – specifically 'La Rousserolle effarvatte' – was like 'a photograph album from bygone times'.[18] In the score we find references to family members, too frequent to be coincidental: the words 'clair', 'pierre', 'loriot' and 'sauvage' appear numerous times. Gilles Tremblay, who experienced Messiaen's teaching of *Pelléas et Mélisande* in class during the crucial years 1954–1957, was in no doubt as to the composer's keen identification between the musical and personal:

His analysis began at the beginning of the work, with the first words [of Mélisande]: 'Do not touch me, do not touch me or I will throw myself into the water.' The class burst out laughing, but then things began to get serious … He

---

[18] Rößler, *Contributions*, p. 68.

Example 3.6 'Le Loriot', p. 2, b. 3

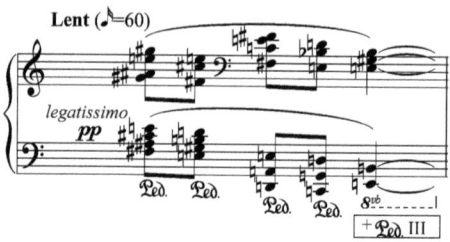

talked of Baudelaire, the jealousy of Golaud – one sensed that he had a profound sympathy with Golaud. I remember that one day he stopped talking, walked around the piano and said: 'I am walking round the piano because I can't carry on. It's too beautiful.' He truly became the characters. Another time, he stopped at the nigh-on blasphemous words of Arkel: 'If I were God I would have pity on the hearts of men.' 'Don't you realise?' he demanded, 'This is awful!'[19]

It comes as no surprise that Debussy should figure in some of the more impassioned moments in *Catalogue d'oiseaux*. The chords on p. 2 of 'Le Loriot' that have been described as Debussian are derived from the declaration of love in Act IV, Scene 4 of *Pelléas* (see Exx. 3.6 and 3.7; the sequence of roots follows a whole-tone scale – an unusual progression for a composer who maintained that Debussy had exhausted everything that could be said with that mode – and the notes of the D^9 and C^9 chords are a precise match with the Debussy).[20] And the upper line of the 'magic hand' cluster chords in 'Le Merle de roche' is, for a moment, a melodic fragment from 'Clair de lune' (Exx. 3.8 and 3.9).

The *Catalogue* is almost entirely referential; nearly every bar represents *something* from nature. The quotations, on the other hand, are occasional, and varied in their presentation: some are submerged (e.g. the chords in 'Le Loriot'), some gild the music ('Le Merle de roche'), some are more prominent (the opening of 'Le Courlis cendré'). Messiaen thereby evokes time by being evocative, as well as by simulating events in their succession. Time is articulated by the concept of 'temps superposés', and enriched by colour, memory and allusion – we don't perceive time in isolation but in relation to a previous week, a month, a year or a life. Messiaen is not unoriginal, but absorbent; this is what enabled him to forge such a powerful musical language.

---

[19] Jean Boivin, *La Classe de Messiaen* (Paris: C. Bourgois, 1995), p. 212. Messiaen's teaching was particularly focused on opera at the end of the 1950s. The scores of *Catalogue d'oiseaux* have a resemblance to vocal scores, with each bird's name placed above the stave, as is a character's before they sing.

[20] Olivier Messiaen, *Technique de mon langage musical*, 2 vols. (Paris: Alphonse Leduc, 1944), Vol. I, p. 59.

Example 3.7 Claude Debussy, *Pelléas et Mélisande*, Act IV, Scene 4

Example 3.8 'Le Merle de roche', p. 2, b. 10

Example 3.9 Claude Debussy, 'Clair de lune', bb. 13–14

Though the *Catalogue* is mainly populated with Messiaen's musical memories, Cécile Sauvage has the last word. The final stanzas of her *L'Ame en Bourgeon*, written while she was expecting her first child, Olivier, read:

So it shall be: the dazzled hour
Of my new-born child decrees it –

> To him the audacity, the madness,
> The mountain, and the wild thyme;
>
> For me the restrained intoxication, which,
> Like foam that rushes forward, first rising,
> Then falls slowly back, dissolves,
> For me the sober truth.[21]

These lines summarise the *Catalogue*'s journey from the Dauphiné of 'Le Chocard des Alpes' to the Atlantic surf in the final bars of 'Le Courlis cendré'. The 'sound of the surf' ('bruit du ressac') with which it ends had been with Messiaen all his life, a life he spent searching for truth (just as Pelléas desired 'la vérité').[22] Writing this extraordinary documentary-in-sound was one way of discovering it.

Catalogue d'oiseaux and the Avant Garde

Although Messiaen largely turned his back on serialism when he devoted himself to birdsong in 1952, he did not entirely abandon its aesthetic. He had spent three years experimenting with this new language – according to Pierre Boulez this was 'a period of intense self-questioning, possibly as a result of the explorations carried out by some of his pupils (of whom I was one) who had made a more-or-less radical break with his personal predilections' – although it had in fact occupied his thoughts since the end of the war, as we know from the planned ballet on the subject of time, and diary entries on serialised tempi in 1945.[23] And in the music of the later 1940s (such as the three 'Turangalîla' movements of *Turangalîla*) it was clear Messiaen was moving in this direction. If Boulez was right about his generation's catalytic effect, then the influence was mutual; *Mode de valeurs et d'intensités* was revelatory for both him and Stockhausen (and others such as Karel Goeyvaerts), making its presence

---

[21] Philip Weller, '*L'Ame en Bourgeon*: Translation and Afterword', in Christopher Dingle and Nigel Simeone (eds.), *Olivier Messiaen: Music, Art and Literature* (Aldershot: Ashgate, 2007), pp. 191–278 (pp. 250–251).

[22] 'There has only been one influence in my life, and it happened before I was born': Messiaen quoted in Dingle, *The Life of Messiaen*, p. 2. The source is Dennis Marks (executive producer), 'Messiaen at 80', TV programme, BBC, 10 December 1988.

[23] Pierre Boulez, 'The Utopian Years', in *Orientations: Collected Writings*, ed. Jean-Jacques Nattiez, trans. Martin Cooper (London: Faber and Faber, 1986), p. 412. In the *Traité*, Vol. VII, p. 44, Messiaen claims to have suggested serialising durations, dynamics, attacks and timbres to his class (Boulez amongst them) as far back as 1942, following an analysis of Berg's *Lyric Suite*. However, as Boulez joined the class in 1944, Messiaen must have misremembered the date.

felt motivically in Stockhausen's *Kreuzspiel* and as the basis for the tone row of Boulez's *Structures Ia*; although Messiaen was never to write total serialism (with all its serialised parameters independent of each other, unlike the fixed sonic entities of *Mode de valeurs*), he played a large part in its inception.

Structures Ia was written after the healing of a rift that had developed between Messiaen and Boulez in the late 1940s, which stemmed in part from Boulez's intense dislike of *Turangalîla*. After their reconciliation (which involved a more recent student, Jean Barraqué, acting as go-between) Messiaen's relationship with the avant garde in Paris was one of mutual support.[24] Boulez has expressed the view that the Domaine musical 'projected Messiaen during this period' (he is referring to 1954–1967, although the elder composer was fully re-established as a leading figure in modern music by the early 1960s), whilst Dominique Jameux's biography of Boulez reminds us that '[Messiaen's] support and participation protected the Domaine musical from accusations of musical Bolshevism'.[25]

Messiaen was also swift to recognise the potential for electronic music to create a more precise rhythmic language than instrumental music could achieve (though he later saw this as an illusion).[26] The pioneers of *musique concrète* recognised the value of his endorsement: 'Concrete music is ready to come out of the laboratory. It is time for musicians to bring it out … The fact that musicians and musicologists such as Roland-Manuel, Olivier Messiaen and Serge Moreux are showing interest gives us hope that this will be the case.'[27] Although the musical value of Messiaen's one contribution to the genre, *Timbres-durées*, is questionable (it was effectively disowned by him), its significance is clear, occupying as it does a pivotal moment in his output. The experience of working with *objets sonores* may well have encouraged him to transcribe naturally occurring sounds for future works (such as the waterfall in *Chronochromie*).[28] More pertinent still is the syntax

---

[24] Barraqué's contemporaneous Piano Sonata (1950–1952) mediates between the underlying concepts of *Mode de valeurs* and *Structures 1a*, vacillating regularly between the concepts of 'note-son' (fixed sounds) and 'note-ton' (variable entities).

[25] Dominique Jameux, *Pierre Boulez*, trans. Susan Bradshaw (London: Faber and Faber, 1991), p. 66.

[26] In the end he felt that this potential for rhythmic super-precision was undermined by the inner rhythmic life of sound samples such as columns of water.

[27] Roger Richard in *Combat* (19 July 1950), quoted in Pierre Schaeffer, *In Search of a Concrete Music*, trans. Christine North and John Dack (Berkeley, CA: University of California, 2012), p. 63. Moreux was later one of the producers of Messiaen's 1956 recordings of his organ works.

[28] The low-fi plumbing effect of many of the *objets sonores* invites ridicule. Pierre Schaeffer was, at the time, surprised by Messiaen's lack of adventurousness in his sound selections. All these

of *Timbres-durées*. As Messiaen refined his *style oiseau* in the latter 1950s he rediscovered the collage textures of early electronic music, and this approach was to inform the majority of future works. The *Catalogue* can be considered a watershed in this respect, and whether or not one hears a narrative behind its frequent splices, the kinship with *Timbres-durées* is unmistakable.[29]

The *cahiers* suggest that these issues were in Messiaen's mind as the *Catalogue* took shape.[30] In the margin of 23044, p. 20, he name-checks the pioneering spirit behind *musique concrète*, Pierre Schaeffer, in addition to Boulez and Stockhausen: 'Catalogue d'oiseaux: write a piece with a series of <u>rhythms</u> – another with a <u>series of sounds</u> – another with series of <u>dynamics and attacks</u> – etc etc (see Boulez, Stockhausen) – make <u>samples</u> [faire des <u>prélèvements</u>] (see Schaeffer)'. The urgency in Messiaen's double-underlining of 'prélèvements' (also meaning a taking or a withdrawal) confirms that sampling of nature – creating musical discourse from 'found' objects – was high on his agenda.[31] On this page we also see an early version of Messiaen's labelling technique – letters and numbers assigned to blocks of musical material. He was looking to exploit music's recent developments on his own terms, overcoming their apparent drawbacks through the potent combination of his musical imagination and Loriod's virtuosity.

In the *Catalogue* Messiaen also demonstrates that serial writing need not be regarded as abstract; in his hands it becomes a metaphor for aspects of nature, beginning with the Alpine landscape of 'Le Chocard des Alpes', which is depicted using twelve-note chordal writing, and independent 'rows' of durations in each hand that contain Greek rhythms. Like Boulez

---

points can be found in Christopher Brent Murray, 'Olivier Messiaen's *Timbres-durées*', in Christopher Dingle and Robert Fallon (eds.), *Messiaen Perspectives 1: Sources and Influences* (Farnham: Ashgate, 2013), pp. 123–142.

[29] As Robert Fallon suggests, it may even have been that pieces such as Schaeffer's *L'Oiseau RAI* (1950) persuaded Messiaen that the time had come to put birds centre stage; in other words, he was being as territorial as his subjects in claiming birdsong as his project. Robert Fallon, 'The Record of Realism in Messiaen's Bird Style', in Christopher Dingle and Nigel Simeone (eds.), *Olivier Messiaen: Music, Art and Literature* (Farnham: Ashgate, 2007), p. 126.

[30] Much later, Messiaen compared his bird style to *musique concrète* (Samuel, *Music and Color*, p. 95).

[31] Thereby overcoming the flaws that he perceived in the *musique concrète* project itself (see Brent Murray, 'Olivier Messiaen's *Timbres-Durées*' for a full explanation). Messiaen's early responses, before his own foray into the medium, and when he was presumably considering its potential, are some of the most interesting. Schaeffer reports that 'Messiaen was shocked by the continuity of the human voice accompanied by concrete music' in response to his 'concrete opera', *Orfée*, in 1951 (Schaeffer, *In Search*, p. 100).

he understood the latent poetry of serialism (although his attitude towards serial music hardened over time, he maintained appreciation of Boulez as 'the great serial composer … the realiser and "surpasser"').[32] The two main organisational procedures of his previous works – modes and permutations – both appear in the *Catalogue*. There is just one example of the former: a mode of pitches, durations and dynamics that evokes 'the night' in 'La Chouette hulotte', similar to *Mode de valeurs* and *Cantéyodjayâ* but specifically tailored to the unnerving circumstances (notes get progressively longer as they go lower, more systematically – or relentlessly, one could say – than in *Mode de valeurs*). The 'interversions' are much more widespread, appearing in seven of the thirteen pieces, including depictions of water and swirling mist in 'Le Courlis cendré' that lead directly to the ultimate climax of the *Catalogue*, the eleven-note chord that imitates the foghorn of the Phare du Créac'h.

The *Catalogue* has its own pitch series, which is subjected to thirty-five permutations using Messiaen's standard method: the same pattern of rearrangement recurs from one interversion to the next. In design and treatment it harks back to the series of *Ile de feu 2*, where the swirling material on page 6 anticipates Book 7 of the *Catalogue* in particular. By the time of *Catalogue d'oiseaux* it was a metaphor waiting to be deployed.

Serial passages occur in all of the *Catalogue*'s books except Book 2 ('Le Traquet stapazin'). Wai-Ling Cheong has written a detailed account of these passages that demonstrates, amongst other things, that the 'cortège' music of 'Le Merle de roche' has special status, using a thirty-two-duration series that was subsequently deployed in *Chronochromie* and other major works up to and including *Eclairs sur l'Au-delà*.[33] The subtle difference in deployment of the cycle's pitch scheme in 'La Buse variable' ('the buzzard glides in circles') and 'Le Courlis cendré' ('the water') is worthy of note: the interversions are superimposed in groups of four (1 and 2 above 3 and 4) in 'La Buse', and groups of two (1 above 2) in 'Le Courlis'. Both arrangements are anticipated in the 'flight of the choughs' in 'Le Chocard des Alpes'. Twelve-note chordal writing is more complex, a phenomenon again demonstrated by the first and last pieces: in 'Le Chocard' the interversions overlap when right and left hands have different rhythms (such as the opening depiction of La Meije) and align when the hands correspond (the central 'Clapier St-Christophe' section). In the passage headed 'the night and the fog close

---

[32] Samuel, *Music and Color*, p. 192.
[33] Wai-Ling Cheong, 'Symmetrical Permutation, the Twelve Tones, and Messiaen's *Catalogue d'oiseaux*', *Perspectives of New Music* 45.1 (Winter 2007), 110–136 (p. 127).

in little by little' from 'Le Courlis' they also align, but the order in which the interversions occur is unruly, and sometimes they are in retrograde. Messiaen's choices seem to reflect what he is depicting: the chough's flight is more skittish than the buzzard; the mist is amorphous, the mountains jagged, the flights continuous.

Messiaen certainly perceived his serial material as having character, if not necessarily colour. His advice to Xenakis 'to love' (or at least 'to know') one's durations harks right back to the idealism of La Jeune France, whose manifesto in 1936 called for a 'living music', away from the 'mechanical and impersonal'.[34] Messiaen's integration of this material into the tapestry of *Catalogue d'oiseaux* is remarkably prescient – prophetic, even – of the more liberated musical language of a later age. The confidence with which he worked is in evidence in the prefaces, which avoid the explaining tendency he showed in earlier scores (such as *Livre d'orgue*, where several movements are headed by an outline of the procedures adopted).

The serial mindset is not limited to individual moments within the *Catalogue*. Juxtaposition of contrasting (or even incongruent) material – the principle on which the cycle is based – reflects both serial thought and *musique concrète*, and it is a useful definition of surrealism to boot. Unlike in *Oiseaux exotiques* it is possible that the featured birds can be gathered in the same place, but how we hear them in *Catalogue d'oiseaux* – orderly and equally prominent – is bizarre and unreal.

Could the choice of thirteen pieces have been an attempt to trump hard-line serialists, some of them habitually reliant on the number 12 even outside the pitch domain? If so, it also speaks of Messiaen's additive tendency: just as the eight movements of *Quatuor pour la fin du Temps* represent the six days of creation, plus the day of rest, then extended to infinity, so the *Catalogue* represents something beyond the emblematic twelve of serial composition – not a retreat from it, but a new realm.

---

[34] André Cœuroy, 'Manifeste et concert des "Jeune France"', *Beaux-Arts*, 5 June 1936; and Iannis Xenakis, *Arts/Sciences: Alloys. The Thesis Defense of Iannis Xenakis*, trans. Sharon Kanach (New York: Pendragon Press, 1985), pp. 31–32.

4 | The First Wave of Composition

'Le Chocard des Alpes' (Alpine Chough)

Strophe: The Alps of the Dauphiné, l'Oisans. Rising towards the Meije and its three glaciers.

1st Couplet: Near the chancel hut: the Puy-Vacher Lake, marvellous mountain vistas, chasms and precipices. An Alpine chough, separated from its flock, cries as it flies over the precipice. The veiled flight, silent and majestic, of the golden eagle, borne on currents of air. Raucous and ferocious cawings and grunts of the raven, lord of the high mountain. Different cries of the choughs and their acrobatic flight (glides, swoops and loopings) above the abysses.

Antistrophe: In front of Saint-Christophe-en-Oisans, the Clapier Saint-Christophe: chaos of crumbled blocks, rocks from Dante put in disorderly piles by the mountain giants.

2nd Couplet: An Alpine chough circles the landscape and flies over the precipices. The same cries and flights as in the first couplet.

Epode: Les Ecrins: the Cirque de Bonne-Pierre, with its immense rocks, aligned like giant phantoms, or like the towers of a supernatural fortress![1]

Messiaen was consistent in his desire for 'Le Chocard des Alpes' to begin the *Catalogue* from the moment he conceived the work. It appears at the head of the list he compiled in the Black Forest in October 1953 ('Birds of the high mountain: Chough'), and was placed first in the six pieces Loriod premiered at the Salle Gaveau on 30 March 1957. One reason may have been that Messiaen wished to start his journey across France from the territory he considered his 'true home', the Dauphiné. Nonetheless, a piece that is so austere and impenetrable raises a question: why does a cycle that heralds a discovery of new forms, a return to tonality as a major structural force and an assertion of artistic freedom courtesy of the birds begin with a stern, atonal Alpine evocation, of which only 56 out of 182 bars contain birdsong?[2]

---

[1] Olivier Messiaen, preface to the published score.
[2] 'Nature, birdsong! These are my passions. They are also my refuge … for me, it is here that music lives: music that is free, anonymous, improvised for pleasure', Messiaen wrote in *Guide du concert* shortly before the full premiere of the *Catalogue* (translation by Roger

Form and Silence

'Le Chocard des Alpes' is dominated by three passages of twelve-note chordal writing that depict Alpine settings: a journey up the Meije glacier, the boulders strewn around the Clapier Saint-Christophe, and the jagged 'supernatural fortress' of the Cirque de Bonne-Pierre. The use of serial procedures to represent landscape – the first of many in the *Catalogue* – is not just an aural metaphor: the topography of the keyboard feels mountainous to the pianist, who has swiftly to navigate the peaks and gullies of black and white notes with regular movements of the forearm. Interspersed with these passages, similarly dissonant material – strident bird-calls and skittish depictions of the choughs' flight – populates the landscape. The alternation between mountains and birds gives rise to a couplet–refrain form, with the bird material (the couplets) in the second and fourth sections: Strophe – Couplet – Antistrophe – Couplet – Epode.[3] Messiaen outlines the form in the piece's preface, although this does not take account of the Epode being closest in content to the Strophe – they are both in 2/4 time, whereas the Antistrophe has constantly varying metre. The sense that the piece has a superimposed ternary shape is also suggested by the respective dynamics of the mountainous passages: f, $f\!f$ and f (a distinction not always upheld by pianists), and was confirmed by Messiaen in conversation with Claude Samuel.[4] Lengthwise, too, the strophes exhibit balance, whereas the couplets expand in the manner exemplified by *Neumes rythmiques* (1949). Balance and expansion, permanence and development, animate and inanimate: these are the opposites that shape 'Le Chocard'.

This formal scheme took shape late in the day. Messiaen's first idea had been a rigorously symmetrical plan, crammed into the sketches that he jotted down between Brittany and Paris in September 1956:[5]

Nichols). Christopher Dingle has already broached the question in *The Life of Messiaen* (Cambridge: Cambridge University Press, 2007): 'The serialism with which cosmopolitan musical thought was obsessed became Messiaen's point of departure for his journey into nature' (p. 152).

[3] Robert Sherlaw Johnson describes the structure as a 'compositional procedure' rather than a form, and identifies its roots as 'variations of the first theme separated by developments of the second', one of the categories outlined by Messiaen in *Technique de mon langage musical*, and the basis of pieces such as 'Fouillis d'arcs-en-ciel, pour l'Ange qui annonce la fin du Temps' (movement 7 of the *Quatuor*) and *Neumes rythmiques*. Robert Sherlaw Johnson, *Messiaen*, 2nd paperback edn, updated and with additional text by Caroline Rae (London: Omnibus Press, 2008 [1975]), p. 23.

[4] 'This is a blend of the couplet–refrain form with the triad form'; Claude Samuel, *Music and Color: Conversations with Claude Samuel*, trans. E. Thomas Glasow (Portland: Amadeus, 1994), p. 117.

[5] 23044, p. 19.

'Le Chocard des Alpes' (Alpine Chough) 73

Figure 4.1 The Meije glacier viewed from La Grave

chough	La Meije *pp*	raven, crow	Clapier St-Christophe *ff*, Cirque de Bonne-Pierre *ff*	crow, raven	La Meije	chough

However, the retrograde treatment of crow and raven may have seemed artificial – the composer organising nature rather than imitating it – and the reprise of a (curiously quiet) Meije section would surely have lacked the vivid impact of the contrasted Alpine images we now have.

'Le Chocard', like *Chronochromie*, has the energy of music that is new and uncompromising. Even the use of silences, formerly harmonious in Messiaen (as in 'Liturgie de Cristal' and 'Regard du silence'), seems dissonant, the fermatas like magnifications of the tiny 'voids' he perceived (and found disturbing) in Boulez's music, or even the troubled silences of *Götterdämmerung*.[6] Wagner is alluded to conceptually and aurally: the mountain-top location and ravens are reminiscent of the scene between

---

[6] Olivier Messiaen, *Traité de rythme, de couleur et d'ornithologie: en sept tomes* (Paris: Alphonse Leduc, 1994–2002), Vol. I, p. 28.

Example 4.1 (a) 'Le Chocard des Alpes': the 'majestic flight of the golden eagle'; (b) Richard Wagner, *Tristan und Isolde*, prelude to Act III

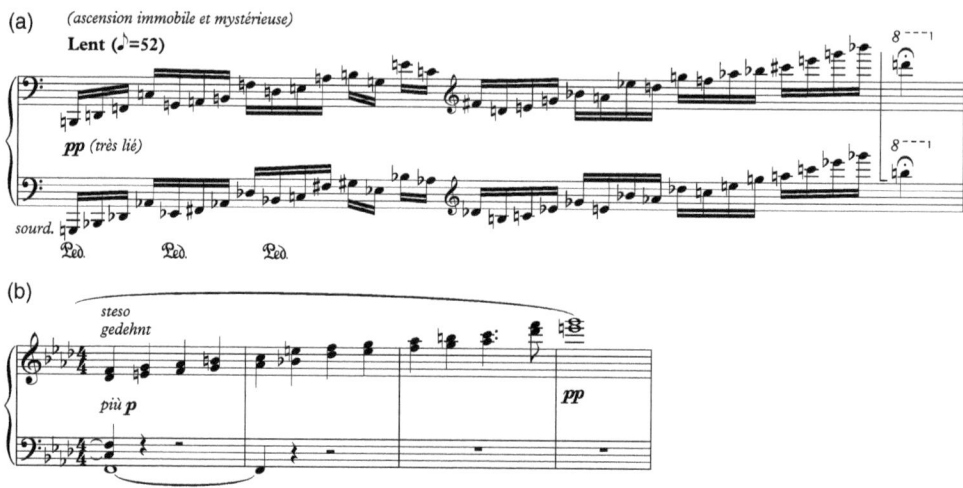

Brünnhilde and Waltraute in Act I of *Götterdämmerung*, and the 'supernatural fortress' that Messiaen saw in the turret-like peaks of the Cirque de Bonne-Pierre is surely a sort of Alpine Valhalla (the preface having already told us that Messiaen imagined giants clumsily arranging the rocks of the Clapier Saint-Christophe – the work of Fasolt and Fafner perhaps?).[7] The rising thirds of the golden eagle's 'mysterious ascent' also bring to mind the clarinets that open the Waltraute scene – even more so the violins that express Tristan's delirium in the prelude to Act III of *Tristan* (and thereby point to the destination of the *Catalogue*, the Brittany coastline that is the setting for 'Le Courlis cendré') (see Ex. 4.1).

It is tempting to see the symmetrical features of *Das Rheingold* as a model for 'Le Chocard', on account of the 'acrobatic flight of the choughs above the abyss' ('vol acrobatique des Chocards au-dessus de l'abîme') – the most frenzied of all the flight depictions – which tumbles down to the piano's lowest note in the first couplet and races up to the highest A in the second, following the musical trajectories of Wotan and Loge's journeys in and out of Nibelheim. References to Wagner are part of the symmetry that connects the first and last pieces of the *Catalogue*, 'Le Chocard' and 'Le Courlis cendré'. Alain Louvier describes the chords that depict 'the night and the fog spread little by little' in 'Le Courlis' as 'the inverse effect of Valhalla's emergence from the mist in the first interlude of Wagner's

---

[7] The nearby Chamchaude was probably not the only peak Messiaen saw as a 'Valkyrie helmet' (23022, p. 2).

Example 4.2 High peaks of the Cirque de Bonne-Pierre

Das Rheingold.⁸ One could add that the foghorn that follows these chords mimics Donner's striking of the anvil at the other end of the opera.

Landscape and Rhythm

Each of the Alpine passages has its own characteristics. In the outer sections – which are in duple metre throughout – there is rhythmic polyphony between the hands, featuring Hindu rhythms (see Ex. 4.3) that are subject to Messiaen's *personnages rythmiques* treatment.⁹ The hands in the central 'Clapier' section are in rhythmic unison, the metre irregular: in this passage the Greek 'cretic' rhythm (quaver-semiquaver-quaver) is heard many times. Their rhythms, chord formations and shifts of register give a strong visual impression of the topography. The 'Clapier' section has a series of tumbling descents suggesting the immensity of the rock piles, while the left hand at the beginning of the 'Cirque de Bonne-Pierre' (the Epode) remains in the treble for some time, suggesting perhaps a high plateau, then plummeting suddenly into the bass (Ex. 4.2). Towards the end both hands start to feature more thirds, recalling the 'statue theme' of *Turangalîla*. The final stratospheric E/G dyad may correspond with one of the cirque's many 'turrets'.

The opening Strophe is an outstanding compositional feat: if *Livre d'orgue* was, according to Messiaen, his 'greatest rhythmic victory', then 'Le Chocard' represents the fruits of the victory.¹⁰ Of the two hands the

---

⁸ Alain Louvier, *Messiaen et le concert de la nature* (Paris: Cité de la musique – Les Editions, 2012), p. 68.
⁹ This is the rhythmic technique that Messiaen claimed to have identified in *The Rite of Spring*, where some repeated rhythmic values remain constant while others steadily increase and/or decrease – see the analysis in Vol. II of the *Traité*, pp. 93–147. The Hindu rhythms Messiaen used are taken from Sharngadeva's table of 120 deçi-tâlas, listed in Appendix II of Sherlaw Johnson, *Messiaen*, p. 219. Messiaen's source was Albert Lavignac's *Encyclopédie de la musique et dictionnaire de la Conservatoire* (Paris: Editions Delagrave, 1924), which he discovered whilst studying at the Conservatoire; his teachers Maurice Emmanuel and Marcel Dupré had particular influence on his rhythmic development.
¹⁰ Messiaen, *Traité*, Vol. III, p. 204.

Example 4.3 Simhavikrama and candrakalâ-lakskmîça

simhavikrama

candrakalâ-lakskmîça

in 'Le Chocard des Alpes'

personnages treatment in the right hand is more regular: a thirteen-duration series starts with seven values that gradually decrease, then three that increase, ending with a long note (dotted minim) with two succeeding values that remain constant. The left hand is a less disciplined presentation of eleven durations (Ex. 4.3). The *Catalogue*, a cycle in which twelve-note music is a recurring presence, therefore opens with an abstract dance around the number 12.[11]

The passage's most memorable bars show us that although the opening of the RH sequence gradually diminishes from 444 to 333, and then 222 to 111, a conventional diminution (4, 2, 1) is normally more perceptible (Ex. 4.4). The diminution from three quavers in the right hand (b. 14) to three semiquavers (b. 20) stands out because both occur after a tie over a barline. Messiaen emphasises the resemblance with his choice of register and pedal changes: the low Es in the odd-numbered bars 13 and 19 suggest an alternation of strong and weak bars, a rarity in his music.[12]

The diminution from three crotchets (b. 1) to three quavers (b. 14) is made even more effective by the left hand restating the three crotchets in bar 13. These left-hand crotchets are especially ambiguous; at first glance they appear to be a continuation of the accumulating *personnages* process at the end of the series (values 9 to 11 in the LH section of Table 4.1).[13] However, they only occur on the downbeat of bar 13 thanks to an eight-duration interpolation that has no other apparent *raison d'être*. The third statement of the LH series has been shunted along, and these three crotchets are its beginning, not its end. As the passage progresses, the whereabouts of the eleven-duration series in the left hand becomes more ambiguous, as the second part of Table 4.1 shows. And unlike the right hand, where the source

---

[11] The left hand can also be understood as a 19-value series that starts with the ninth value in b. 1. In this reading the *personnages* procedure works consistently; candrakalâ-lakskmîça is still split between the series.

[12] The passage is certainly four-square by Messiaen's standards, although the whereabouts of the pulse is not always clear.

[13] The *personnages* features in the left hand are so disparate that the label may seem inappropriate – there only appear to be increasing values, at the beginning and end of the series. But, on closer inspection, there are some recurring values (3, 4, 8 happens twice) and the two 8-note interpolations have a mixture of increasing and decreasing values.

'Le Chocard des Alpes' (Alpine Chough)   77

Example 4.4 Memorable bars in the opening Strophe of 'Le Chocard des Alpes'

(a)

(b)

Table 4.1 Rhythms of the opening 'Meije glacier' section of 'Le Chocard des Alpes' (all values in semiquavers)

simhavikrama (4 4 4 2 6 4 6) with added value in italics

RH												
4	4	4	3	6	4	6	4	2	1	12	2	3
3	3	3	2	5	3	5	5	3	2	12	2	3
2	2	2	1	4	2	4	6	4	3	12	2	3
1	1	1	3	1	3	7	5	4	12	2	15	

candrakalâ-lakskmîça in italics; repositioned series after 8-duration interpolations shown by [ ]

LH												
2	2	2	3	8	3	3	4	*2*	*2*	*2*		
3	3	3	*1*	2	3	4	8	3	3	3		
4	*7*	2	2	3	3	3	3	[4	4	4		
2	2	3	4	8	4	4	4]	5	6	1		
1	2	4	4	[5	5	5	3	2	3	4	15]	

rhythm (simhavikrama) sits within the duration series, here candrakalâ plus lakskmîça lies camouflaged across the boundary between the first and second set of eleven notes. What appears on the page to be a musical abstraction, a game with numbers, turns out to be skilfully wrought counterpoint. The left hand is by turns mysterious, unruly, obliging, cunning and prophetic.

Birds and People

The *dramatis personae* of 'Le Chocard des Alpes' is notable. The first bird to be heard in the *Catalogue* is a single chough that, 'separated from its flock, cries as it flies through the abyss' ('séparé de sa troupe, traverse le précipice en criant' (score, p. 2)). It emits a preliminary 'tragic cry in the solitude'; isolation – splendid or otherwise – is a central theme of this piece. More choughs respond, before the 'tragic cry' returns, this time in a version of expressionist intensity: an elongated, complex, *fortissimo* ten-note chord (see Ex. 3.1b, p. 60).

The combining of an individual soloist with a collective of the same species is unique in the *Catalogue*.[14] Messiaen claimed (in his essay in *Guide du concert*) that the music of the *Catalogue* is faithful to real-life events.[15] The music of the choughs supports this, being based on entries in the *cahier* for 4 July 1955, recorded there in a gripping mixture of prose and notated cries; on that day Messiaen and Loriod ascended the 2,250 metre Croix de Chamrousse (situated to the south-east of Grenoble, halfway to the Alpe d'Huez), returning via the Col des Trois Fontaines in the early evening.[16] The original 'cri', notated in the *cahier* both on the way up and on the way back down, is a stark, five-note chord built round two clashing tritones (see Ex. 3.1a, p. 60); it was eventually lengthened from a dotted quaver to a frozen shard of sound lasting four-and-a-half seconds, the dense and fascinating harmony shown in Chapter 3.

During the descent a chough appeared 200 metres above the pair, setting Messiaen's pen in motion:

A sheet of ice stops me in my tracks – an Alpine chough flies creepingly, then glides, then veers to one side: very black, king of the sky and the abysses. Yellow beak, red feet, plumage ebony black: such is the Alpine chough. In flight: the huge black

---

[14] The collective noun for choughs is in fact a chattering or clattering.
[15] 'Everything is accurate ... the responses, ensembles and moments of silence'; Messiaen, 'La Nature' (translation by Roger Nichols).
[16] 23065, p. 18. Messiaen's verisimilitude is not limited to the number of birds in 'Le Chocard des Alpes'. Just as the *Guide du concert* article claims, their silences as well as their songs are respected – with small tweaks, similar to the pitch material. The chough's cries at the bottom of page 6 (in the score) feature rests that last one, nine and thirteen demisemiquavers; in the *cahier* they last for two, eight and fourteen. The tweaks may be in order to regulate bar lengths.

wings spread, markedly serrated and fringed at the edges – the slender body joined to a powerful beak, more upturned than that of a raven.[17]

It is strange that Messiaen used none of this description for the preface. Indeed, the lack of visual reference to the bird is eerie, as if he were reluctant to focus on his cast. Did this have a private, personal meaning? Perhaps the intensity with which Messiaen studied the sound and motion of the break-away bird surveying the landscape, flying above and below him, suggests a fascination that goes beyond the ornithological to identification with his own isolation. For most of the 1950s his role in the avant garde was poised between leader and dissident. The pointillist pastiche – increasingly a caricature – of the 'vol des chocards' is a giveaway; whereas the rest of the *Catalogue* contains effusive portraits of family and musical friends, 'Le Chocard' has the inquisitorial stare of the self-portrait.[18]

The 'cri tragique'

Messiaen's advice to those who found his music dissonant was that they should 'wash out their ears'.[19] The 'cri tragique' chord is an extreme test of this statement, and it has a complex etymology. The left hand is an E^7 chord over a D♯ bass: a familiar sonority from the French piano music tradition, used by Ravel and Fauré amongst others.[20] As Alain Louvier has recognised, it forms a bridge between the *Catalogue*'s beginning and end, as it is also the lower half of the lighthouse's foghorn blast in 'Le Courlis cendré' – a tragic cry of a different kind.[21] The full 'cri tragique' chord is also related to a

---

[17] 23065, p. 19.
[18] The final 'vol acrobatique' of the choughs before the Epode is a skit on the rapid avant-garde piano music of the time, brilliantly played by Loriod in her first recording. Nowhere is Messiaen's opinion of the Darmstadt collective ('Ils sont tous fous', as reported by Christopher Dingle in *The Life of Messiaen*, p. 152) in plainer view. But there is also a hint of *mea culpa*; as Cécile Sauvage predicted, 'To him the audacity, the madness, the mountain', quoted in Philip Weller, '*L'Ame en Bourgeon*: Translation and Afterword', in Christopher Dingle and Nigel Simeone (eds.), *Olivier Messiaen: Music, Art and Literature* (Aldershot: Ashgate, 2007), pp. 191–278 (pp. 250–251). Original source: Cécile Sauvage, *Œuvres complètes* (Paris: La Table Ronde, 2002).
[19] From a statement made in 1939 in defence of *Chants de terre et de ciel*: 'As for those who bellow about my so-called dissonances, I tell them quite simply that I am not dissonant: if they wash out their ears!' (Olivier Messiaen, 'Autour d'une parution', *Le Monde musical*, 30 April 1939; this translation Stephen Broad, *Olivier Messiaen: Journalism 1935–1939* (Farnham: Ashgate, 2012), p. 10).
[20] See Roy Howat, *The Art of French Piano Music* (New Haven and London: Yale University Press, 2009), p. 67 for a fuller account of its origins, principally in Chopin.
[21] Louvier, *Le Concert*, p. 69.

Example 4.5 (a) Igor Stravinsky's 'Augurs of spring' chord; (b) the 'Golaud' chord from Claude Debussy, *Pelléas et Mélisande*

harmonic type that for Messiaen linked the famous 'Augurs of spring' chord from *The Rite of Spring* (which the 'Courlis' foghorn blast imitates) with Debussy: the 'Golaud' chord from *Pelléas et Mélisande*.[22] Messiaen analyses the latter in *Technique de mon langage musical* as superimposed second inversion chords a semitone apart (A major above B♭ minor, see Ex. 4.5b). In 'Le Chocard' this becomes three harmonies a semitone apart: F♯ minor (second inversion) above G major (first inversion with added sixth) above G♯ minor (second inversion).

Although it is the most expressionist moment in the piece, the 'tragic cry' is a polytonal beacon against an atonal backdrop, an appeal for tonality above the chasm. Its E^7 foundation points not only to the foghorn of 'Le Courlis' but also to the emergence of tonality at the beginning of 'Le Loriot', whose first two chords rise sharpwards from it. A piano chord that sounds momentarily like an organ, it is where eternity and transience, tonality and atonality, Messiaen and Loriod, landscape and birdsong meet.[23]

'Les oiseaux sont émus par la beauté du paysage'

In Volume V of the *Traité* Messiaen describes how birds respond in song to the landscape around them, 'moved by the beauty of the colours'.[24] Hence

---

[22] Messiaen, *Traité*, Vol. II, p. 99.
[23] The chord is reminiscent of the vertiginous opening to 'Les Mains de l'abîme' from *Livre d'orgue*.
[24] Messiaen, *Traité*, Vol. V, Part I, p. 18.

the integration of birdsong and landscape that takes place in *Catalogue d'oiseaux*, which is normally expressed harmonically, or in special cases (such as 'L'Alouette lulu') through a melodic device. 'Le Chocard des Alpes' takes the idea a stage further. Harmonically, the birds sing with a voice that clearly reflects their habitat – dissonance meets with dissonance. The choughs' flight patterns are even more closely matched with the twelve-note music of the strophes – appropriately so, their trajectories being influenced by the surrounding topography.

The topography is also detectable in the metrical structure of the bird-calls. Just as the strophes contrast duple metre (the outer sections) with additive rhythms (the 'Clapier Saint-Christophe' antistrophe), so the bird-refrains constantly move in and out of 2/4. The very first set of calls is a case in point: the 'solo' chough begins with an irregular bar, effectively 11/16, followed by a pause (p. 2, line 3). The flock then responds with a 7/16 and then a brace of 2/4 bars. Another pause, and then the 'cri tragique': this, too, is in a slow 2/4. The raven starts with a variant: 4/16, but its most ferocious music is more irregular. At the bottom of the third page, the chough sings trenchant, intriguing harmonies that are resolutely in 4/8.[25] Similar things happen in the second couplet. This time, rests of a full bar are often two crotchets in length. Even the golden eagle combines four-square and irregular grouping, the contours of its ascent hinting at the groupings on the page. Both times its second bar is more regular, containing constant groups of four semiquavers.

'Le Chocard des Alpes' is filled with singular detail like this, and once understood, this dense, difficult piece comes alive under the fingers. In many ways 'Le Chocard' gives the lie to the view that the birds were a means for Messiaen to escape the avant-garde world in which he no longer felt comfortable. On the contrary, it revisits a place that had inspired a movement from *Livre d'orgue*, one of his most radical works: the Meije glacier, which appears on the cover of the *Livre*. Starting the *Catalogue* at one edge of France was matched by a musical extreme; in the context of the *Catalogue* as a whole, 'Le Chocard des Alpes' ensured that the diversity of the French landscape is conveyed by a diversity of musical means.

---

[25] This short passage is untraceable in the *cahier*.

'Le Loriot' (Golden Oriole)

The end of June. Branderaie de Gardépée (Charente), around 5.30 in the morning; Orgeval, around 6 o'clock; Les Maremberts (Loir et Cher) in midday sunlight.

The golden oriole, yellow-gold with black wings, twitters among the oak trees. Its song, flowing, golden, like the laughter of an exotic prince, evokes Africa or Asia, or some unknown world – filled with a rainbow light, the smiles of Leonardo da Vinci. In the woods and gardens, other birds: the rapid, decisive stanza of the wren, the secretive caress of the robin, the brio of the blackbird, the long-short-long metre of the black-throated redstart, the ritual incantations of the song thrush. For a long while, tirelessly, the garden warblers pour forth their sweet virtuosity. The chiffchaff adds its skipping droplets of water. Drowsy recollections of gold, of the rainbow: the sun seemingly draws its light from the golden rays of the oriole's song.[26]

In 'Le Loriot' Messiaen returned to the setting he knew best from the early *cahiers*, the forest in spring and early summer. The contrast with the *Catalogue*'s opening piece, 'Le Chocard des Alpes', could hardly be more abrupt. The Alpine scenery had been depicted in dissonant black and white, without the colours of diatonic or modal harmonies, and with the birds 'seen' in flight, but heard only in fragmented cries rather than songs. Coming immediately after this, the opening to 'Le Loriot' feels like a fresh start. The oriole's solo, announcing the onset of dawn, suggests a complex of colours, reflected in the songs of the dawn chorus, and eventually, at the centre of the piece, merging with the harmonies of the sun as it rises to its zenith at midday.

'Le Loriot' is thus the first of three pieces in the *Catalogue* to measure passing time through the progress of the sun. But unlike the others – 'Le Traquet stapazin' and 'La Rousserolle effarvatte' – this imaginary day is left incomplete, without a sunset. For the listener who follows the *Catalogue* as a whole the result is to create a sequence, with 'Le Loriot' forming a prelude to the glittering light of the Mediterranean habitats that follow in 'Le Merle bleu' and 'Le Traquet stapazin'. The second of these ends with an extended meditation after the sun sets, leaving the music to contemplate the fading colours of twilight. With darkness regained the trajectory of the *Catalogue* then moves logically into the two nocturnes, 'La Chouette hulotte' and 'L'Alouette lulu', which form the third 'book' of Messiaen's vast design.

---

[26] Preface to the score.

Example 4.6 Notation of a golden oriole, 13 June 1952

Various factors point to 'Le Loriot' being one of the first pieces in the *Catalogue* to be composed. The long gestation of the oriole's song can be traced back to the earliest *cahiers* in 1952. But the ambition to compose a piece about the golden oriole may have been in Messiaen's mind even before that, since his first encounter with Yvonne Loriod in 1941, when she joined his class at the Conservatoire.[27] At the time Messiaen used to spell Loriod's name with a 't'; he must have been delighted by the coincidence that this astonishing young pianist shared the name of one of France's most spectacular songbirds. Seen in this light, 'Le Loriot' is as much about the pianist as it is about the bird. The exceptional virtuosity of the piece, especially in the duet for garden warblers that accompanies the sunrise, is a tribute to her pianism. But the music also has the feel of a portrait, capturing Loriod's mercurial manner and conversation: voluble, high-spirited and laced with gossip. If so, Messiaen's meaning is made explicit by a passage of stillness at the heart of the piece, when a 'souvenir' of the oriole's song, heard in slow motion, is accompanied by a sequence borrowed from *Cinq Rechants*, whose surrealist texts had been inspired by the intensity of Messiaen's feelings for Loriod.

Notations of the golden oriole are frequent in Messiaen's earliest *cahiers* and played a central part in the way he developed his thinking about birdsong. The oriole was the first birdsong to acquire in Messiaen's notations a clearly defined musical personality, quite distinct from the more diffuse transcriptions of robins, blackcaps and nightingales. This is true even in the earliest notation of the oriole, made in Delamain's garden in June

---

[27] See Peter Hill (ed.), *The Messiaen Companion* (London: Faber and Faber, 1995), pp. 288–289.

Example 4.7 Notation of a golden oriole, 15 June 1953

1952 (Ex. 4.6).²⁸ Already this foreshadows the oriole's song in 'Le Loriot', with the fanfare-like insistence on the triad of E major (with added C♯) and phrases ending with jagged falling ninths (B to B♭ and G♯ to G♮). A note added later (perhaps when Messiaen was gathering material for *Réveil des oiseaux*) gives a description of the birdsong's colour and character: 'the timbre is flute-like, slurred together, very loud and cheerful, but unhurried – low flute or horn'.²⁹ A notation made a year later at Orgeval was used in *Réveil*, in the exchanges between the oriole and a blackcap (*fauvette à tête noire*) at fig. 41. Here there is a stronger sense of E as the tonic, as well as being the dividing line between the upper pitches, which use the E major triad plus C♯, and lower pitches (C, A♯, G) that are foreign to the key (Ex. 4.7).

The following year – 1954 – was the first season for birdsong research since Messiaen had outlined his plans (in the Black Forest, in October 1953) for a series of solo piano works on birdsong. During the spring and early summer he made repeated visits to Orgeval, often with Loriod for company. On 22 April Messiaen noted a redstart (*rouge-queue*), the earliest notation to be used in the *Catalogue*, found among the dawn songs in 'Le Loriot' (pp. 2–3), and again towards the end of the piece.³⁰ In June he made intensive notes on a dawn chorus, listing the birds in order of appearance, and timing their songs, always with the oriole very much to the fore.³¹ At the same time Messiaen's perception of the oriole's characteristics had become richly imaginative: 'A royal prince, very colourful, full of laughter. The song reflects the sun of Africa as well as the supernatural influence of another world. Whistling, gliding – always gliding – the timbre is strange: golden,

---

[28] 23079, p. 12.
[29] *Ibid.* Messiaen's term 'louré' indicates a type of bowing in which several notes are joined in the same bow stroke but slightly detached from one another and with each given an individual pressure.
[30] 23085, p. 25. In the *cahier* the redstart is identified as a *rouge-queue de murailles*; in the score it becomes a *rouge-queue à front blanc*.
[31] 23002, p. 13.

Example 4.8 Notation of the golden oriole with harmonies, 7 May 1956

laden with harmonics (all the sounds are complex), brilliant, triumphant, luminous and shimmering.'[32]

Signs that the design of the piece was starting to take shape came in May 1956 in what seems to be a preliminary sketch for the 'souvenir' section (score, pp. 9–10). The oriole's song appears in a three-voiced texture marked 'très loin'. The harmonies form a blend of mode and diatonic scale: the lower line uses the notes of the scale of E major, the upper voices the pitches from mode 2 (on E), in each case also including one 'foreign' pitch, C♮ (Ex. 4.8).[33]

The next and most important source comes from September 1956, the Brittany *cahier*. Here work on 'Le Loriot' commences immediately after the final notation made on Messiaen's trip to Ouessant.[34] First comes a phrase of the oriole's song, with the characteristics already noted, the E major triad and ninths falling to A♯ and G. This is harmonised by an upper layer, marked *mf* against *ff* for the melody. After continuing the page with work on 'L'Alouette lulu' Messiaen had just enough room to develop his ideas for 'Le Loriot', squeezing into the margin a pair of dominant seventh chords on F♯ and G♯ – 'to accompany the oriole's song'. The whole-tone step upwards is then mirrored by a step the other way, down from F♯ to E, but this time coming to rest on a pure triad, not a seventh chord. Below this, in the faintest handwriting, Messiaen lists the sources for the birdsong: Orgeval, for the oriole, along with the wren and blackbird, and the oriole again from Gardépée and from Les Maremberts in the Sologne region.

---

[32] 23086, p. 20.
[33] 23049, p. 9.
[34] 23044, p. 17.

Example 4.9 (a) Golden oriole from the Brittany *cahier*; (b) the opening to 'Le Loriot'

In the event, none of these were used for the oriole's song. Instead, Messiaen turned to the Swedish radio recording, very surprisingly in view of the plethora of 'live' notations. The first phrase of the Swedish oriole turns out to be the same as the sketch in the Brittany *cahier*. The upper (right-hand) strand has subtle differences, however. Example 4.9b shows that three of the notes have been modified: C♮ to C♯, G♯ to F♯, and B to B♯. The effect of these changes is that the harmonisation of the oriole's song now consists of broken chords of dominant seventh on F♯ and G♯, replicating the bass harmonies. The result is three strands of colour: E major and mode 2, overlapping in pitch content with the chords of F♯ and G♯, with the exception of the one 'foreign' pitch C♮ (or B♯).

The opening of 'Le Loriot' proceeds with the oriole's song as a series of variations. One aspect of the process involves the exchanging of pitches between the melody and the descant harmonies. So, for example, the upper strand in the third phrase introduces a G♮ acquired from the melody, while in the subsequent phrase the principal line (the oriole's song) introduces a C♮, reflecting the B♯ from the chord of G♯⁷. An added harmonic subtlety (which will bear fruit later in the piece) exploits the fault lines in the melody between the upper pitches (which outline E major) and the lower dissonant notes (A♯ and G♮). The fifth phrase, for example, ends with a sequence of descending ninths: C♯/C♮, B/A♯, G♯/G♮. These leaps tend to divide the melody: the upper notes comprise E major plus C♯; the lower half, pivoting from the tonic E, gives a harmony of E, C, A♯ (or B♭) and G. In combination, these two harmonies – E^6 and C dominant seventh – form a characteristic sound of the *Catalogue*, found elsewhere, for example, in the music of the spectacled warbler in 'Le Traquet stapazin'. Incidentally, the accents on B and G♯, designed to emphasise the triad of E major, were an afterthought, added by Messiaen when preparing the *Catalogue* for publication.

The introductory dominant seventh harmonies, balanced in favour of the low open fifths, are both mysterious and weighty, not so much drifting up the whole tone as posing a question. The response comes after the exposition of the oriole's song, concluded by the reprise of its opening phrase. We hear the chord of $F\sharp^7$, as if to open a new phase of song, but this time (as in the Brittany *cahier*) the step is downwards, to E: a pure triad that serves both to echo the tonality of the oriole's song and to clear the air, so to speak, suggesting a fresh start. In performance Messiaen suggested the moment be marked by a slight emphasis on the third of the chord of E.[35]

We now come to one of the most beguiling passages in the *Catalogue*, as the dawn chorus gets underway. What is immediately striking is how far Messiaen has travelled in the three years since *Réveil*. Instead of lengthy solos we find vignettes, like a portraitist's pencil sketch, pared to the minimum, but each a sharply rendered likeness. Five birdsongs are used, not in a simultaneous medley, as in *Réveil*, but as a mosaic of contrasted fragments. The piano writing is marvellously resourceful and varied. The redstart is given an almost creamy sonority by a shadowing descant of two-note clusters, a tone apart; the wren ('authoritative, bright, rapid and decided') occupies the highest and most brilliant register as it whirrs and trills, the robin ('tender, confiding') gently cascades into the quieter heart of the piano's middle range, while the blackbird Messiaen thought of as 'like a fanfare'.[36] The quintet is completed by the song thrush (*grive musicienne*), 'active, incantatory' (score, p. 3).

The deftness is something new in Messiaen's music; the freshness and naivety have precedents in his earliest works – such as the *Préludes* or *Trois Mélodies*, and later *Poèmes pour Mi* – but a light touch is not a characteristic generally attributed to the composer of *Vingt Regards* or *Turangalîla*. The humour even extends to a glance at Debussy, in the dominant ninth chords that are a sort of slow-motion echo of the robin's cascade (p. 2, b. 3).

---

[35] To Peter Hill.
[36] To Peter Hill.

The music of the dawn chorus sounds spontaneous but proves to be exquisitely calculated. The first birdsong heard, the redstart, strikes up over the sustained harmony of E major reached at the end of the oriole's solo, and reiterates the modal version on E, its call falling away from B♮, one of the pitches common to mode 2 (on E) and the diatonic scale. The lower note of each shadowing cluster lies a minor sixth above the main melody, the same interval then fixing the gap between left and right hands in the calls of the wren, with B used as the anchoring pitch. For the robin the hands start again a sixth apart (A♭ and C). Flowing downwards, *quasi glissando*, on black keys in the right hand and white in the left, the interval naturally contracts, the cascade coming to rest on what sounds like the subdominant (a harmony of A major, though obscured by Messiaen's enharmonic notation), with A and C♯ (reading upwards) enriched, after an appoggiatura 'chirrup', by G♮, C♯ and F♯. If this is A major, the next move is especially sensitive, turning from A♮ to A♯ (the major third in the dominant ninth on F♯), with the ninth itself (G♯) a reharmonisation of the A♭ that began the robin's *glissando* (Ex. 4.10). This Debussy-like caress was one of Messiaen's earliest ideas for the piece (sketched at the back of the Brittany *cahier*), the bass moving in descending whole tones (F♯, E, D, C). The blackbird that follows ('brillant et gai') also plays around this whole-tone scale, reaching upwards (C, D, E, F♯, G♯) and pitting C major against E, recalling the oriole's solo, with E major winning in the final flourishes.

The dawn chorus concludes with a reprise of the robin, again with the move from A to F♯ major. From here (score, p. 3) a series of chordal progressions depicts the rising sun, the sonority stretched as the hands move in contrary motion. The initiating harmony is once again F♯, but now a pure triad. The first step is to E, but then (as with the robin) the line moves in whole tones via B♭, A♭, C and F♯ to close on A minor, the first minor chord of the piece, and one that both breaks the whole-tone pattern and

Example 4.10 Robin from 'Le Loriot'

contradicts the robin's recent A major. In these senses A minor feels like a modulation, or at any rate a surprise. Alternatively, one could regard the phrase as a whole as a reblending of the whole-tone scale (in the bass) with the soprano line tracking the pitches of mode 2, albeit with the mode in a different transposition from the one encountered so far.

Three more phrases follow, guiding the sun towards its midday zenith. The spaces between are filled with a torrent of song, actually only a duet (for a pair of garden warblers), but at Messiaen's indicated tempo the effect is of a *prestissimo* medley. The warblers' song has repeated notes broken up by sharp accents and broken chords, typically made up of fourths and tritones, with the upper notes of the first warbler inclining towards E major. Other than that there is no consistent attempt to reflect the harmonic or melodic relationships that link the oriole, the birds of the dawn chorus and the sunrise. Instead, the development is taken forward in the phrases of the sunrise chorale. The central two phrases cadence on F♯ (minor) and G♯ respectively, echoing the F♯–G♯ at the start of the piece. The first of these moves through whole-tone steps in both hands, the second takes as its starting point A minor, the harmony that had concluded the sunrise's opening phrase. The longest phrase is the last. It opens with the upper voice moving through the alternating semitones and tones of mode 2, harmonised by a sequence of minor and major chords. After the top of the phrase (*ff*) the dynamic fades, and the harmony switches again to A minor, the hinge in an extended plagal cadence on E, with the intervening steps taken by harmonies on G and F.

The E major chord (p. 8) both represents the point of arrival and, in its spacing, concentrates in one chord the way the music of the opening pages has spread gradually across the piano: here upper, lower and middle registers are all present. Midday in Messiaen is a time of stillness, but musically something has to happen, so that the reverberations of E major are filled with the chiffchaff (*pouillot véloce*), its song an obsessive scrutinising of the smallest intervals, semitones around minor and major thirds in E.

The crucial moment in all this is the final approach to E major, made by a semitone (from F major). Up to this point F♮ has been notably absent. It plays no part, for example, in the oriole's solo, despite being part of the version of mode 2 on which the oriole's song is based. Equally, all the harmonic moves have started from F♯: the pair of chords at the opening, the step down to E, the onset of the sunrise. The final phrase of the sunrise is no exception, again beginning with F♯ (this time minor), with F♮ withheld until the phrase's penultimate chord. Here at last is the missing link in the mode 2 scale, as the tonic E is approached, as it should be in the mode,

Example 4.11 Midday

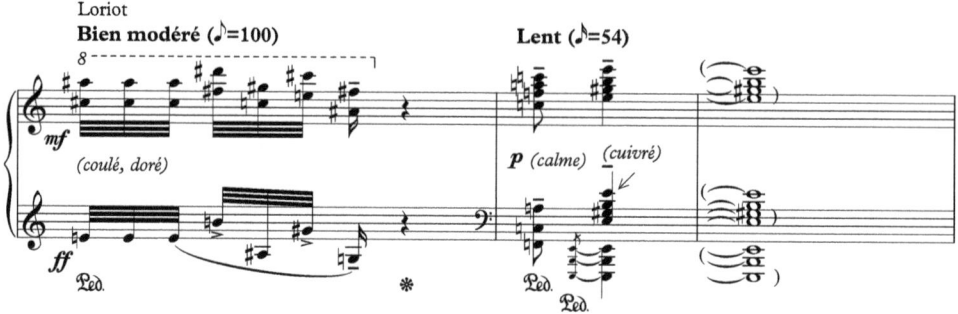

via a semitone. Messiaen now makes his structural and psychological point unmistakable. We hear again the first phrase of the oriole, ending as before with G♮ – dissonant against E major – but this time resolved, as G steps down through F♮ to E, so completing the descending mode 2 scale: B–A♯–G♯–G♮–F–E (Ex. 4.11).

The silence of the forest is shattered by the resumption of the oriole's solo, this time stripped of its introductory harmonies. Its phrases appear in reverse order, the effect oddly disconcerting, like a film run backwards. Two new phrases are inserted: they serve to focus on C♮, cadencing on C where the other phrases all terminate on G. The reason becomes clear in the 'souvenir' that follows, the meditation on the oriole's song, supported by the harmonies borrowed from *Cinq Rechants* – with C♮ acting as a pivot within the undulations of the melody. C also plays a part in the harmony, first as part of a diminished seventh, later as an appoggiatura (a dominant seventh on C) resolving by semitone to B⁷, the 'true' dominant of E major (Ex. 4.12). The dominant sevenths on B complete a progression from whole tone through modal to diatonic. In this way the meditation forms a logical climax to what Paul Griffiths calls the reciprocity between tonal harmony and birdsong, fulfilling the point of the piece as (in the words of Messiaen's preface) 'the sun seemingly draws its light from the golden rays of the oriole's song'.[37] The harmonies in the left hand also make it clear that Messiaen is thinking of Loriod; in *Cinq Rechants* they accompany the words 'Tous les philtres sont bus ce soir' ('All the love potions have been drunk this evening').

---

[37] Paul Griffiths, *Olivier Messiaen and the Music of Time* (London: Faber and Faber, 1985), p. 184. The dominant sevenths arise because the music quoted from *Cinq Rechants* blends two transpositions of the second mode: 2^2 (with E as 'tonic') and 2^3.

Example 4.12 The 'memory of gold and rainbow' in 'Le Loriot'

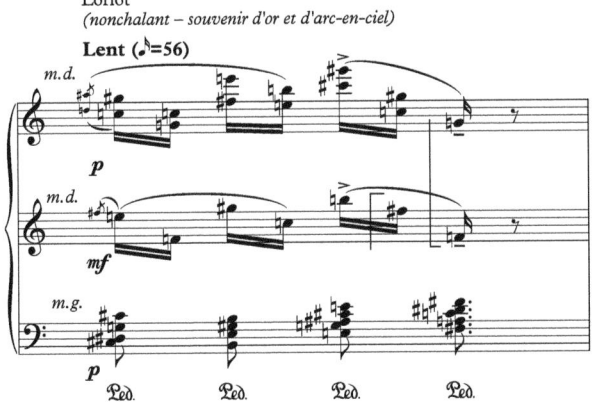

Two interruptions strike a disturbing, anguished note. Both are alien to the carefully constructed harmonic sound-world, the first in mode 3, the second using Messiaen's chords of 'contracted resonance'. Again, one is reminded of Messiaen and Loriod, their predicament as well as the strength of their feelings for one another: 'They were in love – an "impossible love" as Loriod put it – but they were not lovers; they needed frequently to escape from one another, to resist the temptation to defy the moral precepts of their shared faith.'[38]

Then, abruptly, the trance is dispelled. The dawn birds resume – song thrush, redstart, wren – urgently in the present. But on another level the harmonies of the dawn drift, then fragment towards silence, broken by the opening phrase of the oriole, stridently assertive: so that there is no end, only a new beginning, as the cycle of songs resumes.

'La Chouette hulotte' (Tawny Owl)

Plumage flecked with brown and russet; huge facial discs; a look of solemnity, stamped with wisdom, mystery, the supernatural: and even more than its appearance, the voice of this nocturnal bird inspires terror. I have often heard it, in the depths of the night, towards two o'clock in the morning, in the woods of Orgeval, of St-Germain-en-Laye, on the way from Petichet to Cholonge (Isère).

---

[38] PH/NS, pp. 229–230.

> Darkness, fear, a racing heartbeat, mewings and yelpings of the little owl, cries of the long-eared owl; and there – the call of the tawny owl: now cheerless and mournful, now vague and disquieting (with a strange shudder), now shouted in terror like the shriek of a murdered child! ...
>
> Silence. The hooting is more distant, like a bell tolling from another world ...[39]

The earliest sketch for 'La Chouette hulotte' comes from October 1953 in the Black Forest, on the same page of the *cahier* as the list of birds and habitats that was Messiaen's starting-point for the *Catalogue* (See Ex. 2.4, p. 29).[40] The owl's cry is notated as a *glissando*, falling through either a minor third (C to A) or a tritone (C to F♯, A to E♭). Unusually for a notation made at this date, these motifs come with harmonies, all drawn from the modes of limited transposition: parallel chords from mode 3 at first, then a more complex brace of harmonies belonging to mode 7. The cry is then developed – 'always with the same harmonies', Messiaen notes – sometimes with a single grace-note upbeat, sometimes with stuttering repeated notes, and with varied dynamics. The owl's hooting is 'harrowing and mournful'; in other notations Messiaen heard it as 'a terrible moaning' and even 'like a strangled child'.[41]

The notation of the tawny owl made in the Black Forest may well have been Messiaen's direct model for 'La Chouette hulotte'. In the score the tawny owl's first solo (p. 3) begins with repeated cries, each with a different upbeat. These lead to another version, where the passage climaxes on a dense dissonance, followed by further reharmonisations with the left hand descending into the bass; the dynamics (just as they did in the *cahier*) suggest the owl's cry fading into the distance. A difference with the *cahier* is that Messiaen restricts the call to a falling minor third, so that the ear focuses on the variations in the harmonies, reflecting changes in the owl's timbre. The tritones remain but are now located *within* the harmony, so that the upper chord (on C) of the opening cry has a semitone cluster (C/B and C/D♭) plus the tritone (F♯).

The design of 'La Chouette hulotte' is simple: ABA¹B¹ plus coda. The 'A' sections ('la nuit') set the scene, allowing Messiaen to feature the tawny owl as the central character in a nightmare. Darkness is disjointed and menacing, the complementary opposite to 'L'Alouette lulu' (the nocturnal companion-piece in Book 3), where night is a peaceful chorale. There is

---

[39] Preface to the score.
[40] 23001, p. 9.
[41] 23081, p. 10 (27 April 1953); and 23085, p. 42 (23 April 1954).

no doubt that Messiaen had a fascination with the sinister and dark; his mother, Cécile Sauvage, reported the young Olivier as saying that he thought he preferred 'things which make me afraid', and as an adult he retained a penchant for the fairy tales of Perrault (including Red Riding-Hood and Bluebeard), while his leaning was towards *Siegfried* among the *Ring* dramas.[42] Echoes of Wagner's dragon appear in numerous works: the 'statue' theme in *Turangalîla* sounds like a fusion of Fafner and the Commendatore (*Don Giovanni* had been a formative influence during Messiaen's childhood years in Grenoble), and it is doubtful that the contrabassoon that provides the eerie backdrop for 'Lauds' in *Saint François d'Assise* would exist without the example of Wagner.

Messiaen's first idea was to represent night with clusters in the extreme bass of the piano.[43] This was then rejected in favour of revisiting a technique developed in the piano music of 1949, in *Cantéyodjayâ* and in two of the *Quatre études de rythme*, *Mode de valeurs et d'intensités* and *Ile de feu 2*. In 'La Chouette hulotte' Messiaen fashioned a 'mode' that combines three parameters: pitch, duration and dynamic. The first of these comprises a chromatic scale descending from the A above middle C to the A at the bottom of the keyboard. The durations are similarly organised, with the topmost A being a demisemiquaver, increasing by one value with each successive note, so that that lowest A is worth forty-nine demisemiquavers. Dynamics make another 'chromatic scale', as Messiaen termed it, but are limited to seven values, from *fff* to *ppp*, and so form a maverick element that cuts across the smooth progress of the pitches and durations, ensuring that a spread of dynamics is heard in every register. Each octave contains a hairpin: the dynamics descend by step from the top A (*fff*) reaching D♯ (*ppp*), then increase by step, so that the next A is again *fff*. A and D♯ always have these dynamics, wherever they occur on the keyboard; likewise D♮ (together with E♭) is always *pp*, C♯ and F♮ are always *p*, and so on. The result is that each sound is a unique combination of pitch, duration and dynamic (Table 4.2).

Messiaen's innovation in *Cantéyodjayâ* and *Quatre études* had a direct bearing on the integral serialism of the avant garde in the 1950s. The difference with Messiaen is that the order of events is usually freely chosen, not governed by a series, so that the term 'quasi-serial' is used to describe

---

[42] Sauvage, *Œuvres complètes*, p. 244, cited in Christopher Dingle, 'Sacred Machines: Fear, Mystery and Transfiguration in Messiaen's Mechanical Procedures', in Christopher Dingle and Robert Fallon (eds.), *Messiaen Perspectives 2: Techniques, Influence and Reception* (Farnham: Ashgate, 2013), pp. 13–32 (p. 15).

[43] 23044, p. 19.

Table 4.2 Pitches and dynamics in the 'mode' of 'La Chouette hulotte'

A	G♯	G	F♯	F	E	D♯	D	C♯	C	B	B♭	A
fff	*ff*	*f*	*mf*	*p*	*pp*	*ppp*	*pp*	*p*	*mf*	*f*	*ff*	*fff*

pieces such as *Mode de valeurs* and 'la nuit' in 'La Chouette hulotte'. In 'La Chouette' this freedom finds its counterpart in a world of threat and terror, inhabited by hunting owls and their prey. The effect is a tapestry of unpredictable 'points' of sound, congealing into pools of stillness thanks to the longer durations in the bass of the piano, and interrupted by sudden bursts of activity in the treble.

The second 'night' section is more than double the length of the first. This climaxes at the exact centre of the passage (effectively the mid-point of the piece) when the A at the bottom of the piano is sounded for the first time. The moment is prepared by a sort of gravitational pull on the surrounding notes, which are dragged towards the lowest octaves of the piano, intensifying the nocturnal gloom. At the same time the A is preceded in the lowest register by C♮, so echoing the tawny owl.

This climactic moment is indicative of a strong sense of integration throughout the material for 'La Chouette hulotte'. One element in this is the octave, which links pitches by dynamic in the 'night' sections, as well as through doublings of the owl's minor-third motif (p. 3, b. 12). The stratified dynamics that are such a feature of the way Messiaen orchestrates the tawny owl's call are pushed to extremes in the 'night' music, where there is a change of dynamic on every note: the pianist has to articulate each one, even where two notes have to be played simultaneously by the same hand (the combination of *fff* and *ppp* – p. 5, b. 19 – can be solved by dividing the notes between the hands, with the bass B♭ sustained by the third pedal). A further pianistic problem in the 'nuit' passages concerns timing the release of notes: again, a creative approach to fingering and distribution pays dividends, as Ex. 4.13 shows.

The minor-third motif that integrates 'La Chouette hulotte' points to another source. This is the stick-cutting scene (Act I, Scene 2) from Alban Berg's *Wozzeck* – an opera that Messiaen deeply admired, and that figured regularly in his teaching – in which a chilling atmosphere is created by falling minor thirds, with chromatic steps filled in by oboes, piccolos and xylophone (just as they are filled in by Messiaen on p. 4, b. 1 and p. 9, b. 1 of his own score). Moreover, the chord ('étrange, inquiétant') that is repeated *pianissimo* as a sort of shudder at the end of the tawny owl's solos (also

Example 4.13 Possible hand distribution on p. 4 of 'La Chouette hulotte'

p. 4 and p. 9), is a direct borrowing – as Messiaen admitted freely to his students – of the major-minor mixture on a low C with which Berg begins the stick-cutting scene.[44] The same harmony (with the addition of a D♭) occurs in 'L'Alouette lulu', where it represents the mysterious repetitions of the nightingale (the timbre being 'like a harpsichord blended with a gong'), so forming a link between the two nocturnes in Book 3 of the *Catalogue*; and the minor third (stretched out over more than two octaves) between the top and bottom notes is of course a transposition of the owl's cry.

A further reference to *Wozzeck* comes in the repeated low Cs that begin each of the B sections, introducing the owls with a motif that Messiaen labels 'la peur' (see score, pp. 2, 5–6), a clear echo of Berg's 'invention on a rhythm' from *Wozzeck*. The direct source for Messiaen's 'fear' motif is quite different, however, and somewhat bizarre: a notation of a long-eared owl from the Swedish recordings, in which the repeated Cs are Messiaen's way of describing the beating of the owl's wings. Messiaen turned to this page of notations when composing the motifs for the long-eared owl, and opportunistically borrowed the Cs as a metaphor for the racing pulse of the hunted animal, and also, perhaps, of the human spectator – a rare instance in the *Catalogue* of an emotion being directly invoked.

If 'La Chouette hulotte' really was the second piece to be composed, then the coda is where Messiaen signals unambiguously that the *Catalogue* is dramatic as well as descriptive. Usually in the *Catalogue* passages that Messiaen marks as a 'souvenir' (or that one may understand as such) characterise the step into an interior world with quietness. Here the opposite is the case: after the thrumming repetitions of the *Wozzeck* chord, the cry of the tawny owl rears up, grotesquely magnified, then reiterated. Messiaen's

---

[44] According to George Benjamin, cited in Julian Anderson, 'Olivier Messiaen and the Notion of Influence', *Tempo* 247 (January 2009), 2–18 (p. 14).

direction makes it clear that this is a step from reality into the imagination: 'like the cry of a murdered child' ('comme un cri d'enfant assassiné'). The cry fades into the night, each step deeper into the darkness measured by meticulous voicing of the harmonies, finally slowed almost to a standstill. Ideally, pianists should play the two pieces in Book 3 as a pair, 'L'Alouette lulu' following without a break. The music seems to want this: the B♮ in the bass of the final chord of 'La Chouette hulotte' reaches forward through the long pause, resolving (to B♭) in the chorale ('la nuit') that follows.

'L'Alouette calandrelle' (Short-Toed Lark)

(Provence in July. Les Baux, Les Alpilles: arid rocky terrain, with broom and cypress. The Crau, a stony wilderness. Fierce light and heat.)

2 p.m. The piping call of the short-toed lark. Chorus of cicadas, the *staccato* alarm of the kestrel, the dull long-short-long of the quail. A two-part invention for the short-toed lark and the crested lark. Silence. The cicadas, kestrel, quail.
4 p.m. Alone in the heat and solitude of the mid-afternoon the brief phrases of the short-toed lark.
6 p.m. The skylark erupts in song, vehement, jubilant. Again, the short-toed lark … [45]

'L'Alouette calandrelle' is the simplest piece in the *Catalogue* in terms of Messiaen's research. The source is the *cahier* Messiaen took with him to Provence and the Camargue in July 1956, with all the birdsong for the piece coming from just two pages, notated to the east of Arles around the Abbey of Montmajour and in the nearby Désert de la Crau. In the absence of sketches it is impossible to know for certain when the piece was composed: 'L'Alouette calandrelle' is not included in the pieces outlined in the Brittany *cahier*, and this might suggest that it had already been written, during the summer break at Petichet in 1956. However, the sophisticated handling of birdsong and environment makes it unlikely that the piece predates the obviously experimental work at the back of the Brittany cahier, and it seems more probable that it comes from towards the end of the first wave of composition, which resulted in the six pieces performed by Loriod in March 1957.

The *cahier* enables us to follow Messiaen's progress through an afternoon of searing heat and sunlight. He began at Montmajour at 1.30 p.m., devising a transcription of the cicadas. A kestrel flew from its perch in the Abbey's tower, before Messiaen turned his gaze to the distant hills of the Alpilles,

---

[45] Preface to the score.

towards Les Baux. At 4 p.m. he notated a crested lark (*cochevis huppé*). Then an hour later he heard the short-toed lark (*alouette calandrelle*). Messiaen's notation of the lark falls into two sections, each with distinct characteristics. The first corresponds to the lark's three quieter solos (score pp. 1, 2–3 and 7), the remainder used for the livelier central part of the piece. In the lower half of this page of the *cahier* is the monotonous long-short-long rhythm of the quail, Messiaen reminding himself of its kinship with Greek and Hindu rhythms (the Amphimacer and the Dhenkî, both long-short-long); the sound is like 'large droplets of water or clicking tongues'. Finally, at 6 p.m. comes the explosive solo for the skylark that will be used at the end of the piece to interrupt the song of the short-toed lark before it recedes into the enveloping silence of the landscape.

'L'Alouette calandrelle' is therefore the only piece in the *Catalogue* notated entirely from nature without recourse to recordings. Moreover, the songs in the *cahier* are used in their entirety – not selectively, as had been Messiaen's practice since *Oiseaux exotiques* – and are transferred note-for-note into the score: the few changes are made for pianistic reasons or to avoid unwanted octave doublings or unisons. The way Messiaen uses his notations looks back to the era of *Réveil des oiseaux*, except that where *Réveil* and most of the pieces in the *Catalogue* are compiled from multiple sources, with 'L'Alouette calandrelle' Messiaen seems to have had a remarkably clear conception of the piece in mind even as he was making his notations. For the first time there is no clear separation between research and composition, making a foretaste of Messiaen's trip to the Roussillon coastline the following summer, where he both researched and to a large extent composed the music of 'Le Traquet stapazin' and 'Le Merle bleu'.

The shape of the piece may be summarised: Exposition (first solo for the short-toed lark) – Interruption (cicadas, kestrel and quail) – Variation 1 – Variation 2 (duet with crested lark) – Variation 3 – Interruption (extended) – Recapitulation – Skylark – Coda. The opening sounds unusually understated for Messiaen; one would have to go back to the 'Regard du Temps' (from *Vingt Regards*) to find anything comparable. The sense of reticence is beautifully caught, the 'heat and solitude', within which 'the tiny phrase of the short-toed lark alone inhabits the silence'. The harmonies – on G♯ and F♯ – are close to the opening of 'Le Loriot' (Ex. 4.14). In 'Le Loriot', however, the chords have sevenths and seem to float in suspension, resolved by E major at the end of the oriole's first solo; here, as pure triads, they form a 'sigh', an appoggiatura and its resolution (with F♯ as the tonic), the point confirmed by the semitone clash (C♯/B♯) at the top of the first chord. As in 'L'Alouette lulu' the relationship between chords

Example 4.14 Opening of 'L'Alouette calandrelle'

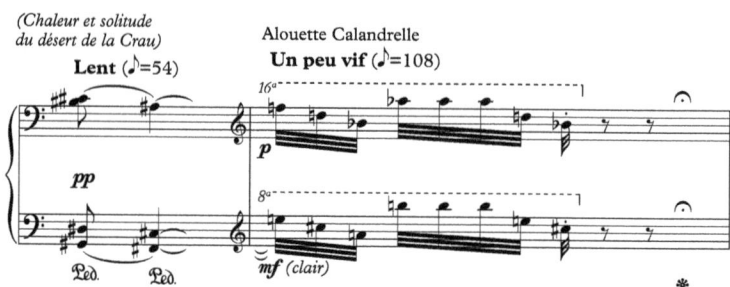

and birdsong is ambiguous – an accompaniment to the birdsong, but at the same time setting the music's slow, hypnotic pace.

The way chords and birdsong interact is very precisely imagined. The lark's song (exactly as it occurs in the *cahier*) is taken by the pianist's left hand, outlining A major with an upper B♮. The A♮ sounds bright ('clair') against F♯ major; but as so often in Messiaen a harmony can be heard in two ways, either as A major, or as a minor harmony with A, C♯ and E ascending in thirds from the bass F♯. In a similar way, the right hand that shadows or 'colours' the birdsong also connects with the underlying harmony, with the A♯ (of the chord of F♯ major) understood as the root of the B♭^{7} harmony in the upper line.

The trance-like repetitions of the cadence recall the darkness in 'L'Alouette lulu', as does the convergence of tempo between background and foreground (♪ = 54/108). Movement is kept to a minimum as the lark stays within its limited repertoire of pitches. Melodically, however, the song starts to develop, and as it does so the five phrases seem to preview the future trajectory of the piece: if the first phrase is the opening statement or 'theme', the three that follow are variants, each with a little more movement and variety than its predecessor; the fifth phrase at last introduces a new pitch (F♯), acting as a tiny coda that, in keeping with the prevailing mood, is terse and laconic.

The music that follows is another metaphor for the arid environment, stark and monolithic: the cicadas and the strident alarm call of the kestrel, followed by the dull cluck of the quail. The contrast is abrupt, but at the same time Messiaen seems intent on building bridges with linear connections. For example, the C♮ at the top of the first chord of the cicadas harks back to the B♯ of the opening harmony (see Ex. 4.14; Messiaen's fingering, with the thumb on the B♯, suggests this should be slightly emphasised). The kestrel continues with a chromatic descent, with its B♮/B♭ combining with the C♮ (from the cicadas) in the harmony Messiaen then devises for the quail.

After this interruption the line of development that began in the lark's exposition (p. 1) resumes in the first of three sections, which form a continuity running through the piece rather like a set of variations. At the start of the first variation (score, p. 2) the lark picks up the F♯ introduced in the coda to its first solo, adding to this a G♯ (a reference, perhaps, to the G♯/F♯ of the opening chords). Change also comes in the surrounding texture, where Messiaen may be imagining (though he doesn't say so) the wind in the desert, whispering or in sudden gusts ('le vent souffle', he writes in the *cahier*). The harmonies come from Messiaen's paintbox of colour chords: 'contracted resonance' and 'turning chords', together with sturdier chromatic sequences (one of which will be reused to stand for the terraced vineyards in 'Le Traquet stapazin'). The most developed of these interjections, in a significant move, reconnects firmly with F♯ major, answered at the end of the variation by the four chords of Messiaen's 'transposed inversions' ('renversements transposées') sequence, on the dominant (C♯) – in effect like an imperfect cadence, as if poised for further action.[46]

The short-toed lark's second variation takes the form of a duet with the crested lark (*cochevis huppé*). The new birdsong brings an increase in tempo (♪ = 132) and a new style, jaunty compared with the short-toed lark, but well short of the exuberance of the skylark, which at the end of the piece will trump the gradual increase in energy of the variations; compared to the skylark (as Messiaen notes in the *cahier*) the crested lark is 'lighter, its joy gentler, and its melody more monotonous'.

The bass harmonies, together with the tonic F♯, now drop out. Instead, the crested lark takes over the original repertoire of pitches (A, C♯, E and B), with the short-toed lark moving to the second half of its long solo from the *cahier* (Ex. 4.15). For the first time Messiaen has to make changes from the notations in the *cahier* in order to avoid doublings, with the effect of further enriching the soloist's repertoire of pitches, as Messiaen alters As to B♭s, Bs to C♮s. Another adjustment is needed when the crested lark runs

---

[46] The 'turning chords' are first heard in *Visions de l'Amen* (1943) and have been identified by Julian Anderson ('The Notion of Influence', p. 3) as originating in Jolivet's *Cinq danses rituelles* (1939). Messiaen's 'contracted resonance' progressions feature compressed sonorities where resultant tones are transposed up into the range of the chords that generate them. His 'transposed inversion' progression features four harmonies that are transpositions of each other with notes rearranged over a common bass note (hence the name). They are described in full in the *Traité*, Vol. VII, and have a strong relationship with the 'chords on the dominant' outlined in the preface to *La Nativité*. Christopher Dingle, *Messiaen's Final Works* (Farnham: Ashgate, 2013) also has a useful summary, pp. 15–19.

Example 4.15 Notations for 'L'Alouette calandrelle', including the short-toed lark, skylark and quail (facsimile)

out of material: it simply goes back to the beginning of its song, Messiaen underlining the suggestion of recapitulation by making the short-toed lark do the same, though for one phrase only. The two birdsongs are kept distinct in terms of register and pitch content, but similarities of motif create a dialogue, the high repeated Bs of the crested lark echoed by repeated G♯s (short-toed lark), the G♯ neatly filling the gap in the ascending chain of thirds observed earlier – A, C♯, E, (G♯), B.

The enrichment of the pitch repertoire continues in the third variation, the lark's climactic solo. The shift is towards D, with descending thirds, making seventh or ninth chords in either hand. The flickering interjections are a return to the first variation, but the resonant bass notes are new, stepping finally to A at the bottom of the piano: this is perhaps the moment when the A major tonality of the lark asserts its independence from the F♯ major of its environment.

At this point the music changes course abruptly, interrupting again the line of development, with its incremental release of energy from one variation to the next, as Messiaen returns to the music of the cicadas, kestrel and quail, now considerably extended ('developed' would be the wrong word, since they remain essentially static). Strategically, this has the effect of absorbing the energy built up during the variations, so that the song of the short-toed lark can be brought back in its original reticent form. Space and stillness return with the quail, its rhythm repeated with quiet insistence and surrounded by silences.

In Messiaen's design we have now reached the recapitulation. The lark resumes, in the manner of its opening solo, extended this time to seven phrases, and drawing on the pitches acquired during the middle part of the piece. G♯ and F♯, for example, are present, while the repeated A♭s in the upper voice remind us of the repeated G♯s in the duet with the crested lark. The penultimate phrase (p. 7, line 4) contains pitches from the climactic variation (p. 5), the dip to E♭ and C♮ resolving with the E♮ and C♯ of the final phrase of this passage.

The music has come full circle, and the pianist can deceive us into thinking this is the end of the piece by not anticipating the ambush that follows. With the sudden eruption of the skylark ('jubilation véhémente'), the pianist has to go from absolute stillness to uninhibited (though disciplined) virtuosity and back again, almost as if nothing had happened.

The purpose of the skylark's solo within Messiaen's structure is intriguing. In one sense it exists because it was there: as the *cahier* shows, the skylark really did rocket heavenwards in a torrent of song at the end of a long hot afternoon. By now, however, Messiaen was long past the stage of

Example 4.16 Skylark

including a birdsong purely for ornithological reasons. Musically, the skylark (*alouette des champs*) shares characteristics with the other two larks, a further variation added to theirs, confirmed by the repeated leaps to the high B (now pinging right at the top of the keyboard), underpinned by A major and with pitch content based on the third variation (the climactic solo of the short-toed lark), including the chains of thirds, now rising, which have been anticipated in the penultimate phrase for the short-toed lark in the solo just heard. In another sense the ruthless, mechanical virtuosity of the skylark links it with the cicadas and kestrel (Ex. 4.16).

Above all, the whirr of unrestrained energy has a psychological impact, setting in relief the previously carefully measured release of momentum, and thereby underlining the point of the piece. Remarkably, Messiaen's structure works not only as music but also as his imaginative response to the spirit of the place, the heat-drugged landscape irrigated by the trickle of vitality that is the lark's song. Ceaselessly inventive, the only example of a phrase being repeated comes at the very end, in the coda, the final bar resuming the opening bar of the piece. Messiaen's preface describes this as a 'souvenir', a hint of nostalgia perhaps; in performance he permitted a slight easing of tempo and dynamic (not indicated in the score) to suggest the lark fading into the distance.

'Le Courlis cendré' (Curlew)

The island of Ouessant, off the west coast of Brittany. On the headland of Pern one can see a large bird with streaked plumage and russet markings, a grey-brown bird standing upright, with a long beak curved like a sickle or yataghan: the curlew![47]

---

[47] A yataghan is a mid-length Ottoman sabre.

This is its song: sad, slow tremolos, chromatic ascents, wild trills, and a mournful repeated *glissando* that expresses all the desolation of the seashore. On the headland of Feunten-Velen, lashed by the noise of the waves, the cries of water birds: the cruel call of the black-backed gull, the rhythmic horn calls of the herring gull, the fluted melody of the redshank, the repeated notes of the turnstone, the piping trills of the oystercatcher, and others besides: the little ringed plover, the common gull, the guillemot, the little tern and the sandwich tern. The water extends as far as the eye can see. Little by little, fog and darkness spread over the sea. All is dark and dreadful. From amidst the jagged rocks the lighthouse of Créac'h sounds a dismal boom: it is the alarm! Again, a number of birdcalls, and the lament of the curlew, repeated as it flies far away ... Cold, black night, the splash of surf ...[48]

Although it is the final piece in the *Catalogue*, 'Le Courlis cendré' belongs to the first group to be composed, completed by the end of February 1957. In this earlier version of the *Catalogue*, performed by Loriod in March of that year, 'Courlis' ended Messiaen's journey from the Alpine peaks of the south-east to the island of Ouessant, the most westerly point of Brittany and the end of France (Finistère).

Two years later, the ordering in the expanded and finished *Catalogue* enriched the symmetries between the work's end and its beginning. By then three more sea pictures had been added, the sea variously turbulent ('Le Merle bleu'), a mirror to light and colour ('Le Traquet stapazin'), or sparkling (in the 'powdering' of the waves in 'Le Traquet rieur'). 'Le Traquet rieur', chosen as the work's penultimate piece, sees Messiaen at his most subjective. More than any other piece in the *Catalogue*, the music evokes the composer's feelings about the scene in front of him rather than its reality: whatever the score may say, the 'joy of the blue sea' is clearly Messiaen's joy. In its very personal approach 'Le Traquet rieur' makes a close counterpart to the love song in 'Le Loriot', now placed second in the *Catalogue*. In the first and final pieces, however, the opposite approach is taken: nature is seen at its most grim and unforgiving, as Messiaen finds an impersonal way to describe the environment of mountains or sea, in some of the most powerful and impressive examples of twelve-note writing in the *Catalogue*. In 'Le Chocard' the mountains are an implacable presence; in 'Courlis' the sea is a more active threat, coiling and uncoiling, like the dragons Messiaen imagined in the silhouetted shapes of the rocks bordering the Atlantic. Two-thirds of the way through the piece the wildness of the waves – a furious, anarchic force – becomes disciplined into serial permutations, used for

[48] Preface to the score.

the water's ebb and flow, and – as the permutations stack into chords – for the descent of darkness and fog.

Before this, the central part of the piece (pp. 5–13) is a tumult of piercing calls and cries, a mosaic of hard-edged fragments very much of the type used earlier by Messiaen in *Cantéjodjayâ*. The technique here is to assign the birdcalls different roles. Some are static; others, like the herring gull and oystercatcher, develop, while a quiet perspective comes from the rather wistful sighing of the redshank, which acts as a refrain. An opening trio (p. 5) sets the tone, with the mercurial black-headed gull flanked by the insistent cries of the sandwich tern and the repeated swirls of the little ringed plover, beating against a high B, as do many of the birdcalls.

Another recurring pitch reference is at the other end of the piano, the bass F♯ that initiates the music of the waves. The shorter appearances of the waves act as urgent punctuations, a constant reminder of the sea's presence. But twice they erupt, rearing up into mountainous breakers, the pianistic pattern alternating black and white keys, as Messiaen would do later when he composed 'Le Merle bleu'. Incidentally, Messiaen wanted these cadenzas played 'very, very quickly'.[49] The pianist can gain extra power by reorganising Messiaen's fingering so that that topmost cluster is taken by the left hand, even (in the second cadenza) using the fist.

The first of these cadenzas divides the central medley into two. The first half settles on developments of the herring gull, ending with a flourish (p. 7, b. 3) that acts as an upbeat to the first cadenza. A new energy comes in the second half, as the music drives towards a crisis (culminating in the second cadenza of the waves), gaining momentum (in the music of the oystercatcher) from repeated crescendos and from the repetitions, growing in number, of a thrummed chord (p. 12, bb. 6, 8 and 10).

The bird conspicuous by its absence from the central medley is the curlew itself. Messiaen's decision to make the soloist a lone voice seems to come from his earliest notation of the curlew, made (probably in 1954) from Ludwig Koch's *More Songs of Wild Birds*: the notation comes with a comment that perfectly foreshadows the spirit of 'Courlis' – the curlew's cry 'expressing the loneliness and desolation of darkness descending over the sea'.[50]

The notation from Ludwig Koch is in three sections. The first has a timbre somewhere between a 'musical barking' and a 'squeaking pulley', with oscillations that are just recognisable as the forerunner of the opening phrases

---

[49] To Peter Hill.
[50] 23037, pp. 18–19.

Example 4.17 Notation of a curlew from *More Songs of Wild Birds* (Ludwig Koch)

of 'Courlis'. Next comes the curlew's insistent cry, sliding upwards: the pitches are close to the finished score, though as yet without the parallel harmonisation in the left hand. Lastly comes the 'wild nuptial song', with hesitant upbeats that coalesce and sweep forward into a tremolo, marked in the score 'savage and passionate' (Ex. 4.17). The most significant difference between *cahier* and score is the change in order, with the nuptial song placed second, so that the curlew's solo ends with its cry swelling and fading, followed by a long silence that separates it from the medley of sea and seabirds that follows.

The upward chromatic shifts in the tremolo of the nuptial song also characterise the wheedling oscillations of the opening figure (marked 'flûté, triste') as it curls chromatically inwards. The next example shows the genesis of this opening phrase. After the notation from *More Songs of Wild Birds* came a harmonised version of the curlew made in Brittany (see Ex. 4.18a).[51] A further preparatory step seems to have come from Messiaen's idea for harmonising the song of the redshank (*chevalier gambette*),[52] found among the earliest notations he made on Ouessant (see Ex. 4.18b): the combination of an E major triad with C♮ is a consistent feature of the redshank that found its way into the upper strand of the curlew's song (see Ex. 4.18c). This becomes a defining sound that drifts through the piece, hauntingly reiterated at the start, and carried forward during the central section in the redshank's refrains. Its final appearance (see Ex. 4.18d) is especially exquisite: coloured by quieter upper harmonies, and at a significantly slower tempo than before, this suggests a 'souvenir', giving a sense of unreality to the final calls of the curlew that follow.

The minor triads in the bass that accompany the curlew's song can be traced to Messiaen's earliest sketch for 'Courlis', where he imagined ending with resounding chords of C minor;[53] an echo of this remains at the beginning of the piece, where minor triads accompany the curlew's song. This diatonic harmony is strikingly at odds with the harmonies of the remainder of the piece, and another way in which Messiaen kept the curlew's solo separate. At the same time the most important pitches in the opening solo combine to outline the chromatic space that the piece will inhabit. Nine notes of the chromatic scale come from the three minor triads used for the three phases of the curlew's song – E♭ minor, E minor and D minor – while the three remaining are prominent in the curlew's song: C♯ anchors the tremolo in the 'wild, nuptial song' (p. 2, b. 7), while C and G♯ start the upwardly sliding motifs (p. 4).

More than anything, the gaunt eloquence of the curlew's song seems to encapsulate the spirit of the place, the intensity of the musical image matching the words Messiaen used in the *cahier* to convey his impressions of the

---

[51] 23044, p. 6.
[52] *Ibid.*, p. 8.
[53] *Ibid.*, p. 19.

Example 4.18 (a) The curlew harmonised; (b) the redshank; (c) the opening of the curlew's song in the score; (d) the redshank in the score

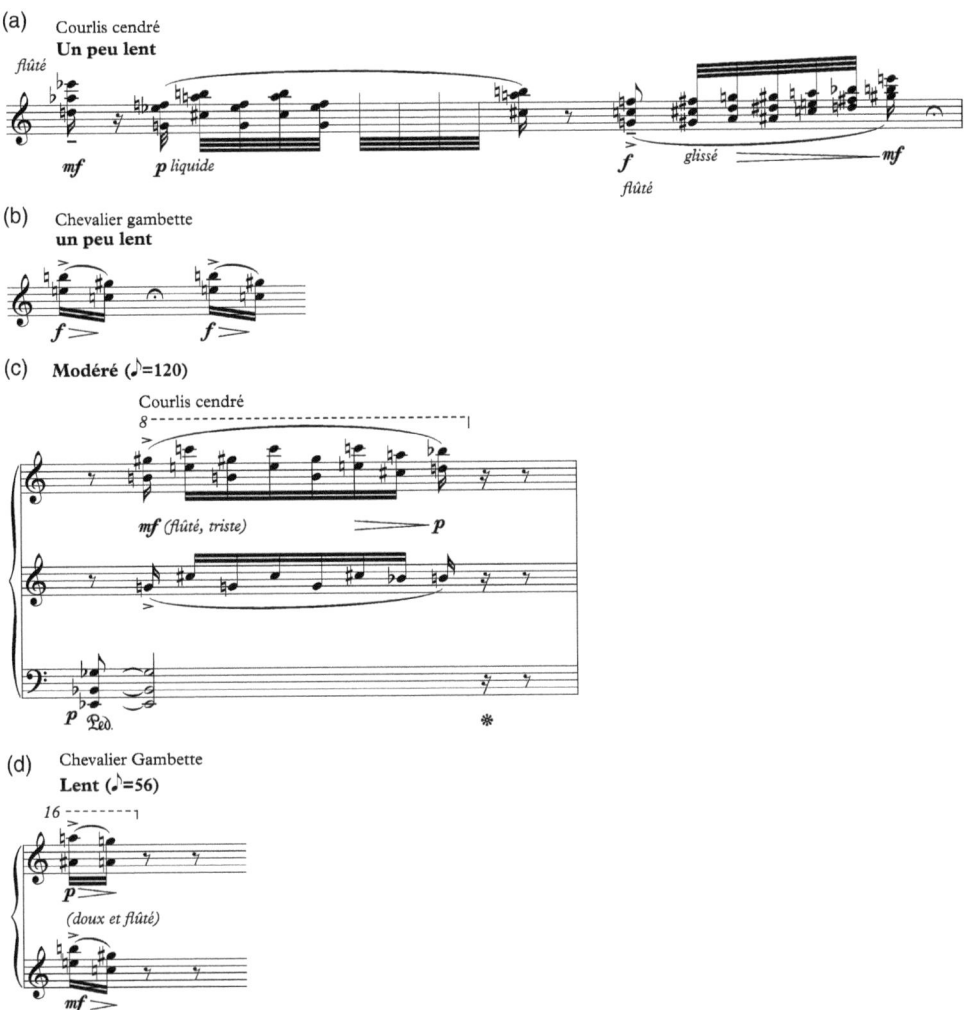

sea, sky and shoreline. In the distance was the line of the horizon ('silvery white, shining, luminous, separating sea from sky'), in the foreground rocks piled into fantastic forms:

Chaos of overhanging rocks … Terrible! The rocks are grey, green, black, brown ochre, jagged … like the teeth of a lion, dragons' tongues, the snouts of hippopotamus, the jaws of crocodiles … Ovoid pebbles, white, pale blue, pink. The smaller rocks are entirely covered with brown algae, like hair – the hair has the fetid, salty smell of the sea gods … Rocks like decayed molars, grotesquely shattered … a veritable cathedral of columns – phantoms or iguanodons, upright with index finger raised. The sea is Prussian blue or purple – the waves leap furiously around the rocks, which are surrounded by water, leaving great wakes of white foam, the waves like horses with white manes! Opposition of the active sea, constantly at work, agitated, furious, and the still, motionless, cold fury of the rocks …[54]

From the headland tongues of stone stretch out into the sea like crocodiles … a complete architecture: pointed columns like organ pipes, or overlapping steps … others cut into shapes: the head of an eagle or dog, or a Druidic deity …'[55]

[6 p.m.] Now it is grey and cold. The sea is grey, black in the foreground, blue-grey at the horizon … cold and sad. A large tongue of rocks, streaked yellow and black, advances into the black water like an enormous prehistoric monster, a diplodocus with head outstretched … Others are like a castle from the planet Saturn, or the spread wings of an eagle, or the Winged Victory of Samothrace![56]

The consequence of keeping the curlew apart from the rest of the piece is the strangest design in the *Catalogue*, with the soloist heard in a continuous solo at the opening (pp. 1–4), and then only once more, in a flashback just before the end of the piece. In each section Messiaen's strategy is to concentrate and simplify ideas. In the opening pages the music of the curlew is reduced to a single motif, the repeated ascending *glissandi*; in the central section the scattered cries of the seabirds are ultimately absorbed into the exasperated cadenzas of the waves. Disorder then gives way to the controlled unfolding of twelve-note permutations, the eddying of the water, gliding and slithering under the pianist's fingers, the hands moving in opposite directions, with occasional movement in similar motion, rising and falling to suggest perhaps waves in slow motion. Finally, the linear movement of the permutations congeals into huge chords, representing the descent of fog and darkness. Ultimately this vast curve of development is concentrated into a huge sonority, an eleven-note chord followed by the A at the bottom of the piano.

This chord, representing the boom of the lighthouse siren, is the climax of the piece, arguably of the whole *Catalogue*. The coda is beautifully imagined. The chord becomes itself a refrain, interleaved with fragments of earlier birdcalls, with the redshank reduced to an echo (described earlier),

---

[54] Ibid., p. 5.
[55] Ibid., p. 1.
[56] Ibid., p. 6. The Winged Victory of Samothrace, depicting the Greek goddess Nike, is in the Louvre.

connecting back to the opening sonority of the piece and at the same time creating a moment of stillness before the curlew's final solo. This is another simplification, just the final element of its song, the upward *glissando*, which fades into the night – 'cour--lis, cour--lis', as Messiaen noted in his *cahier*. The last word is given to the sea, drawing on the final notation made on the beach at Ouessant, a great crashing wave, now reduced to fragments, the muted splash of the surf.

The first pieces composed for the *Catalogue* were complete by the end of February 1957, Messiaen noting in his diary that Loriod had been given copies of six of the pieces:[57] these were the five for which Messiaen had sketched his first thoughts in the back pages of the Brittany *cahier*, together with 'L'Alouette calandrelle'. The much longer 'La Rousserolle effarvatte', eventually the centrepiece of the *Catalogue*, must have been finished shortly afterwards because it is included in the premiere of 'extracts from the *Catalogue d'oiseaux*' given by Loriod on 30 March.

There must have been doubt about whether she would manage to learn 'La Rousserolle effarvatte' in time, because in his diary Messiaen considered two possible orders. The one without 'La Rousserolle effarvatte' shows him trying out symmetries and oppositions: it begins and ends with the two larks, 'L'Alouette calandrelle' and 'L'Alouette lulu', representing sunlight and darkness, while the middle two pieces make a similar contrast of day and night ('Le Loriot' and 'La Chouette hulotte'). The other ordering (printed in the programme for the concert) has all seven pieces, strangely with 'Le Loriot' as the centrepiece. Otherwise the layout anticipates the completed work by beginning and ending with 'Le Chocard des Alpes' and 'Le Courlis cendré', placing 'L'Alouette lulu' and 'La Chouette hulotte' side by side (though the wrong way round) and 'L'Alouette calandrelle' in the second half, after 'La Rousserolle effarvatte'. In the event Loriod omitted 'La Rousserolle effarvatte', which she had been unable to memorise in time. Messiaen subsequently revised the piece, which was eventually finished later in the year, on 4 October.[58] The revisions and additions must have been considerable because at the time of the concert in March Messiaen had timed 'La Rousserolle effarvatte' at fourteen minutes; even allowing for underestimate, it seems that the piece grew by at least a third.[59]

---

[57] OMR, p. 94.
[58] *Ibid.*, p. 101.
[59] *Ibid.*, p. 105.

Loriod's performance was warmly praised by Suzanne Demarquez, writing in the *Guide du concert* on 12 April 1957, who noted the change that had come over Messiaen's music under the influence of birdsong:

> Messiaen, no doubt freed long ago from principles and theories, seems to me to have followed the advice of Debussy, who found it more worthwhile to admire a sunset than to go to a concert. He has travelled by day and night from the Alps of the Dauphiné to the island of Ouessant, by way of the Crau. He has listened to numerous birds of which we know nothing … and he has translated their songs for us thanks to his knowledge of the piano, from which he draws hitherto unimagined sonorities, thanks also to Yvonne Loriod, that fairy with the magic fingers.[60]

'La Rousserolle effarvatte' (Reed Warbler)

The whole piece is a great arc lasting twenty-seven hours, from midnight until three in the morning, the events of the afternoon and night repeating in reverse order the events of night and morning. The piece is dedicated to the reed warbler, and more generally to the glory of the birds of the reeds, lakes and marshes as well as neighbouring birds in the woods and fields.

Midnight: music of the lakes, followed by a chorus of frogs, the booming notes of the bittern.

3 a.m. A long solo for the reed warbler, concealed among the reeds, rasping in timbre (like a xylophone, a squeaking cork, pizzicati on strings, a harp *glissando*), with something of that savage obsessiveness found only in reed birds. Cymbals, gongs and trombones – interspersed with a confusion of sounds from the marsh – mark the solemnity of night. Silence.

6 a.m. Sunrise: pink, orange, mauve over the lake of the waterlilies. A blackbird duets joyfully with a red-backed shrike. A chuckling solo for the redstart. The chords of sunrise intensify.

8 a.m. The yellow irises. A medley of incisive calls: the raucous pheasant, the reed bunting, weird laughter of the green woodpecker, the whistling *glissando* of the starling, the great tit, nervous fluttering of the white wagtail (exquisite in its garb of half-mourning).

Midday: the interminable insect trills of the grasshopper warbler.

5 p.m. Return of the reed warbler, alternating with the powerful tremolos of the sedge warbler; the harsh, obstinate call of the great reed warbler; the singing harmonies of the purple foxgloves and the waterlilies. The dry, flabby croak of a frog.

---

[60] Suzanne Demarquez, 'Premières auditions … Domaine musical (Gaveau 30.3)', *Guide du concert* 151 (12 April 1957), 893.

> A black-headed gull gives chase. A coot – black, its forehead marked with white – clucks sharply (a sound like stones dashed together), then tootles its little trumpet. A long, syncopated duet for two reed warblers.
> 6 p.m. The yellow irises, and again the high trills of the grasshopper warbler. The skylark rockets heavenwards in jubilation, answered by the frogs in the lake. A water rail, unseen, screams like a strangled pig – falling, fading ... silence.
> 9 p.m. Sunset: red-orange, violet over the lake of the irises. The bittern booms, a solemn, awesome blast. The blood-coloured disc is mirrored in the surface of the lake: the sun merges with its reflection as it sinks into the water. The sky is a deep violet ...
> Midnight: the darkness is profound, like the resonance of a tam-tam. The nightingale strikes up, its phrases by turn biting, mysterious. The confused sounds of the marsh ... a frog stirs ... the cymbals, gongs, trombones.
> 3 a.m. Another scherzo for the reed warbler. Chorus of frogs. The mysterious, brittle music of the ponds fades into the mist. The bittern booms ...[61]

Messiaen composed with renewed impetus after the 1957 premiere, and a further boost was the acquisition of a Gaveau piano at Petichet – an instrument 'assez bon', though with a sound that could hardly be contained within his small, uncarpeted room.[62] The time that Messiaen didn't spend composing, swimming in the lake or planning his *Traité* that summer he could be heard playing works such as *Gaspard de la nuit* for the birds of the Lac du Laffrey. According to Loriod's diary, the sound of the new piano immediately brought about some inspired writing for the instrument.

'La Rousserolle effarvatte' could be considered Messiaen's finest hymn to the sounds and rhythms of nature. Its tonal variety – from the pounding 'solemnité de la nuit' and the xylophonic 'music of the ponds' to the pungent harmonies portraying the rising and setting sun – allied with its ingenious design across a thirty-minute span are justification enough for this view. The variety is heard in microcosm in the 'grande diversité d'attaques' of the reed warbler's solos, and in her 1959 recording of the *Catalogue* Loriod capitalises on this, imbuing 'La Rousserolle' with the thrill of the avant garde; it could be that, in Messiaen's 1956 plan for a serially organised *Catalogue*, this piece was linked to the 'série d'attaques' – although the eventual compositional basis was quite different, serial writing only being present in the first two and last two pages. Its bold spirit, nevertheless, fired Boulez's enthusiasm at the piece's premiere, in a Domaine musical concert on 25 January 1958.[63] In the opening 'music of

---

[61] Preface to the score.
[62] The piano was the same make that had featured in the Salle Gaveau concert.
[63] OMR, pp. 109–110 reports that Boulez was 'enchanted', and that Messiaen was particularly encouraged by the enthusiasm of Walter Goehr, who conducted *Turangalîla* 'with much passion'.

the ponds', in particular, Messiaen adopts the vein described appreciatively by Boulez in 'The Utopian Years': 'There are without doubt two different desires in Messiaen himself. He wants discipline, a discipline that transcends his own personality ... to decipher in his own way the secrets of the universe ... but at the same time he wishes to express himself with greater immediacy.'[64]

Messiaen completed the revised version of 'La Rousserolle' on 4 October 1957 and gave it straight to Loriod, who learnt it during a particularly busy period that included recordings of works by Couperin, Debussy (the *Etudes*) and Schumann (an idiosyncratic version of the *Novelettes*), plus Jolivet and Boulez in recital. The variety of touch required for 'La Rousserolle' must have nicely complemented this diverse repertoire.

The Two Reed Warblers

The revised version surveys twenty-seven hours of passing time, from midnight to 3 a.m. One consequence is that (in contrast to a more obvious twenty-four-hour span) the reed warbler is heard twice singing at 3 a.m. The effect is to create an arch form; outside the solos sit the 'music of the ponds', a bittern with its repetitive call and a chorus of frogs. Between them further symmetries exist, most notably the chorale-like sunrise and sunset passages. The central piece of the *Catalogue* therefore condenses the symmetrical structure of the whole cycle. Viewed this way the virtuoso reed warbler duets at the heart of the piece become the focal point of the entire work.

Messiaen's programme notes for the March 1957 concert reveal the outline of the first version of 'La Rousserolle'; his moment-by-moment summaries allow us a clear view of how the piece would later need to evolve:[65]

The marshes, the ponds, the reeds of the Sologne. Midnight: the chorus of frogs. 3 o'clock in the morning: the reed warbler, hidden in the reeds, emits a long solo with a scratchy timbre and wild rhythm, a mixture of xylophone and pizzicato. The night is solemn, like the resonance of a tam-tam. 6 o'clock in the morning: sunrise over the pond of waterlillies. The birds of the woods and fields are also there: blackbird, red-backed shrike, redstart, starling, green woodpecker, great tit. 5 o'clock in the afternoon: other birds of the reeds: sedge warbler, great reed warbler. 6 o'clock in

---

[64] Pierre Boulez, 'The Utopian Years', in *Orientations: Collected Writings*, ed. Jean-Jacques Nattiez, trans. Martin Cooper (London: Faber and Faber, 1986), pp. 411–417 (p. 415).

[65] There is no recording of the 1957 premiere, though there was of the first half of the programme: Berio's *Serenata I* and Boulez's *Sonatine* were issued on Vega.

Table 4.3 The two versions of 'La Rousserolle effarvatte'

First version	Revised version
Midnight: music of the ponds, frogs	**Midnight:** music of the ponds, frogs and bittern
3 a.m. Reed warbler solo, night	**3 a.m.** Reed warbler solo, night
6 a.m. Sunrise, birds of woods and fields	**6 a.m.** Sunrise, birds of woods and fields
	8 a.m. Yellow irises, medley of pheasant, green woodpecker and starling
	Midday: grasshopper warbler
5 p.m. Other warblers	**5 p.m.** Other warblers, gull, coot, purple foxgloves and waterlilies, reed warbler duets interspersed with sedge warbler
6 p.m. Coot, skylark, water rail	**6 p.m.** Yellow irises, grasshopper warbler, skylark, frogs, coot, water rail
9 p.m. Sunset	**9 p.m.** Sunset with bittern, nightingale and 'souvenir'
Midnight: nightingale, frogs	**Midnight:** night, nightingale, 'souvenir', frogs
3 a.m. Reed warbler solo, music of ponds, bittern	**3 a.m.** Reed warbler solo, frogs, music of the ponds, bittern

the evening: the coot seems to blow a small, pointed trumpet; a skylark rejoices in the clear air; the water rail gives out the cries of a pig having its throat cut, a howling that gradually subsides. 9 o'clock in the evening: sunset, red, orange, violet, over the pond of irises. Midnight: the nightingale begins its strophes. A frog rustles some bones. 3 o'clock in the morning: new solo of the reed warbler. Music of the ponds and boom of the bittern…

Both versions have a symmetrical structure, a reflection of the diurnal cycle (Table 4.3).

The preface for the revised version contains small mistakes as a result of retaining text from the earlier version. The coot blows its 'small, pointed trumpet' twice, in the 5 p.m. and 6 p.m. sections in the later version, but Messiaen only tells us about its second appearance in the text; he normally highlights events when they first occur. Similarly, the nightingale is a significant presence during the long sunset passage, but the preface matches the earlier programme note in stating that it begins at midnight.

Messiaen may well have felt that the reed warbler was under-represented in the first version. The missing ingredients are its short contributions to the 5 p.m. sequence and the three central duets; in addition there is no mention in the first version of the grasshopper warbler trills at midday and 6 p.m., and perhaps most importantly the various passages devoted to flowers.

Example 4.19 (a) *Turangalîla* material in *La Transfiguration de Notre-Seigneur Jésus-Christ*; (b) opening of *La Fauvette des jardins*

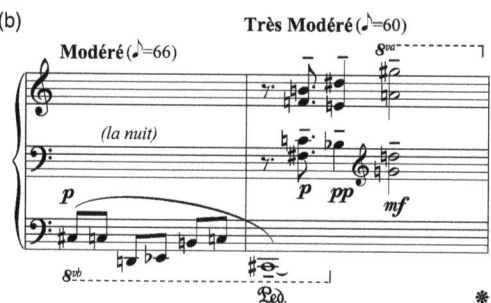

For the flower music Messiaen used melodies borrowed from the 'Tristan' trilogy (see Ex. 2.2, p. 20), and the extra expressive dimension they provide raises 'La Rousserolle' to the level of a masterpiece. The yellow irises have particular resonance, as Messiaen would later use their melodies in *La Transfiguration* (the cello solo and female voices singing 'Candor est lucis aeternae' ('Wisdom is a reflection of eternal light') in 'Quam dilecta Tabernacula Tua' ('How lovely are your tabernacles')), and the music of the night that opens *La Fauvette des jardins* (Ex. 4.19). Like many of Messiaen's devices, their expressive potential proved to be diverse.

Sources

Messiaen first seems to have encountered the song of the reed warbler during his studies of the 'Disques Angleterre'; it was the first bird on 'disc B', alongside the sedge warbler – anticipating the conjunction of their songs in the 5 p.m. section of 'La Rousserolle effarvatte'. Apart from the pitches of the reed warbler's opening tritone (E♮–B♭), which matches the later sources and the score, there is no material of direct relevance to 'La Rousserolle' except for a momentary down-and-up arpeggio flourish, out of which the 'comme un glissando de harpe' figure on p. 18 of the score may have developed. As there is no water rail on the English discs, however, it is unlikely that Messiaen's plans for a piece for 'birds of the reeds and ponds' were far advanced at this point.

Messiaen and Loriod visited the piece's eventual setting, the Sologne, in June 1955, but there are no surviving *cahiers* from this trip. Two principal sources *do* exist, however: the Swedish discs, which are the source of the opening reed warbler solo and also produced detailed harmonisations of the water rail and great reed warbler; and one of the richest of all the *cahiers*, 23043, compiled during the couple's tour of Provence and the Camargue in July 1956. Although many of the species from 'La Rousserolle' appear in this notebook, the songs themselves are rarely utilised. The material from 23043 that does survive is scattered around the central reed warbler duets – sometimes as several phrases, sometimes a short arabesque. On the shores of the Etang de Vaccarès Messiaen also witnessed a sunset that clearly transfixed him; the sky was aglow with colours familiar from the sunset in 'La Rousserolle' (and sunsets since time immemorial). His description contains some vivid detail:

Pink, red, orange and violet sunset, framed by grey-mauve clouds. A fiery orange stripe reflects the sun and crosses the water of Vaccarès – above the intermingled green and grey of the water, a great band of lilac cloud, grey-mauve, almost like a pigeon's wing – humid weather – some tamarisk of salicornia – in the thick phragmite bushes (big green reeds) the chorus of great reed warblers (ten to twenty) salute the setting sun.
  The sun is a blazing disc of orange and gold, breaking through the violet clouds, leaving in the sky a memory of dreamy red and pink fire … stormy heat, wind, mosquitoes. A tiny piece of the sun's red fire passes beneath the large cloud, springs back, and the whole of the sun's disc sinks into the water – all is violet, purple and lilac – the wind stirs the reeds and silences the choir of great reed warblers![66]

The second paragraph of his description suggests that the 'sunset' chords in 'La Rousserolle effarvatte', which occur *after* the sun has sunk below the horizon, and which Messiaen refers to as a 'souvenir de coucher de soleil – violet sombre' in the score (p. 42), are a response to a witnessed event – the afterglow, or a visible 'memory' of the sunset – rather than a product of his imagination, as with the other 'souvenirs' in the *Catalogue*.

Messiaen does not mention the Swedish discs in the 'reed warbler' section of the *Traité*, merely implying that he heard the bird in the Sologne with the comment 'Restons en Sologne'. There are no specific notations from the Sologne in the *Traité*, suggesting that *cahiers* from this trip never existed, or were lost some time ago. What is clear is that he used the Swedish discs to fashion the piece's distinctive musical environment, perceiving a correspondence between the sounds of wetland birds that lends it timbral

---

[66] 23043, p. 19.

Example 4.20 Notation of a bittern from the Swedish discs (23045, p. 50)

coherence. He made two attempts at transcribing the bittern (23045, pp. 36 and 50), and the second – where a 'lowing' semitone is transformed into a booming tritone – became a fitting gesture for the piece's final bar. In both versions his imagination was at work straightaway, likening the call to a tuba ('or a 16-foot bassoon stop on the organ'), and making the distinctive gesture seem like a bridge between the music of Fafner the dragon from Wagner's *Siegfried* and the eerie sounds that open the 'Lauds' scene (on tuba and contrabassoon) in *Saint François d'Assise* (Ex. 4.20).

The reed warbler also specialises in tritones, a tendency Messiaen decided to capitalise on. In the Swedish disc notation, bars 10–13 were transcribed from the record as a repeated B♮; they become B–F–B in the right hand, and C♯–F♯–C♮ in the left (b. 10 on p. 4 of the score) (Ex. 4.21). This bar is a distillation of the sound-world of 'La Rousserolle effarvatte'. Tritones paired with perfect intervals are the timbre and the ambience of the Sologne landscape, and this compound sonority is so ubiquitous – both harmonically and as a melodic cell – that an account of all its appearances would require a lengthy appendix. Paul Griffiths identifies it as a recurring *style oiseau* motif that can be traced back to Messiaen's earlier music – for example the symmetrical sequence of four pitches (G, high C♯, A♭, low D) that opens *Les Corps glorieux*.[67]

---

[67] Wai-Ling Cheong also demonstrates its importance in the pitch rows that are used in the *Catalogue*; Wai-Ling Cheong, 'Symmetrical Permutation, the Twelve Tones, and Messiaen's *Catalogue d'oiseaux*', *Perspectives of New Music* 45.1 (Winter 2007), 110–136 (p. 116). Griffiths mentions the melodic cell in *Olivier Messiaen and the Music of Time*, p. 173.

Example 4.21 The source of the first reed warbler solo in 'La Rousserolle effarvatte' (23045, p. 22)

Here the link between the vocalise/monody writing of the 1930s and the later *style oiseau* is made plain – a transition undertaken in reverse in the first two movements of the *Quatuor* (compare the angel's slow vocalise with the violin's nightingale). It is also the chord that marks Loriod's entrance into Messiaen's life, a constant presence in the

Example 4.22 Notation of the grasshopper warbler from the Swedish discs (23045, p. 27)

piano 1 part of 'Amen de la Création' (the first movement of *Visions de l'Amen*).

'La Rousserolle effarvatte' is the apotheosis of this melodic and harmonic idea. One of the most spectacular uses is Messiaen's original 'hearing' of the grasshopper warbler, notated on p. 27 of 23045 (Ex. 4.22). This shimmering, complex sonority (a 'super-high tremolo' as Messiaen describes it) was eventually replaced by a compact double trill that symbolises the 'sizzling weariness' of nature under the midday sun. Messiaen then moved the original harmonic idea into the bass: it becomes a tam-tam, held by the pedal throughout the thirty-second 'grillotement' (chirping) of the warbler, providing an extra dimension for this moment of stillness. The chords sound particularly gong-like if the pianist follows Messiaen's instruction to play the grace notes quickly (Ex. 4.23).[68]

The tritone is also a telling presence in the harmonies of sunrise and sunset. As the sun goes down Messiaen embarks on a series of twenty-four consecutive parallel chords with tritones at both top and bottom (in a footnote

---

[68] The tam-tam chords are also heard immediately before the iris melody, further anticipating the sound-world of *La Transfiguration*.

Example 4.23 'La Rousserolle effarvatte' p. 18, bb. 7–9

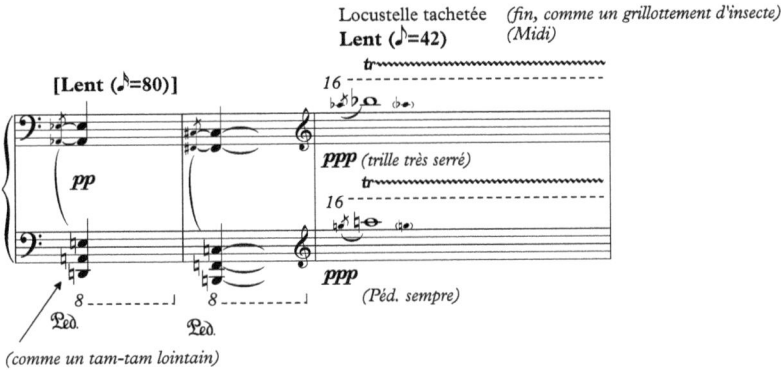

on p. 39 of the score he suggests that the timbre of the chords should change at the start of this sequence from string quartet to a 'sad and sombre' oboe and cor anglais). The sunset lasts longer than the sunrise, building through long phrases coloured red, orange and violet. Eventually they too outline a diminished fifth, cadencing on E♭ minor, then C minor, and finally A minor as the sun 'rejoins its reflection and sinks into the water'. The core interval is writ large across the scene.

Ingenuity of Design

Were it not for the bittern's final call, 'La Rousserolle effarvatte' would end as well as begin with the music of the ponds. The best way to view its monumental design is to peel away the layers, working gradually inwards. The opening music is a rich and complex metaphor: Messiaen creates a self-contained ritual that is sharp and ingenious, evoking a still landscape, teeming with life. The two hands follow contrasted schemes: the right hand alternates two repeated dyads that follow a 'scissor' scheme of durations (1, 13, 2, 12, 3, 11 […] 13, 1); the left hand is isorhythmic, combining nine chords with seven durations.

An additional complication to the scheme is that the sixth value in the isorhythm increases by one semiquaver each time, which heightens the opposition between the mysterious left hand and the mechanical right. The challenge for the performer is to maintain their independence, particularly tricky when the accented changes of dyad coincide with a left-hand chord (which must resist accentuation). If anything, concentration must be focused on the left hand. Its full cycle takes slightly less time to complete than that of the right, so there is time for its first statement to be almost completely reiterated. The ticking of the right hand stops just before the last left-hand chord can be played, leaving the familiar tritone-plus-perfect-fourth sonority (B, F, C) hanging. The immediate impression is of an arbitrary resting-point; nevertheless, the piece's emblematic harmony creates a muted sense of expectation.

Though the rhythms of the two hands are independent, their pitch material is complementary: three black notes in the right hand (G♭ and A♭, A♭ and B♭), and the other nine chromatic pitches distributed across chords of subdued hue in the left. Many of these harmonies – especially the first one – reflect the perfect interval/tritone dichotomy of the piece to come, and the moment when the dichotomy is resolved, chord three (F, C, G), is also the moment when the span of the left hand mimics the right: a major ninth. This mirroring comes and goes repeatedly, making the landscape breathe in an apparently arbitrary but ordered way, as if the water is ebbing and flowing gently (Ex. 4.24).

In this finely tuned system there is a more chaotic element: the pedal, which always changes when the third left-hand harmony returns. The combined effect of the augmenting rhythmic value and the isorhythmic treatment means that the steadily increasing gaps between pedal changes start to decrease again just before the passage ends; this phenomenon gives the music a further respirational quality (the sustaining pedal acting like a pair of lungs).[69]

When this music returns at the end of the piece it begins as an exact reversal of the opening. The difference is that the process is not worked through, but hinted at – we only get five fragments of the right hand, separated by silences that increase in length. These silences, Messiaen told Peter Hill, signify mist obscuring the water.

Moving inside this outer frame we find a different view of night, to which all the surrounding music (with the exception of the reed warbler solos) is subordinate. Messiaen has in mind the 'solemnity' of the night, represented by cymbals, gongs and trombones – a dark counterpart to the blinding cacophony that would later open 'Christus Jesus, splendor Patris' and 'Perfecte conscius illius perfectae generationis' in *La Transfiguration*. The creatures also contribute to this character – the heaving *ostinato* of the frogs and some unspecified 'sounds of the marsh'.

This second night music forms a frame within a frame, since embedded in it are the first and last solos of the reed warbler. These are sculpted in sharp relief, being spikey, abrasive, hyperactive – everything that is unmysterious.

---

[69] The lengths of the pedals are, in order, 4, 17, 21, 22, 22, 23, 31, 26 and 16 semiquavers.

Example 4.24 The opening of 'La Rousserolle effarvatte'

The next step inside the symmetrical structure is marked by a further huge contrast, from blackness to colour, as the *Catalogue*'s most impassioned sunrise gathers and intensifies. The chords have the even pacing of a hymn, and the pauses are filled by a dawn chorus: blackbird, red-backed shrike and redstart. These birds are not specifically inhabitants of the water margin, and musically they provide an intermezzo, a kind of gentle scherzo, between the reed warbler and the medley of other reed birds that begins at 8 a.m.

At the other end of the piece the events are reversed, but with inevitable differences. The only sounds accompanying the sunset, at first, are three punctuations from the bittern. The sun's morning ascent is mirrored by the falling harmonies, but its symmetry is brutally obliterated by the nightingale: 'brusque, incisive, biting'. During its second intervention Messiaen begins the passionate 'souvenir' of the sunset; this moment has a big impact on any performance, partly because of the absence of any birdsong to carry forward the slow-moving harmonies. It is the only time a *fortissimo* is heard during either sunrise or sunset.

All the music discussed so far forms a vast frame to the main body of the piece, which takes place between the end of sunrise at 8 a.m. and the eruption of the skylark at 6 p.m. – a dynamic part of this great structure that counterbalances the static masses on the outside. The 5 p.m. reed warbler duets play a dual role within this: as a climax at the centre of the form, but in a more immediate context as part of a build-up of energy. This accumulates gradually, starting at 8 a.m., through a series of verses, each of which is more active than its predecessor, and culminates in the triumphant peroration of the skylark. Not even the grasshopper warbler, which pipes up for a second time just before the lark's arrival, can disrupt the gathering energy.

The first birds to stir after the sunrise are a disparate group, providing comic relief: the grotesque double cry of the pheasant, the weird laugh of the green woodpecker, and the effervescent starling. The musical ordering of the calls is entirely unpredictable and capricious and – most importantly – without direction. This is the kind of music we would find if the *Catalogue* really were a 'catalogue'. Though only a brief episode, it has its own miniature frame in the music of the irises.

Within two minutes we have progressed from 8 a.m. to 5 p.m., via the static grasshopper warbler at midday. But now the music begins to move. Initially this is through a series of variations. The first is brief, equally divided between the reed warbler (which with the resumption of song in the late afternoon seems to have caught the fantastic tone of the starling) and the clankings and whirrings of the sedge warbler. With each variation the sedge warbler expands its expressive range, winding itself up in a series of tremolos; in the third variation it is joined by a new character, the great reed warbler, even more obstinate than the eponymous bird. The level of hysteria that has been reached is neatly encapsulated in a short coda, juxtaposing a mad dash for the blackheaded gull with the coot's trumpet.

The great reed warbler is one of the most impressive of all Messiaen's transcriptions from the Swedish discs, both visually and texturally – it already looks like the manuscript copy of a piano piece.[70] Having worked out this texture, however, he then sourced the gruff set of calls on p. 22 of

---

[70] 23045, p. 25.

Example 4.25 'La Rousserolle effarvatte', p. 25, bb. 11–14

the score from the Etang de Vaccarès notations, the only other remnants (alongside snatches of reed warbler) from the trip to the Camargue.[71]

The last of the flower music (waterlilies) that precedes the central 'concert' of reed warbler duets is the most intriguing of the floral interludes. A melody that is especially prominent in *Turangalîla* (played by bassoon and flute in the second movement, for example) is combined with an early version of Messiaen's 'turning chords' (Ex. 4.25). It is certainly an evocative juxtaposition.

The central 'concert' is a breathless alternation of reed warbler duets – sometimes verging on slapstick – and sedge warbler solos (the fingering of the frantic scales in the duets emphasises their tritone patterns). The sedge warbler provides a necessary foil in its 'simple' gestures, but there is no let-up in the tension. The reed warbler duets become less concerned with metrical interplay and more with accents and articulations (the second, on p. 32, is marked 'éclaboussant' – splashy), and they eventually take over

[71] 23043, p. 9a.

from the sedge warbler. As they do so they become ever more light and intricate; the concluding duet has the feel of a coda that cuts off suddenly, plunging abruptly into the reflective music of the flowers and the grasshopper warbler.

The passage that now concludes the events of the day balances the 8 a.m. 'medley'. As in 'L'Alouette calandrelle' the skylark plays a spectacular role, but with a different purpose. Whereas in the former its song was used explosively, as a way of emphasising the silent void, here what counts is the obsessiveness of its patternings; from the most intense musical mobility, in the duetting of the reed warblers, we move to the most decisive of musical certainties. The water rail upends the scenario one final time with its cry 'of a pig having its throat cut, a subsiding howl'.

Once the events of the evening have played themselves out, the 'lowing' bittern in the final bar confirms that we have come full circle ('the piece as a whole follows a great curve'). Given that the flower melodies inherit themes from *Cinq Rechants*, it makes sense to relate this concluding sound to the end of the fifth and final *Rechant*, 'Mayoma kalimolimo, mayoma kalimolimo', which explores the magical properties of love in an arch form, with 'Tristan' trilogy melodies submerged in the verses. Its Introduction and Coda both conclude with a melodic rising semitone that resolves on a bare tritone: 'Dans le passé' in the Introduction, 'Dans l'avenir' in the Coda. There is no denying the evocative power of the tritone here: the *Rechant* is poised between past and the future (life with Claire Delbos and Yvonne Loriod?). 'La Rousserolle effarvatte', similarly, looks all around: at the rest of the *Catalogue*, and the ongoing life cycle of the Sologne.

5 | The Second Wave of Composition

'La Bouscarle' (Cetti's Warbler)

The last days of April. Saint-Brice, La Trache, Bourg-Charente, the banks of the Charente and of the Charenton, a small tributary.

A sudden burst of violence: the enraged call of a Cetti's warbler, hidden in the reeds and brambles. A moorhen cackles. Sharp cries, then a flash of colour as a kingfisher skims across the water. A fine day of light and shadow. The willows and poplars are reflected in the green of the water. Rich chords hymn the calm flow of the river: joyful fanfares of the blackbird, the blue-green shimmer of the kingfisher, the pearly cascades of a robin.

Again, the furious Cetti's warbler. And what is this strange noise – a saw? A scythe being sharpened? The scraping of a güiro? It is the corncrake, repeating its iambic rhythm in the tall grasses of the meadow. The song thrush adds its fierce incantations. Accents and tremolos from the little wren.

The river continues calmly, its phrases interspersed with a medley of song. The chaffinch exclaims in triumph. A blackcap adds its flute-like descant. The muffled rhythm of the hoopoe. A halo of harmony (like a harpsichord blended with a gong), distant lunar chords and piercing flashes: the nightingale.

Nuptial flight of the kingfisher, its colours spinning in the sunlight – forget-me-not, sapphire, emerald. Intense, nervous rustlings of the sandmartin. A last cadence for the river, a gentle secretive cadenza for the robin. The yellow wagtail, its head coloured ash-blue, steps elegantly along the bank. The kingfisher dives, then arrows past in a jewelled blur. Silence. A final tirade from Cetti's warbler.[1]

The early months of 1957 were difficult for Messiaen. A simmering row with his publisher, Durand, came to a head in a 'dreadful scene'.[2] Messiaen's health was poor, with disorders of the stomach and gall bladder for which a strict diet was prescribed. A break listening to birds in the forests around Orgeval, to the west of Paris, did him good, and he and Loriod decided to take advantage of the Easter holiday to travel south to the Charente, staying in a hotel in Jarnac a few kilometres from Gardépée, the former home

---

[1] Olivier Messiaen, preface to the published score.
[2] OMR, p. 95. Messiaen believed Durand were failing to promote *Réveil des oiseaux*. The details are in PH/NS, p. 222.

of Jacques Delamain (who had died in 1953). This was Loriod's first visit to Gardépée, which she later remembered as 'a sort of pilgrimage'.[3]

The abundance of springtime bird life was a spur to Messiaen's imagination. Many of Messiaen's observations were made at Gardépée, as they had been in 1952; nearby is a prehistoric dolmen, which Messiaen described at twilight, and which possibly gave him the idea for the 'magic hand' in 'Le Merle de roche'. What particularly caught his attention, however, was an area on the south bank of the River Charente opposite Saint-Brice, where a narrow stream encircles a large meadow: this is the Charenton, the 'petit bras de rivière' described in Messiaen's preface to 'La Bouscarle'. The essential features of the piece are squeezed into a single page of the *cahier* as Messiaen followed a path alongside the Charenton, the water lined with willows and poplars (Ex. 5.1).[4] The page contains five of the birdsongs that feature prominently in the piece: several of the abrupt, impatient phrases of the Cetti's warbler, all of which would appear in the score; the energetic motifs of the song thrush (*grive musicienne*); and the three birdsongs that would be used as descants to the music of the river. Of these the blackcap and blackbird as they appear here are not quoted literally in the score, but the *cahier* already has the characteristics of their songs. The solo for the robin in the cahier is very much as it will appear in the score (see score, pp. 9–10; the passage ringed on the right-hand side of Ex. 5.1 appears in the score on p. 20).

Messiaen climbed the hillside behind the meadow, his description capturing the spirit of the place and of the piece: 'Before me the valley, from which rises, muted, the songs of blackbird and blackcap … The river Charente – peaceful, and green with the reflection of trees – and beyond it the Charenton, hidden by willows and poplars, while still further away climb immense vineyards and blue hills'.

It was to be another two months, however, before he began composition. The evidence comes in a *cahier* (23056(1)), dating from two months after the research in the Charente, which Messiaen used during his trip to the Mediterranean coastline near Banyuls in late June.[5] This contains three pages with musical sketches for 'La Bouscarle'. Some ideas are obviously at a preliminary stage, including a discarded sketch for the kingfisher's virtuoso 'vol nuptial';[6] others are almost exactly as they will appear in the finished

---

[3] Yvonne Loriod, letter to Jean-Pierre Valion, dated 18 February 1995. Copy in the Messiaen Archive.
[4] 23009, p. 19.
[5] 23056 contains two *cahiers*, designated here as 23056(1) and (2). The second of these contains Messiaen's prose plans for 'La Bouscarle' and 'Le Traquet stapazin'.
[6] 23056, p. 20.

'La Bouscarle' (Cetti's Warbler) 127

Example 5.1 Birdsongs for 'La Bouscarle' (facsimile)

Figure 5.1 The Charenton

score: the nightingale (score, p. 15), and the music of the river in the passage that modulates to the dominant (score, pp. 12–13), together with descants for the blackcap that come complete with details of fingering.

The Banyuls *cahier* also contains several pages of prose plans (in 23056(2)), in which Messiaen first outlines and then refines the structure of 'La Bouscarle'. Messiaen's initial idea gives a remarkably exact summary:

A little piece for a bank of a river; the Charente and the Charenton. Entitled La Bouscarle. With yellow wagtail, kingfisher, Cetti's warbler, moorhen and hoopoe, corncrake, etc. The wind – reflections of trees in the river – willows – poplars, aspens. Reflections of the green water of the Charenton – blue and green (azure/emerald) flight of the kingfisher – Look for polymodality for the blue and green. Birds from recordings: Swiss – see sandmartin, blackcap; for moorhen – English discs.

This outline is then developed into a detailed plan that offers a fascinating insight into Messiaen's working method. The plan begins with a medley of birdsongs that includes refrains for Cetti's warbler and the flight of the kingfisher. Next come the reflections of trees in the river, the second section, which are portrayed through a musical metaphor: Greek and Hindu rhythms in rhythmic canon, with the left hand adding a semiquaver to each value, reflecting (as it were) the right. The central part of the plan is the music of the river, which will recur (as a 'rondo'), its third appearance modulating to the dominant, before returning to the tonic. The river is the continuity at the heart of the piece, almost like a little sonata form, while the subsequent coda suggests a symmetry, with its reprise of ideas from earlier in the piece – the reflections of the trees, the flight of the kingfisher, and the refrain of Cetti's warbler.

Messiaen was drawing on three sources: the notations made in the Charente, imaginary depictions of the watery environment – the river and the reflections of trees in the water – that had not yet been composed, and finally his extensive library of notations made from recordings. Example 5.2 shows the kingfisher (*martin-pêcheur*) from the Swedish radio recording, which Messiaen immediately developed on the same page of the *cahier* into a pianistic version, harmonised and with fingerings (see also the treatment of the blackcap in Ex. 2.11a (p. 43)). When working out the structure of 'La Bouscarle' he returned to the *cahier* and identified each phrase of the kingfisher with letters, which in the plan form a sort of mosaic: 'Moorhen from a to c / chord z below the kingfisher / chord p kingfisher b / chord o kingfisher c / chord j kingfisher d / kingfisher x / blue-green arrow [flight] of the kingfisher / [silence] / Cetti's warbler (4), etc'.[7] This comes from the part of the plan that deals with the first section of the piece. The main outlines are clear, the refrains by Cetti's warbler framing the kingfisher, which takes two forms: its flight (a 'blue-green arrow') and its brief staccato calls. Already one can see Messiaen organising his large cast of birds according to the characteristics of their song. In this first section the birdcalls are all quick and active, and mostly high-pitched; later in the piece the more lyrical songs – of the blackbird, robin and blackcap – are used as afterthoughts to the music of the river.

The rhythmic canon for the reflections ('the water reflects the willows and poplars') is worked out on a separate page of the *cahier*. The sequence of durations opens (in the right hand) with three rhythms, two being Greek (a dactyl and third epitrite), the other consisting of three durations, each of three semiquavers; the pattern then repeats – 422 (dactyl), 4424 (third epitrite), 333, 422 etc., followed by the Hindu râgavardhana. Three further rhythms form a middle section (gajalîla, lakskmîça and iamb, beginning at the tenth bar of the passage) before the first group is repeated, coming to rest on the long final value of the râgavardhana (twelve semiquavers) (see Ex. 5.3).

[7] 23056 (2), p. 5.

Example 5.2 Kingfisher

(a) Martin-pêcheur

(b) Cri du Martin-pêcheur

Example 5.3 Part of Messiaen's sketch for the reflections, from 23056(2), p. 7

Dactyl	♩ ♩ ♩
3rd Epitrite	♩ ♩ ♩ ♩
Râgavardhana	♪ ♪. ♪ ♩
Gajalîla	♪ ♪ ♪ ♪.
Lakskmîça	♪ ♪. ♩ ♩

The harmony for this passage was devised from the basic twelve-note series used in the *Catalogue*. Example 5.4 shows the opening bars, which use the first three interversions (score, p. 2).[8] From this we can see that in contrast to the rhythm, where right and left hand are separate strands, the interversions are used as 'vertical' segments (i.e. chords shared between the hands) rather than as linear counterpoints: this enables Messiaen to infiltrate his twelve-note texture with occasional startlingly consonant chords – dominant sevenths, for example – rather like objects reflected in water swimming in and out of focus (the A major sound in the second bar of Ex. 5.4 is a case in point). Messiaen described his use of the series here

---

[8] The first three interversions are: F♯ C♮ B♮ E♮ B♭ D♭ G♮ D♮ A♮ E♭ A♭ F♮ / G♮ F♯ F♮ B♭ A♭ C♮ D♮ B♮ E♭ E♮ A♮ D♭ / D♮ G♮ D♭ A♭ A♮ F♯ B♮ F♮ E♮ B♭ E♭ C♮. See Wai-Ling Cheong, 'Symmetrical Permutation, the Twelve Tones, and Messiaen's *Catalogue d'oiseaux*', *Perspectives of New Music* 45.1 (Winter 2007), 110–136 (pp. 118, 121–123).

Example 5.4 'La Bouscarle': 'The water reflects the willows and poplars'

(l'eau reflète les saules et les peupliers)

as 'not fierce', and this was perhaps a way of suggesting the muted greens of the trees (in contrast, for example, to the decidedly fierce use of twelve-note writing that gives rise to the darkness of 'La Chouette hulotte'). Messiaen's performance instruction ('liquide et fluide') encourages the performer to create an effect of gliding through the sonorities, minimising any percussiveness of attack, the pedal producing a subtle wash of sound, yet clean enough to avoid undue blurring.

The next part of the plan outlines the music of the river. Its 'theme' (as Messiaen calls it) would recur as a rondo, with two strophes, both in the tonic (A major), then a modulation to the dominant that will be followed by a cadenza for the kingfisher ('passage de virtuosité: vol nuptial du martin-pêcheur – long!'). Then comes the reprise of the river in an extended version in the tonic. The remainder of the piece is headed 'coda', and brings a return to the events of the opening section, within which would be the music of the reflections (this time, Messiaen notes, with the same rhythms but different series) – thus making overall a clear ternary shape to the piece.

Almost immediately, as he was sketching the coda, Messiaen seems to have had second thoughts. His first revision was to cross out the extended reprise of the river and transfer it (in a shortened form) to the coda, situated between a third and final 'nuptial flight' of the kingfisher and a refrain for Cetti's warbler that would end the piece. This overlapping of the music of the river with the birds of the coda was the start of a series of modifications to Messiaen's original plan.

In the finished piece the neat sections of the plan are still discernible but are now interleaved so as to create a triple structure. The soloist (Cetti's warbler) acts as a refrain, recurring regularly throughout, and beginning and ending the piece. The symmetry is emphasised by the music of the reflections, divided between two passages that are placed near to either end of the piece, while the third element of the design is the purposeful, developing role played by the music of the river.

Another type of evolution comes with the progress of the piece, which involves a gradual departure from the crisply differentiated sections of the first few pages. To this end Messiaen drastically streamlined the opening section, so that it became essentially a solo for the kingfisher, framed by the refrains of Cetti's warbler. The kingfisher becomes the active ingredient in Messiaen's design, playing a maverick role as it darts through the piece in a series of spectacular 'nuptial flights'. In one sense the kingfisher belongs to the sharp, decisive music of the refrains; in another it connects through its blue-green colouring with the music of the river, using harmonies that mirror the river's – mode 3, A major and E^7.

The two passages of water music – the 'reflections' and the river – are placed side by side, separated only by a short silence, in a telling contrast. The first strophe of the river comes in four phrases (score, pp. 4–6): statement, variant, development and a coda that moves in calm circles before ending with an eloquent cadence. The initial phrase makes a plagal cadence, from D to A, expanded in the third phrase. Key (A major) and mode 3^3 combine, so that the resolution to the tonic gives a particular glow because approached by semitone from notes from the mode (B♭, F♮) that are foreign to the key. Messiaen encouraged the pianist to explore the balance within these chords, slightly emphasising (for example) the outer pitches in the second chord (A♮ and F♮) and the C♯ in the chord of A major; similarly, in the second phrase the minor third (C♮) is important (Ex. 5.5).

Between the third and fourth phrases Messiaen introduces an interruption, a refrain (for Cetti's warbler) together with the first 'vol nuptial'. Placing the kingfisher within the music of the river emphasises their shared tonality. (The right hand, incidentally, recalls the undulating figuration of Chopin's *Etude*, Op. 10, no. 10, and is much harder to play than it looks, especially at Messiaen's precipitate tempo and muted dynamic.) In another sense the interruption proves prophetic, as the river, in its second strophe (score, pp. 7–9), has to compete with increasingly varied and assertive birdsongs – a trio of low, medium and high calls (corncrake, song thrush and wren) and the developments of the 'vol nuptial' as these become increasingly virtuoso. Messiaen's original sectional design has become a richly detailed fabric with different strands, existing in its own space but connected by refrains and reminiscences.

The climax of the river comes in its lengthy development (score, pp. 12–13), in which varied transpositions of mode 3 give the dominant seventh (and ninth) harmony (of A major), expanding into a leisurely swing to the

Example 5.5 The river

'dominant of the dominant' (as Messiaen termed it). As it does so, the interplay between setting and birdsong comes into balance, with the phrases of the river complemented by the fragile lyricism of the blackcap, considerably extended compared with the descants for blackbird and robin in the earlier strophes.

A further page in the Banyuls *cahier* (23056(2)) shows Messiaen refining the closing pages of the piece. The coda became in effect a recapitulation, as the watery music dissolves away, with the rhythmic canon of the reflections fragmented by silences, the river returning to the tonic but now represented only by its final phrase, though with the cadence extended for quiet emphasis, and giving way to an exquisite solo for the robin.[9] The creeping silence is perhaps Messiaen's memory of the twilight by the Charenton. Messiaen resists the temptation to end quietly, however. The kingfisher ducks and dives before flashing past, using the same harmonies as on the first page of the piece; and the last word is with Cetti's warbler, a final tirade that seals the piece's symmetry while suggesting the cycle of songs will recommence.

'Le Traquet stapazin' (Black-Eared Wheatear)

Late June. Roussillon, the 'vermilion' coast near Banyuls. Rocky cliffs, mountains, the sea, terraces of vines. At the roadside a black-eared wheatear. Proud, aristocratic, he stands on the rocks, in his finery of orange silk and dark velvet – a black inverted T dividing the white of his tail, a mask of deepest black covering eyes, face and throat. He might be a Spanish nobleman going to a masked ball. His song is loud, brusque, abrupt. Not far away, among the vines, an ortolan bunting launches ecstatically its flute-like repeated notes, with their

---

[9] Messiaen's revised plan for the coda identifies the solo for the robin as having been notated beside the Charenton on 25 April at 10.15 a.m.

melancholy cadence. This is the 'garrigue': a landscape of low, prickly plants. The exquisite song of an unseen spectacled warbler. Flying high and far out over the sea two herring gulls utter cruel cries, dry, percussive sniggers. A trio of ravens fly above the rocky cliffs with powerful and deep cawings. The bell-like tinkling of the little goldfinch …

Five o'clock in the morning. The red and gold disc of the sun rises from the sea and climbs into the heavens, at its summit a gold crown that increases until the sun is entirely yellow-gold. The sun climbs higher, a band of light forming on the sea. Nine o'clock. In the light and heat a succession of new voices. Paired, flute-like notes of the Orphean warbler, the glinting crystal of the corn bunting, the unreal laughter of the rock bunting, the voluble melodious warbler – while on the wing, the scintillating, exultant song of the Thekla lark, mingled with sharp cries. Several black-eared wheatears respond.

Nine o'clock in the evening. Drenched in blood and gold the sun sinks behind the mountains. The peaks of the Albères mountains seem on fire. The sea darkens. The sky changes from red to orange, then is stained a dream-like violet … Final verses of the spectacled warbler. Three notes of the ortolan bunting, among the darkened vines. Again, a black-eared wheatear, far away on the road. Dry percussive note of a herring gull, far out over the dark sea. Silence … Ten o'clock. Total darkness. A memory of the spectacled warbler …[10]

Messiaen's first visit to the Mediterranean coast of Roussillon came in June 1957. The sea, cliffs and rocky coves, sparkling in the sunlight of a midsummer morning, left an indelible impression. The setting initially inspired two pieces for the *Catalogue* – 'Le Traquet stapazin' and 'Le Merle bleu', with a third piece, 'Le Traquet rieur', added after a return visit the following year. His base was Banyuls, just north of the border with Spain, the most southerly of the small towns that grew up behind bays or inlets on this rugged coastline. In between these settlements one can clamber up cliff-top paths, through vineyards planted in steep terraces, fringed by meadows scented with wild herbs, very much as described in Messiaen's preface to 'Le Traquet stapazin'. Messiaen must have been struck by the juxtaposition of the orderly vineyards and the wildness of the shoreline, with waves breaking on jagged rocks at the foot of sheer, fissured cliffs. This scenery suggested a contrasted pair of pieces, one set mainly on the land – 'Le Traquet stapazin', the more lyrical of the two – while in 'Le Merle bleu' the song of the soloist, the blue rock thrush, competes with the piercing cries of seabirds and the turbulence of the surf.

All the pieces in the *Catalogue* considered so far were written as imaginative recreations of the birdsongs and landscapes that had been recorded

---

[10] Preface to the score.

Figure 5.2 The coastline at Banyuls

earlier in Messiaen's *cahier*. 'Le Traquet stapazin', on the other hand, seems to have been composed at least partly in situ, in an extraordinary burst of inspiration. The two *cahiers* he used give an exceptionally full picture of how the piece was composed, containing not only notations of birdsong and descriptions of habitat, but also compositional sketches, complete with indications of dynamic, pedalling etc., and a series of prose plans in which Messiaen developed his ideas for the structure.[11] Taken together these give a uniquely detailed insight into the ways Messiaen tackled the fundamental challenge of the *Catalogue*, on the one hand sharply differentiating the birdsongs, on the other finding ways to link his disparate material into musical continuities.

From an early stage in his researches for 'Le Traquet stapazin' Messiaen seems to have divided the birdsongs into two categories: those that were harsh and abrasive (the herring gulls; raven; and the soloist, the black-eared wheatear) and birds such as the ortolan bunting and spectacled warbler whose

---

[11] 23056 and 23057. The prose plan is contained in 23056(2).

melodies seemed like a reflection of their sun-drenched surroundings. This opposition is laid out on the first page of the piece, which is headed by a brief, almost laconic indication of the setting, in a sequence of chords that represent the vines growing on terraces that step down the hillside towards the sea. The opening medley of birdsongs is the first of three verses, or 'couplets', in each of which the sequence of songs is repeated but always varied and with different birds given prominence. These three couplets form what Messiaen calls the exposition. The development begins with the sunrise, painted in the rich colours of Messiaen's chords of 'transposed inversions', which rise in sequence towards the birdsongs of morning and midday: the climax to this section is a cadenza for the Thekla lark, halted abruptly by a long silence.

Up to this point in the piece composition seems to have gone smoothly and rapidly. But the final section of the piece caused Messiaen significant trouble. Initially, he had in mind ending with a few fragmentary recalls of the earlier birdsongs. The sketches and prose plans show how this grew gradually into the eventual solution, which combines elements of recapitulation with a drawn-out coda, closing a symmetry that had begun in the darkness before dawn with the fading colours of twilight.

The first notations in the *cahiers* are brief, as Messiaen started to gather impressions of birdsong and setting. Gradually, over a period of several days (22–30 June), he achieved a sharper, surer characterisation of each birdsong; at the same time a consistency of approach started to form, so that birdsongs appear to be variants of the same melodic and harmonic template. The line between research and composition starts to blur: at times one can see a reciprocity between the two, as the characteristics of a particular birdsong become modified, in the act of notation, in order to fit with the emerging musical idea.

Messiaen began, on 22 June 1957, by getting his bearings, facing the Mediterranean at Cap l'Abeille, with Cap Rederis to the south, Cap Béar to the north.[12] This page of the *cahier* starts with four notations of birds with important roles in 'Le Traquet stapazin' (see Ex. 5.6). Even at this early stage a family of pitch relationships starts to take shape, commencing at its simplest with the pure E major of the ortolan bunting (Ex. 5.6a). Subsequently, the perfect fifth – B to E – extends downwards by a tritone to B♭, in the songs of a Thekla lark and of the soloist, the black-eared wheatear (b and c). A notation of the spectacled warbler enriches the collection of pitches further, though is still clearly related to the previous birdsongs (d).[13]

---

[12] 23057, p. 21.

[13] The kinship may be partly because Messiaen initially mistook the song of the spectacled warbler for that of the ortolan bunting. See 23057, p. 21.

'Le Traquet stapazin' (Black-Eared Wheatear) 137

Example 5.6 (a) Ortolan bunting (*bruant ortolan*); (b) Thekla lark (*cochevis de Thékla*); (c) black-eared wheatear (*traquet stapazin*); (d) spectacled warbler (*fauvette à lunettes*); (e) Thekla lark; (f) spectacled warbler; (g) goldfinch (*chardonneret*); (h) rock bunting (*bruant fou*); (i) Thekla lark; (j) spectacled warbler (facsimile)

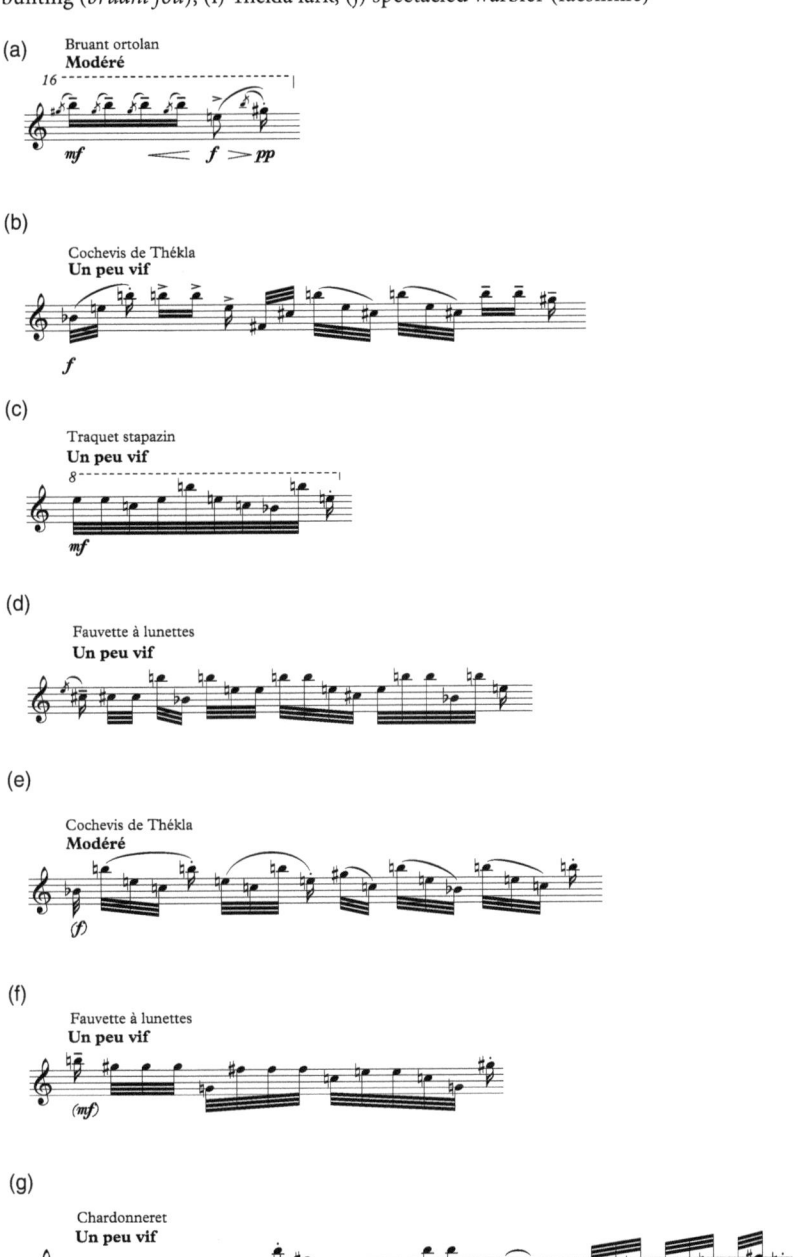

Example 5.6 (cont.)

(h) Bruant fou
Un peu vif

(i) Cochevis de Thékla
Un peu vif

(j)

The following day (23 June) saw the first notations to be used in the finished score: the Thekla lark (e: the passage commencing in the score on p. 17, last system) and the spectacled warbler (f: score, p. 25).[14] Both notations were made in the evening: 'the mountains darken, the sky and sea are blue and pink, a pink that becomes fiery red, then ash-violet'. A further variant of the family of pitches comes the following day (24 June) with the goldfinch, whose contribution is to extend B–E down a fifth to A, and to create broken chords out of a fifth plus a tritone (g).[15] The pitch material for the rock bunting (*bruant fou*) is closely related to the goldfinch, and would become closer still when in the finished score Messiaen altered the C♮s (at the beginning of the second group, for example) to C♯s (h).[16] This notation would be used for two solos (score, pp. 10–11, 14), with the order of events indicated in the *cahier* by letters and ligatures.

A few days later (28 June) the fifth/tritone relationship (B–E/E–B♭) and the harmony on C or C⁷, found earlier with the spectacled warbler, feature in the song of the Thekla lark, which would form the closing stages of the lark's solo (score, p. 18, last system; and p. 19) (i).[17]

By 30 June ideas for the first couplet were taking shape: goldfinch and wheatear, side by side, are as they will appear in the score, while Messiaen has already devised the harmonies of the gulls and raven. The most important notation, however (j), is a long solo for the spectacled warbler (30 June), here a continuous song that would be broken up, with its phrases scattered through the early part of the piece (score, pp. 1–8). In a note Messiaen reminds himself how this should be done: 'In each strophe the first two sounds are separated, *mf*, flute-like; the remainder is a twittering, fairly rapid though less hurried than a whitethroat, the timbre gentle and charming.' The song forms in effect a chain of variations, starting in its simplest form, before being gradually infiltrated by pitches outside the key of the E major – F♮, B♭, C♮ etc. – with the cadence also varied as the song proceeds.[18]

As well as birdsong, Messiaen made notes on the landscape, the vineyards and the stony *garrigue*, speckled with wild flowers. Beyond was the Mediterranean, pale in the dawn light:

The sea is silvery grey. In the far distance, close to the horizon, the water is pink. The line of the horizon is blue-black, ash-grey; the base of the sky is mauve,

---

[14] *Ibid.*, p. 22.
[15] *Ibid.*, p. 12.
[16] 23056, p. 31.
[17] *Ibid.*, p. 7.
[18] *Ibid.*, p. 6.

pink, or like a pigeon's breast. The sun rises from the sea, fiery red, translucent red. Its blood-red disc is decorated with a band of gold at the top. Out of the fire, and gradually as it rises, the disc becomes entirely yellow, gold and orange. Immediately in front of the sun a golden band in the water extends into a thousand flecks of light.[19]

At the other end of the day, Messiaen recorded the colours as the sun set behind the Albères, the range of mountains at the eastern end of the Pyrenees:

Golden, red, gilded, pink and mauve, the vineyards in shadow, the sea a silvery pale blue. A band of mist, ash-blue, at the horizon ... Scent of thyme ... Quiet ... At 9.30 darkness falls over the vineyards and the sea. An umbrella pine extends its dark silhouette over the hillside. The mountains are consumed in fire – red, orange, violet – as the setting sun dies behind the mountain ... the lighthouse at Cap Béar, silence, the air still warm, the first star![20]

It must have been clear from an early stage that sea and sky would play a part in framing the birdsongs and shaping the progress of the music. Initially, indeed, it seems that Messiaen envisaged something similar to 'Le Loriot', the music beginning at dawn and developing through depictions of the sunrise.[21] One obvious difference with 'Le Loriot', however, is the role of the soloist, which in 'Le Traquet stapazin' (as also in 'La Bouscarle') is used as a brief and forceful refrain – Messiaen described its song as consisting of short, abrupt phrases, well-spaced and loud, with a 'rather metallic' timbre.[22] As such the wheatear forms the initial birdcall in the succession of three 'couplets' that open the piece (see the score, pp. 1–8).[23]

The first couplet forms a seedbed of motifs and relationships that will be developed throughout the piece; the harmonic connections are intricate and imaginative, so are worth examining in detail. Underlying them is the contrast (already noted) between the dissonant calls and cries – of the wheatear, gulls and raven – and the lyrical songs of the ortolan bunting, spectacled warbler and goldfinch, all characterised by their E major colouring. Both strands of harmony are present in the two introductory bars, the 'vignobles en terrasses'. In the first bar the harmony combines fourths and tritones, a variant of the fifth-plus-tritone observed earlier in

---

[19] Ibid., p. 6.
[20] Ibid., p. 7.
[21] Messiaen's prose plans for 'Le Traquet stapazin' come in a nine-page supplement to 23056, which we refer to as 23056(2).
[22] 23056, p. 2.
[23] See 23056(2), pp. 3–4. This also contains a draft of the title page and of the preface.

Example 5.6: for instance, in the song of the Thekla lark. In bar 2 we find the same chord-type (E–A♯–D♯), but this time combined with a harmony of E minor – answered, in the second half of the bar, by a pair of Messiaen's chords of 'contracted resonance' (Ex. 5.7a). The call of the wheatear (Ex. 5.7b) continues with the same chordal geometry (G–D–G♯, B♭–E♭–E), the G♯ in the melody being especially telling, after the earlier E minor harmony (Ex. 5.7a). Meanwhile, the tritone of the cadence (E to B♭) reverses the bass line in b. 2 (Ex. 5.7b).

The next birdsong, the ortolan bunting (Ex. 5.7c), has a similar chromatic shift from G♮ to G♯. This time the preliminary harmony (related, perhaps to the 'Wozzeck' chord found in 'La Chouette hulotte') builds on a low C, combining the tritone-plus-fourth (A–E♭–A♭) with rising perfect fifths, which extend logically into the ortolan's song – at the close of which E–B cadences downwards on to G♯. The descant in the right hand creates a blend of tonal colours – reminiscent of the oriole from 'Le Loriot', or the curlew and oystercatcher in 'Le Courlis cendré', with hints of triads on C, B, F♯ and D♯.

E major is given a new twist with the spectacled warbler (Ex. 5.7d), sunny ('ensoleillé') where the ortolan bunting was secretive ('flûté, mélancolique, extatique'). Again, the song is coloured by its introduction (b. 7), the two-note upbeat harmonised by a chord of 'contracted resonance' borrowed from bar 2, with the bass register once more filled with perfect fifths, again with a chromatic resolution, as G shifts up to G♯, C to C♯, and F to F♯. Meanwhile, the cadence – G♯ to E – completes the triad started by the ortolan bunting (B to G♯). Messiaen allows the harmony to linger (b. 9), gently imprinting on the mind what will become the defining sonority of the piece. Incidentally, his pedal marking leaves the pianist in some doubt: should one detach the E? Or sustain it in the pedal? Perhaps a middle way is best, allowing the pedal to catch the E but only as a 'shadow' sound.

The herring gull and raven (bb. 10–13) continue with fourths (or fifths) plus tritone; bar 12, however, is triadic, borrowing from the ortolan bunting (C major/D♯ minor). Finally, the goldfinch, in a descant of perfect fifths (A–E–B), embellishes a further cadence for the spectacled warbler. The warbler's last two phrases (p. 2, bb. 1 and 4) are the first sign of what will become a thread of development; here its melody suggests a triangular relationship between E and C^7 (and perhaps also $F\sharp^7$), all prefigured in the harmonies of the ortolan bunting.

A similar web of cross-references continues in the second and third couplets. In these the same birds are heard, but varied and with different songs given prominence. The second couplet, for example, sees a brief but brilliant episode for the goldfinch, supported by harmonies of

Example 5.7 (a) Harmonies from the first two bars; (b) wheatear (right hand); (c) ortolan bunting with introductory harmonies; (d) spectacled warbler with introductory harmonies; (e) herring gull and raven

(a)
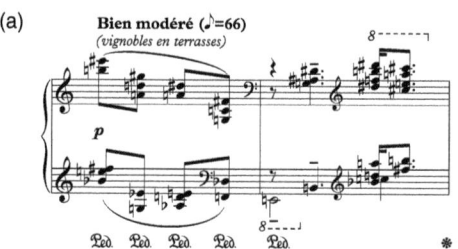

(b)

(c)
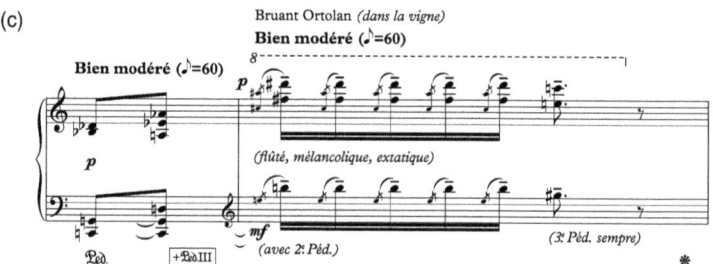

(d)

(e)

'transposed inversions'; these connect forwards with the middle part of the piece because Messiaen uses the same harmonies for the sunrise.

The development is divided into four sections (corresponding to pp. 8–19 of the printed score). The first and third of these sections (pp. 8–10 and 12–14) portray the sunrise, interrupted by the black-eared wheatear – whose calls have the effect of carrying the music forward through the long pauses. Between the two phases of the sunrise comes a trio of new birdsongs: rock bunting (with rapid repeated notes); the Orphean warbler, with its springing rhythms; and the high-lying corn bunting, its trills 'like splinters of crystal'. The last section of Messiaen's development (score, pp. 14–19) further extends these three birdsongs, culminating in the Thekla lark singing in flight, cut off by a long silence. This perhaps stands for midday, although the effect in performance is quite unlike the stillness in 'Le Loriot' or 'La Rousserolle effarvatte': a dramatic silence, quivering with possibilities.

The difficulty now was how to end. Messiaen's first idea was to bring back the birds of the opening couplet ('all different, but brief') and to conclude the piece with a coda, consisting of reminiscences of the Thekla lark and black-eared wheatear, finishing quietly with the ortolan bunting. This feels perfunctory, and must have seemed so to Messiaen, because immediately he had a new thought: 'perhaps a sunset? – a retrograde of the sunrise, with the chords only' (omitting, in other words, the interjections for two wheatears that had punctuated the sunrise). A musical sketch follows, headed 'Continuation of the coda: the sky red and violet, as the sun sinks behind the mountain'.[24] The sunset is represented by five chords – using only the first of Messiaen's 'transposed inversions' sequence – which reverse the sunrise by descending through a diminished seventh (the bass on C♯, B♭, G, E, C♯). Fragments of birdsong follow, no longer with the ortolan bunting but with a 'souvenir' of the spectacled warbler in slow motion (an idea retained in the final line of the finished score).

An interesting sidelight on Messiaen's working method is that these fragments, though not yet positioned as they will be in the final score, are meticulously finished. He has even gone to the trouble of indicating fingering for the slow-motion warbler, solving the awkwardness in the left hand of sustaining the harmony while sharing the melody with the right hand. He also details a subtle and exquisite effect whereby the melody is played without pedal, which is added in the final bar to give a just-detectable glow to the fading sound.

---

[24] 23056, p. 15.

Even so, this second solution seems unbalanced when set against the long process of development in the earlier part of the piece. And the ornithology is unconvincing, as Messiaen admitted, somewhat pedantically, in a note in the *cahier*: 'For formal reasons, the musical text does not always follow the chronology of the day's events.'[25] In other words, truth to nature has given way to the musician's desire for a sense of recapitulation.

Messiaen now embarked on a thorough revision. Originally, the closing section was to be announced by the wheatear; now he decided to introduce these phrases by returning to the music from the very beginning of the piece. The quiet sequence – the 'vignobles en terrasses' – steals into the long silence that halts the spectacular solo for the Thekla lark; the effect is formal, signalling both the start of a recapitulation of some sort, but also reconnecting with the landscape, the unchanging backdrop to the mercurial, ever-varied birdsongs.

What follows is a further variant on the sequence of songs found in the opening page of the piece. The one important difference, for reasons that will become clear, is that the spectacled warbler is omitted. Compensation comes with the goldfinch, the final song in the original strophe, now transformed into a scintillating duet, a tour de force of trills, broken chords and sharp interjections. (The sources for the duet suggest a later revision: the right hand is adapted from a recording, the left hand from a notation made at Petichet a few weeks later – proof that although much of 'Le Traquet stapazin' may have been composed at Banyuls the music was completed at Petichet later in the summer of 1957.)[26] The purpose of this episode for the goldfinch becomes clear in performance, as it gives a spurt of momentum that carries the music irresistibly into the music of the sunset. Unlike the slow unfolding of the sunrise, the sunset bursts in, the sun at its zenith, and musically the apex of the rising sequence left incomplete several pages earlier (score, p. 13).

In all likelihood Messiaen must have realised that a full-scale sunset – as in 'La Rousserolle effarvatte' – would have dissipated the momentum built up in the central part of the piece. The answer was a ruthless abbreviation, using (as already noted) only the first of the four chords of 'transposed inversions' found in the sunrise, and reducing the sequence of harmonies from five (in the original sketch) to three. The bass descends – C♯, B♭, G – with the expected arrival on E delayed by fragments (wheatear, Orphean

---

[25] It seems likely that Messiaen initially intended using this remark as a disclaimer in the preface. See 23056(2), p. 3.

[26] The recording is labelled 'Suisse 6', 23040, p. 8; the notation at Petichet is in 23052, p. 4.

Example 5.8 Harmonic progression, sunrise to sunset

warbler, ortolan bunting) (Ex. 5.8). When resolution arrives it does so unexpectedly, with E transformed, no longer the root of a chord of 'transposed inversions' but as the root of E major, warmed, as it has been throughout, by an added C♯. E major has been a colour and a point of reference, a link between birdsongs; now, finally, it is established as the home tonality. While E major (plus C♯) chimes below and above, the melody outlines a reminiscence, quoting 'Jardin du sommeil d'amour' from *Turangalîla*.

Coming at the end of what can now be seen as a huge arc of development, this is one of the great moments in the *Catalogue*, the start of a sublime contemplation on the fading colours of the sky – 'Use at the end', Messiaen reminds himself, 'the sunset at Cap l'Abeille, 28 June at 8.30, with the Thekla lark, corn bunting, ortolan, the Albères mountains, red and violet, the first star, the sun setting behind the mountain'.[27] To the listener this is so obviously a step into an interior state that we willingly understand birdsong and setting as merging in the mind and memory of the spectator, dream-like, as the day fades.

'Le Merle bleu' (Blue Rock Thrush)

June. Le Roussillon, the Côte Vermeille. Near Banyuls: Cap l'Abeille, Cap Rederis. Overhanging cliffs above a Prussian, sapphire-blue sea. Cries of swifts, splashing of water. The capes stretch into the sea like crocodiles.

The blue rock thrush sings, echoing in a rocky cleft. Its blue contrasts with the sea: purple blue, blue-grey, satin, blue-black. Almost exotic, recalling Balinese music, its song merges with the sound of the waves. We also hear the Thekla lark, fluttering in the sky above the vines and wild rosemary. Herring gulls scream far out to sea. The cliffs are fearsome. The water comes to die at their feet, a memory of the blue rock thrush.[28]

---

[27] 23056(2), p. 3.
[28] Preface to the score.

Messiaen's first visit to Banyuls also precipitated the final piece in Book 1, 'Le Merle bleu'. His *cahier* entries upon arrival show that he was immediately struck by the contrasting shades of blue: 'On the left, a mountain summit (1,000 m) – in strong sunlight – and another dark blue summit – in the clouds and golden sky. The Madeloc, with a lignite tower at its summit: the Tour de la Madeloc. On the right: the ash-blue sea, flecked with white horses – we are in a stony garden surrounded by vines.'[29] In the *Traité* he recalled his first sighting of a blue rock thrush:

> The place is extraordinary, it combines six landscapes in one: the mountain, the ash trees, the terraced vineyards, the scrubland with thorny vegetation, the rocky cliffs, the blue sea, surrounded by splashes of silver. This is where I encountered my first blue rock thrush. It was 22 June, it must have been 7 p.m., a kind of glorious sunshine gilded part of the sea and covered the cliffs in pink. Still, on the edge of a rock, a superb blue rock thrush.[30]

One of the innovations of 'Le Merle bleu' is the varied manner in which the blue rock thrush's song is set, reflecting the constantly changing light of the Côte Vermeille, the bird's song echoing in the rocky crevices ('anfractuosité'), and its blending with the sound of the sea. The writing for piano marks a step forward, showing a sophisticated acoustical imagination at play; it is as if the instrument is a resonant 'cave', a metaphor for the sights and sounds Messiaen encountered.

The piece is, above all, a meditation on the colour blue. The chordal refrain depicting 'la mer bleue' is a highlight of the *Catalogue*, contemplative and consolatory. The blues are contrasting: the sea is Prussian blue, sapphire-blue: the bird, by contrast, purple blue, blue-grey, satin, blue-black. There are, similarly, several 'shades' of song: at a gentle pace with a halo of upper resonance; steady and drawn-out with a tam-tam accompaniment; *très vif*, joyous, with a 'Balinese' ensemble of gongs in the bass; steady again, underpinned by the 'echo of rocks, turning resonance'. Add to these the thrush's introductory calls and drawn-out 'souvenir' on the hushed final page, and we have a unique variety of 'hearings' of a single bird.

These are partly responses to the different qualities of song Messiaen heard as he moved location down the coast. His appreciation of these qualities is also recorded in the *Traité*: 'The blue rock thrush's song is characterised firstly by its great purity of timbre and a certain naivety of contour. Which is not to suggest that it is entirely simple. On the contrary,

---

[29] 23057, p. 19.
[30] Olivier Messiaen, *Traité de rythme, de couleur et d'ornithologie: en sept tomes* (Paris: Alphonse Leduc, 1994–2002), Vol. V, Part I, p. 94.

the bird retains the same basic formula in order to vary its decoration: testimony to a highly developed artistic sense.'[31] The *cahiers* reveal the extent to which Messiaen worked with the blue rock thrush in two locations in order to recreate this 'artistry'. Their phrases are assigned numbers, shuffling them into an order that matches the score – a deft leap from transcription to final product. The second of the two thrushes, heard at the Cap Rederis on 25 June, is more consistent with the *Traité* description: it adheres to the pentatonic 'formula' Messiaen eventually adopted throughout the piece for this bird (A B C♯ E F♯). The first blue rock thrush notations, on 22 June at Cap l'Abeille, contain a more varied selection of pitches, with C♮, D♮ and G♯ making frequent appearances – Messiaen eventually ironed these all out to C♯, E or F♯, allowing musical considerations to take precedence over ornithology. The two locations then became the basis for the piece's form, which, in one reading at least, constitutes four verses framed by an introduction and coda. The phrases from Cap Rederis are used in verses 1 and 4, and those from Cap l'Abeille in verses 2 and 3 – like a holiday diary, one might say. The more diverse song of the Cap l'Abeille thrush, though altered to fit the pentatonic plan, nevertheless inspired the colourful tam-tam-and-gong accompaniment – just as Messiaen's original harmonisation of the grasshopper warbler was converted into a gong-like sonority in 'La Rousserolle effarvatte'. In both cases the composer was able to be true to his source whilst adapting it to suit his broader vision.

The Hybrid Form of 'Le Merle bleu'

Though apparently simple, the structure of 'Le Merle bleu' is in fact one of the most complex in the cycle; as the third piece in Book 1 it stands at the opposite extreme to the block-like 'Le Chocard des Alpes' and the succession of morning calls in 'Le Loriot'. Though the cast is small – four birds in all – their cries are interspersed with music representing the coastal surroundings, arranged into a synthesis of an arch form (i.e. a symmetrical structure), a reprise-based form (returning to earlier material – and the original location – in verse 4), and the strophic structure described above and tabulated here in Table 5.1. A prominent feature of the strophic aspect is that each verse concludes with the stirring 'la mer bleue' passage (Ex. 5.9) – the pun on the title is surely deliberate and an acknowledgment of the symbiosis between bird and surroundings.

[31] *Ibid.*, p. 76.

Table 5.1 The strophic structure of 'Le Merle bleu'

Section	Birdsongs	Nature	Blue rock thrush *cahier* notations
Introduction (p. 1 to p. 3, b. 8)	Swifts Blue rock thrush ♪ = 92 Thekla lark	Water Cliffs	Cap Rederis, 25 June 1957
Verse 1 (p. 3, b. 9 to p. 6, b. 4)	Blue rock thrush ♪ = 80 (with upper resonance)	Resonance of bells ('ambiance') Water The blue sea	Cap Rederis, 25 June 1957
Verse 2 (p. 6, b. 5 to end of p. 9)	Blue rock thrush ♪ = 132 (with tam-tam lower resonance) Herring gull	Waves Resonance from rock faces The blue sea	Cap l'Abeille, 22 June 1957
Verse 3 (p. 10 to p. 19, b. 11)	First Thekla lark duet Blue rock thrush ♪ = 184 (with Balinese accompaniment) and ♪ = 80 ('écho des rochers' – most phrases a repetition of ♪ = 184) Herring gulls Second Thekla lark duet	Lapping of the waterwaves (with A⁰ climax) The blue sea (apotheosis)	Cap l'Abeille, 22 June 1957
Verse 4 (p. 19, b.12 to p. 23, b. 3)	Blue rock thrush ♪ = 80 (reprise of upper resonance)	Waves Resonance from rock faces (with A⁰ climax) The blue sea (fragment)	Cap Rederis, 25 June 1957
Coda (p. 23, b.4 to end)	Blue rock thrush ♪ = 92, 63 and 25 (tending towards 'souvenir') Swifts	Cliffs (with A⁰ climax)	Cap Rederis, 25 June 1957

Example 5.9 'La mer bleue'

These progressions, which conclude with three brilliant bitonal arpeggios ('clair, perlé') – the sun glinting on the waves – strongly influence the tonal argument of the piece, which vacillates between A major with a strong added sixth flavour (when the rock thrush is singing) and the keys of F♯ major and minor, both used to evoke the landscape. As each 'mer bleue' refrain cadences, the right hand is instructed to play 'pouce couché' (thumb under the hand): thumb on A above second finger on F♯. Observing this instruction is important, as it both symbolises and subtly reinforces the tonal argument. In verse 1 the left hand plays A major second inversion under this dyad; in verse 2 F♯ major second inversion; verse 3 climaxes on a heartfelt cadence from F♯ major with added thirteenth to the same A major second inversion as verse 1. Verse 4 cuts off abruptly without cadencing. The sea-refrain therefore creates a sense of tonal return at the end of verse 3, establishing reprise or recapitulation form as an undercurrent to the strophic surface.

The distribution of tempi for the rock thrush (seen in the metronome marks in Table 5.1), along with the placement of the two Thekla lark duets around the central 'Balinese' section (which is the most energetic music in the piece), *and* the locations and times at which the calls were collected, all contribute to the arch form. The early return to the ♪ = 80 of verse 1 in the middle of verse 3 creates a false sense of reprise – convincing enough that, when it arrives, the second Thekla lark duet can sound misplaced, like a kaleidoscope turning back to an earlier pattern. Messiaen immediately counteracts any confusion with the most lengthy and climactic 'mer bleue' passage – suddenly he is at his most teleological.

Robert Sherlaw Johnson subscribes to the strophic view, but his analysis stops short of differentiating the blue rock thrush calls and ignores the final 'mer bleue' fragment, presumably considering it too short to be important.[32] The fragment is only three bars long, but Messiaen's avoidance of cadence – cutting suddenly to the atonal music of the cliffs – is his way of depicting the landscape's variety within a 360-degree sweep, and of keeping sentimentality at bay.

In the last three sections of the piece depictions of various 'characters' from nature – waves, rocks and cliffs – reach climaxes on the lowest notes of the piano, the most telling being the 'resonance from rock faces', for which it is possible to imitate the clangorous bass sonorities achieved by Loriod in her recordings by playing the B♭ within the cluster with the right hand thumb, as the score suggests. Handling this succession of climaxes is one of the challenges of 'Le Merle bleu' (they are gesturally similar). Loriod, typically, avoids any sense of lingering; this, allied with keen judgment of tone colour, is the most effective strategy.

The contrast between simplicity (the 'holiday diary') and subtlety in this hybrid form chimes with what Messiaen calls the 'aesthetic' of the blue rock thrush: the notion of naivety concealing art.

Thekla Lark Counterpoint

The Thekla lark duets in verse 3 are a sophisticated example of Messiaen's contrapuntal *style oiseau*. They are more varied and more pianistic than, for example, the garden warbler duets in 'Le Loriot', the latter featuring awkward repetitions of notes. Dynamics are also an important feature of the duets: in contrast with the 'luminous' blue rock thrush the calls of these birds 'sizzle' and tremble with joy as they perform their 'butterfly-like' flights above the cliffs (all of these are Messiaen's descriptions).

The two birdsongs, one in each hand, come from two virtuoso transcriptions in the Banyuls *cahier*, 23057 – the first lark, which became the lower part, heard at 8 p.m. on 27 June, the second at 9 the following morning (Ex. 5.10). Messiaen modified both, as can be seen almost immediately. In the

---

[32] Robert Sherlaw Johnson, *Messiaen*, 2nd paperback edn, updated and with additional text by Caroline Rae (London: Omnibus Press, 2008 [1975]), p. 145.

Example 5.10 Thekla larks in 23057, p. 37 (a); p. 40 (b)

cahier both birds begin their cadenzas in similar fashion, and tremolo on an E♮/E♭ midway through the first line. Messiaen avoids the chance to create imitative counterpoint from this, instead fast-forwarding the lower part to a flourish at the end of the line – one of the few gestures in this passage that are totally faithful to the *cahier* (Ex. 5.11). Manipulations of a similar kind continue throughout the duets. The song of the evening lark is more repetitive, and this makes it somehow more appropriate for the left hand – more invention can be heard in the right hand's brilliant register. The message in all of this is sheer joy, the celebration of nature by man and bird.

Memory and 'Souvenirs'

A similarly imaginative use of the *cahier* material is found in the slow-motion 'souvenirs' that end the piece. *Cahier* 23057 confirms Messiaen's claim in the *Traité* that he used one phrase from the Cap Rederis for these; this is the second of the two, which is also heard as the bird's second phrase in the introduction.[33] The first 'souvenir' phrase is nowhere to be seen, and may well have been crafted by the composer himself as a memory of the preceding music. It shares characteristics with the bird's very first call on page 1 – both these phrases have seven notes, and open with a descending seventh, with the first note as the highest note, appearing with an

[33] 23057, p. 25.

Example 5.11 Opening of the first Thekla lark duet in 'Le Merle bleu', p. 10

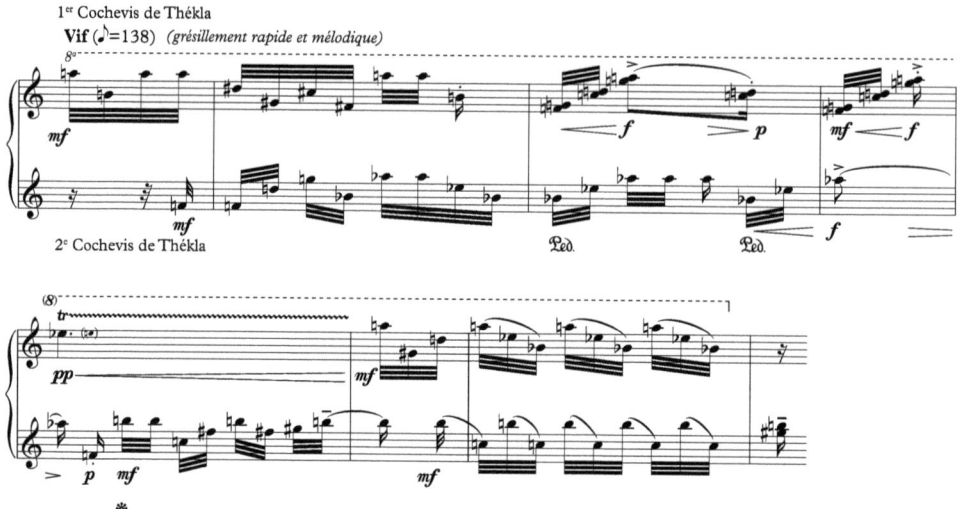

immediate repetition later in the phrase.[34] The same 'souvenir' phrase also includes references to the piece's supporting cast: the falling seventh loosely mimics the swifts (or the other way round), and is closely related to the first Thekla lark's opening motto. As the Thekla lark was notated on 28 June, the day before Messiaen left Banyuls, the impression is that he gathered all his material before choosing the souvenir phrases – or perhaps his memory of the thrushes influenced how he heard the larks. This is one of the appealing riddles that the *cahiers* highlight but cannot solve.

'Le Merle bleu' is an exhilarating synthesis of the two other pieces in Book 1: the craggy atonal music of 'Le Chocard des Alpes' and the tonal warmth of 'Le Loriot'. Whilst Messiaen continually looks to his musical past in the two earlier pieces – the avant-garde pastiche in 'Le Chocard des Alpes', the quotations of Debussy (and himself) in 'Le Loriot' – his joy of discovery on the Côte Vermeille means that 'Le Merle bleu' is almost exclusively absorbed in the here and now.[35]

Until, that is, the final page. Blending, in the stillness of the evening, the A- and F♯-based sonorities that are heard throughout the piece, the souvenirs are marked 'very pure, like a choir of female voices in the distance'. Messiaen could have had in mind either the added-sixth harmonies of his *Trois petites Liturgies* or the offstage voices in Debussy's 'Sirènes' (from *Nocturnes*), or

---

[34] Another implication of arch form.
[35] Nevertheless, 'Le Merle bleu' is a worthy successor to the great Debussian seascapes: *La Mer* and the last scene of the first act of *Pelléas et Mélisande*.

both. In 'Sirènes', and in the third scene of Act I of *Pelléas*, the voices are heard towards the end of the third panel of a triptych, just as in 'Le Merle bleu'.

A more precise model may be *Das Rheingold*, which featured regularly in Messiaen's teaching in the later 1950s. The melodic formulae of the Rhinemaidens as their voices emerge from the prelude match the pentatonic mode from which the souvenir's harmonies are built. Even Messiaen's harmonic progression echoes Wagner.[36] The blue of 'Le Merle bleu', paired with the sunlight of 'Le Loriot', matches the colours of Wagner's title, 'Rhinegold', and the modal ending means Book 1 is left poised, the distant voices stilled as the water glints below.

'La Buse variable' (Buzzard)

In the Dauphiné, la Matheysine. The broad open countryside of Petichet, at the end of the Lac de Laffrey, beneath the bald mountain of the Grand Serre.
Introduction. The cry of the buzzard as it flies to and fro. It circles, the orbits of its flight covering the whole landscape. It descends slowly.
1st couplet. Chaffinch, yellowhammer. Mewing of the buzzard. Refrain of the mistle thrush.
2nd couplet. The same, also with the goldfinch. Refrain of the mistle thrush.
3rd couplet. The swallows. A red-backed shrike gives the alarm. Combat: six carrion crows mob the buzzard for its prey. Deep ferocious cawings from the one, grated fluttering and weird mewing for the other. Refrain of the mistle thrush. Hurried strophes of the whitethroat.
Coda. The cry of the buzzard: it circles slowly, soaring upwards.[37]

'La Buse variable' begins the seventh and final book, bringing the *Catalogue* full circle back to Messiaen's home territory, the Lac de Laffrey and the fields of Petichet; closer to home, indeed, than 'Le Chocard des Alpes'. If anything, however, the mood of the piece is more inscrutable; for long periods there is little comfort to be found on the shores of the lake. In contrast to every other piece in the *Catalogue* – as well as the next Petichet-inspired work, *La Fauvette des jardins* – there is no music that specifically describes the scenery. As if to compensate for this, 'La Buse variable' has a set piece at its core that animates the form: a confrontation between the

---

[36] Woglinde enters on an F, coinciding with the first harmonic shift in the *Ring* cycle, from E♭ to A♭ with added sixth, and anticipating the next move to a chord of F minor – Messiaen follows the same course (a semitone higher) with the last chord of 'Le Merle bleu'. The light harmonic touch marks out both passages.
[37] Preface to the score.

buzzard and some belligerent crows. It is the one piece in the *Catalogue* that features overt interaction between birds, with the red-backed shrike a bystander that 'sounds the alarm' at the beginning of the episode.

Around this centrepiece is the familiar combination of symmetrical design and one-off events, a combination that as always serves to illustrate the passing of time: some birds return later in the day, others do not. In 'La Buse variable' a delightful assortment of birds sing before the fight: chaffinch, yellowhammer (later associated with closure in Messiaen, so that retrospectively we can hear it as acknowledgment that the final *livre* has begun), mistle thrush, goldfinch and swallow.[38] Of these the mistle thrush, yellowhammer, goldfinch and buzzard return after the conflict, and are joined by the voluble whitethroat, a member of the *fauvette* family (*fauvette grisette*) given a piano texture not unlike the one that dominates *La Fauvette des jardins*. The outermost sections are where the symmetry is strongest. Here Messiaen depicts the buzzard's spiralling flight in two hypnotic, monorhythmic passages of twelve-tone material that slowly crescendo in the introduction and diminuendo in the coda until the final two notes of the piece are played *sans pédale*, the buzzard becoming a receding speck far above.

The angular and registrally extreme lines that depict the buzzard's flight contain no actual counterpoint, merely constant reordering of a series of dyads with octave transpositions to provide variety. Each tone row occupies a bar of 12/8, though the barlines only reflect the organisation rather than dictate the flow, which is inexorable. Rather like Harrison Birtwistle in *Silbury Air*, Messiaen invents a scheme for which rules seem to exist, but remain obscure. Five of the twelve dyads in each bar are perfect fourths, and the only other interval represented more than once is the minor sixth.[39] The first bar of spiralling consigns four of the perfect fourths to the last four quavers.[40] These do not seem like chance happenings; they hint at the ultimate goal for right hand of the mistle thrush, whose *nostalgique* music is the most stylised in the whole piece – a powerful, emotive backbone to the entire structure.

---

[38] The yellowhammer has the last word in several of the *Méditations sur le Mystère de la Sainte Trinité* (1969) for organ.

[39] Having the same set of dyads in each bar is a consequence of there being interversions (of the *Catalogue*'s governing 'scheme') in each hand that are always the same distance apart – in this case interversions 1 and 3, 2 and 4, and so forth, as Wai-Ling Cheong has shown ('Symmetrical Permutation', pp. 124–127).

[40] This is a difficult passage to bring off in performance, as each note is so exposed; imagining *portamenti* between them is one way to create line and atmosphere.

Like the varying proximity of the buzzard's flight, the character types of the accompanying cast are expressed through dynamics: from the naive, *pianissimo* octosyllable of the yellowhammer to the optimistic *crescendo* of the chaffinch; the streetwise contrasts of the red-backed shrike; and the aggressive *fff* cawing of the crows. Most of these sounds were collected in the first ten days of Messiaen's 1957 summer break – in *cahier* 23052, to be precise, between 12 and 21 July.[41] There was certainly interaction, if not outright confrontation, between two buzzards and a number of crows on the very first day, and perhaps this was the event that persuaded Messiaen a buzzard piece was dramatically viable.[42]

The mistle thrush is the odd bird out, both musically speaking and in terms of its origin. Thrushes had been on Messiaen's mind throughout the spring and summer months, since a trip to Orgeval in early March. Song- and mistle thrushes sang that day for fully six hours, copiously recorded in the *cahier*, the latter's strophes being described as 'very strong – very clear – courageous and sad'. Brief snippets of this music are heard on pages 3 and 4, harmonised conventionally in three and sometimes four parts. Further notations were made in late April in Lèves, to the west of Paris, during the recuperative trip Messiaen took immediately after the premiere of the first six pieces. By this point the timbre had become 'nostalgic' and even 'mighty' (*puissant*). The material from Lèves is treated in a far more epic manner, the mistle thrush's song being transformed into a sonorous refrain, beginning on page 3 of the score and marked 'strong, clear, brassy timbre – like a courageous, sad fanfare'.

Later in life Messiaen confirmed in conversation that he had a tendency to create an 'idealised' song for any given bird, based on 'the best passages' that he had transcribed.[43] The mistle thrush at Lèves seems the epitome of Dukas's advice: 'Listen to the birds, they are great masters.'[44] Its melodic detail is exquisite, and bears hallmarks of Messiaen's style, in particular reinterpretations of earlier phrases that incorporate an added value (*valeur ajoutée*) (Ex. 5.12).[45]

Phrase 3 repeats the rhythm of phrase 1, with an added demisemiquaver. Phrase 4 has elements of all the preceding three – embellishment of

---

[41] The buzzard's tumbling call (p. 5, b. 4) is to be 'like a moaning woman' ('comme un gémissement de femme') in 23052, p. 1.
[42] *Ibid.*, p. 2.
[43] Olivier Messiaen, 'Entretien avec Claude Samuel: réalisé à Paris en Octobre 1988', liner note to Erato/Warner CD, trans. Stuart Walters.
[44] See Stephen Broad, *Olivier Messiaen: Journalism 1935–1939* (Farnham: Ashgate, 2012), p. 82.
[45] This is perhaps unsurprising, as it is Messiaen who transcribed it! But there is so much material for this bird that does not quite reach these heights, it's possible that he only realised its quality in retrospect.

Example 5.12 The mistle thrush in 23051, p. 6 (a); as realised in the score, p. 5 (b)

the high G♯ that features in phrases 2 and 3; the reintroduction of B♭ from phrase 1 – and it finishes with a combination of the endings of phrases 2 and 3. The bird seems well versed in Messiaen's techniques of composition.

Messiaen clearly admired what he heard at Lèves, because having presented these phrases in gradually accumulating blocks in the first half of 'La Buse variable' he repeated them together after the fight between the buzzard and the crows, adding a seven-bar coda. Formally, this resembles the treatment of the golden oriole's song in 'Le Loriot', and it comes as no surprise that in mid 1957 Messiaen sketched in the back of his diary a brief outline for a mistle thrush piece set in Herbeville and Orgeval on a tempestuous day ('matin – avant l'orage/fin d'après-midi, avant l'orage'). Directly underneath this is a thumbnail sketch of a chaffinch's refrain, heightening the impression that 'La Buse variable' is a metamorphosis of this initial idea. It seems the birdsong collecting of July 1957 awoke Messiaen to the possibility of writing a Petichet piece, and this became an alternative habitat for the mistle thrush, with force of nature replaced by a violent scene.

Though deprived of a title role, the mistle thrush is still entrusted with an important task: it sets out a tonal basis for the rest of Book 7. The fanfare music is accompanied in the left hand by a succession of major and minor chords that span a tenth (too wide a stretch for Loriod – Messiaen didn't always take his dedicatee's physiology into account). The chords vacillate between C major and E♭ minor before eventually reaching D minor (p. 14, b. 6) – the second and third of these chords being

Table 5.2 The tonal structure of Book 7

Catalogue d'oiseaux, Book 7	'La Buse variable'	'Le Traquet rieur'	'Le Courlis cendré'
Tonal centres visited	C major, E♭ minor, D minor	A major	E♭ minor, E minor, D minor
Structural characteristics	Twelve-note passages frame the piece; tonal sections within this	Strophic structure with consistent tonal underlay	Tonal passages frame the piece; twelve-note central section

precisely the left-hand notes above which the curlew gives vent to its 'tragic and desolate' *glissandi* in 'Le Courlis cendré'. These harmonies also create a link with 'Le Traquet rieur', which is firmly rooted in, and glowing with, A major – the dominant of D minor and tritone-dominant of E♭ minor. In 'La Buse variable' the tonal passages are bookended by the atonal flight of the buzzard; in 'Le Courlis cendré' the opposite occurs: the tonal call of the curlew surrounds the more dissonant shrieks of the other birds and the twelve-note sea, mist and foghorn.

The overall scheme for Book 7 is illustrated in Table 5.2. All of the books of the *Catalogue d'oiseaux* could be said to have their own internal logic, and tonal forces are strong in Books 1 (across 'Le Loriot' and 'Le Merle bleu') and 2 (throughout 'Le Traquet stapazin'), and in a more localised way during the sunset in 'La Rousserolle effarvatte' and the river music in 'La Bouscarle'. Book 7 is nevertheless the most balanced and teleological in its tonal design, with each individual key having a strong emotional impact. The issue of Messiaen's reluctance to write music directly portraying a landscape so dear to him remains. Throughout 1957 his wife, Claire, was in an especially fragile state (necessitating a change of nursing home in the autumn of that year). Perhaps memories of time spent with her at Petichet were simply too fresh to write the warmly affectionate portrayal that eventually emerged in *La Fauvette des jardins*. Messiaen may even have felt incapable, at the time, of capturing this landscape in music; his language was about to enjoy a period of considerable enrichment.

Philip Weller expresses the situation vis-à-vis Claire with typical eloquence; he is referring to 1948 rather than 1957, but his description is surely an enduring one: 'Claire's frail yet continuing presence, however tenuous and psychologically fragile, and however absorbed into a beyond of distracted suffering, was not to be simply eclipsed by the phenomenon of Loriod, the initially unwitting agent (as she was soon to become) of Messiaen's artistic and psychological (self) renewal.'[46] It may even be that 'La Buse variable' is a piece for the Claire of the 1950s, and 'La Bouscarle' a more idyllic recollection of the 1930s (the 'nuptial flight' of the kingfisher in the latter contains reminiscences of the *Thème et Variations* and *Poèmes pour Mi*).[47] Just as the golden oriole is associated with Loriod, so the buzzard and the mistle thrush could be said to represent Claire. The mistle thrush's song is 'strong, bright ['clair'], nostalgic, courageous and sad'; the slow orbits of the buzzard evoke her worsening condition (crescendo) and growing distance from her family (diminuendo).

Messiaen's description of the buzzard's call in the *cahiers* as otherworldly and feminine ('un cri étrange – cri de femme') does nothing to dispel this impression.[48] In both 'Le Chocard des Alpes' and 'La Buse variable' the principal bird's flight is described as receding ('s'éloigner'), an evocative verb that also inhabits Boulez's 'Bourreaux de solitude' ('Hangmen of Solitude') – a René Char setting that shares the latent resignation of the two *Catalogue* pieces.[49] 'Bourreaux' is the most conventionally serial movement of *Le Marteau sans maître* (particularly its durations, which range from one to twelve semiquavers) and, having recently been composed, premiered and recorded, was a work that was prominent in Domaine musical circles at the time:

Le pas s'est éloigné le marcheur s'est tu
Sur le cadran de l'Imitation
Le Balancier lance sa charge de granit réflexe.

The step has gone away the walker fallen silent
On the dial of imitation
The Pendulum casts its load of granite in reverse.[50]

Something similar can be found in Paul Eluard's *Présence*:

Lorsque tu es parti à cause d'un accident,
Ils t'ont tous éloigné du monde des vivants

---

[46] Philip Weller, 'Messiaen, the *Cinq Rechants* and "Spiritual Violence"', in Christopher Dingle and Robert Fallon (eds.), *Messiaen Perspectives 1: Sources and Influences* (Farnham: Ashgate, 2013), pp. 279–312 (p. 282).

[47] 'Et la voilà, verte et bleue comme le paysage!' is a line from 'Paysage', the second of *Poèmes pour Mi*. Green and blue are the colours of 'La Bouscarle'.

[48] For example 23052, p. 2.

[49] These are the two pieces in *Catalogue d'oiseaux* where the time of day is unclear – it has been omitted in the prefaces, giving these two Dauphiné pieces a further reflective quality.

[50] Translation by Paul Griffiths.

Et, avec de la terre ils t'ont bien recouvert.
Pour eux, quelle évidence, tu n'étais plus présent.

When an accident caused you to leave,
They all banished you from the land of the living
And completely covered you with earth.
For them it was clear you were no longer there.[51]

If there is an acknowledgment of Claire's distant situation – and even, in the conflict with the crows, recognition of her demons – the mistle thrush from 'La Buse variable' could not pay a finer conjugal tribute; at the very least, it confirms that *something* in the human realm is being powerfully expressed.

The Final Pieces: 'Le Merle de roche' and 'Le Traquet rieur'

On 12 September 1958 Messiaen showed Loriod the last pieces to be completed, 'Le Merle de roche' and 'Le Traquet rieur'. It was a joyful occasion: for Messiaen this was not just another completed work, but the culmination of years of research. The preceding months had brought further enrichment of his musical language. In 'Le Merle de roche', the rock thrush – its song and its plumage – shines out against the jagged limestone backdrop of the Cirque de Mourèze, its blue-orange feathers and radiant harmonies belying its shy nature. The black-and-white 'Traquet rieur' (black wheatear) is the most richly harmonised of all the *Catalogue*'s birds. These are the first pieces in which we hear birdsong being coloured by chords of transposed inversion, which had already played an important illustrative and structural role as the rising-sun harmonies in 'Le Traquet stapazin'; they therefore mark a new phase in the integration of birdsong and scenery. Just as the *Catalogue* lays down a marker for Messiaen's approach to form in his subsequent works, so these two radiant pieces anticipate the harmonic palette of the 1960s and beyond. In a sense they are the *Catalogue*'s own late style. Small wonder that there was elation when Loriod picked up the scores for the first time.[52]

---

[51] Eluard, along with Pierre Reverdy, was an inspirational poet for Messiaen, as acknowledged in the preface to *Technique de mon langage musical*.

[52] The sense of culmination and achievement must have been heightened by the surrounding events: Messiaen had bought a 565 m^2 field at Petichet two days earlier, and the next day he and Loriod returned to Paris for the season's first concerts, the summer over.

Messiaen and Loriod's excursions throughout 1958 had generated reams of material, and some powerful new impressions. The most extensive trip, at Easter, was to southern France: a grand tour taking in Béziers, a return to Banyuls, and the Gorges de Galamus and du Tarn, before looping round to Pézenas, which they used as a base for exploring the Hérault region in the company of the ornithologist François Hüe.[53] While Messiaen found stimulation for his colouristic imagination, Loriod studied the timbre of the birds (larks, owls and warblers prominent amongst them) and drove the two enthusiasts on an itinerary that criss-crossed the area.

'Le Merle de roche' (Rock Thrush)

May. The Hérault. The Cirque de Mourèze. Chaos of dolomite, rocks in fantastic forms. Night, moonlight. Dominating all the other rocks, an immense stone hand! Towards the end of the night the eagle owl hoots, low and loud – his female answers with smothered tapping: sinister hilarity, the rhythm of which merges with frightened heartbeats. Dawn breaks: varied cries of the jackdaws. Then the black redstart begins its monotonous song: in the middle of the strophe, noise that evokes pearls being shaken, paper crumpling or the swish of silk. The rocks are terrifying: prehistoric stone animals, stegosaurus, diplodocus appear to be standing guard – a group à la Max Ernst: cowled stone phantoms, carrying a dead woman whose hair trails along the ground …

Perched on a spit of rock, a rock thrush! How handsome he is! Blue head, red tail, black wings, bright orange breast. He sings in the hours of sun, warmth and light: ten in the morning, five in the afternoon – and his song is luminous orange, like his plumage! The moments of silence are rhythmicised and numbered in slow durations. The black redstart reprises its sound effects. Last cries of the jackdaws. End of dusk: the eagle owl hoots, and his voice resonates amongst the rocks, bringing darkness and dread. Night, moonlight. The gigantic hand is always there, towering above the stone monsters, a magic sign![54]

'Le Merle de roche' is the least often performed of the three pieces in the *Catalogue* that occupy a *livre* of their own. The scene-painting is dissonant and dense, and it is difficult for a performer to establish momentum

---

[53] A long-time birdwatching companion of Messiaen, Hüe was the co-writer (with R.D. Etchécopar) of the immense *Les Oiseaux du Proche et du Moyen Orient* (1970), 948 pages that contain English and German indices of birds as well as a French/Latin integrated one (cf. *Catalogue d'oiseaux*). The authors carried out their fieldwork between 1964 and 1969, so it seems likely that Hüe was a factor in Messiaen's discovery of birds from that region in the late 1960s. He was killed in a car accident in 1972.

[54] Preface to the score.

Figure 5.3 The Cirque de Mourèze

because of the shyness of the rock thrush (there are many long silences) and the rigidity of the rhythmic series that depict the bizarre dolomite formations of the Cirque de Mourèze. Nevertheless, the rock thrush is one of the most colourful of all the title birds, and the piece has an air of mystery and fascination, with Messiaen's surrealist imagination to the fore – all qualities that are evident in the preface.

The piece's gestation is framed by two visits to the Cirque de Mourèze in 1958. The first was as part of the 'grand tour' of the spring, on the evening of 7 April, and the composer was immediately struck by the 'extraordinary chaos of eroded stone – a lunar landscape, or Dante-esque inferno'. Three of the four main characters of 'Le Merle de roche' were encountered that day: jackdaws circling the Mount Saint-Jean-d'Aureilhan; eagle owls nesting on a suspended pathway; and a rock thrush, whose luminous orange breast offset the crepuscular surroundings.[55] In each case Messiaen went

---

[55] Volume V, Part I of the *Traité* (p. 63) contradicts this somewhat, as Messiaen there claims that he heard his first rock thrush on 26 May 1958 in Banyuls. But there is unmistakably one present on this *cahier* page, 23065 p. 15, from 7 April.

on to draw on previous notations, some already pianistically developed and seemingly earmarked for use when the opportunity arose. This is the case for the first and last birds to be heard in the piece, the male and female eagle owls, which are drawn from the detailed 1956 notations from the Swedish discs in 23045. They are a comical pair – the female's 'sniggering' (or 'sinister hilarity') even lower than the baritone male's hooting – and are the only birds already assigned fingerings in this extensive *cahier*.[56]

The evidence suggests that the jackdaws were originally to enjoy a starring role in the cycle, in a piece that melded their cries with the bells of Chartres Cathedral. Lengthy notations were made in *cahier* 23051, in April 1957, when Messiaen and Loriod passed by the cathedral twice in the space of ten days; on the outward journey Messiaen observed that 'the jackdaws are influenced by the bells!' (23051, p. 11). In both 23051 and 23063 they are often written in three parts, 23051 containing some unpianistic triple *glissandi*. Perhaps Messiaen ultimately felt, after his Mediterranean epiphany, that their cries were lacking the colour required for a major piece. Nevertheless, having rejected this initial idea he grasped the chance to bring them into the Mourèze tableau, spurred on no doubt by their presence in this new landscape.[57]

The rock thrush is an elusive bird, and its sources equally so. Even though Messiaen made several notations of rock thrushes from the Swedish discs and *en plein air* up to 1958, little of this surviving material found its way into 'Le Merle de roche'. In the *Traité* Messiaen states that its typical song contains 'two-by-twos' similar to the woodlark, but 'diatonic', as opposed to the lark's chromatic descents.[58] These tendencies are in evidence in 23045 and the notations made at Mourèze, but not so much in the piece itself (only on p. 16 and in the 'idealised' song on p. 19). Instead the bird has a motto theme that returns in various guises (Ex. 5.13).

The valedictory music for the title bird is the 'idealisation of the rock thrush – glorification of the orange-blue of its song and plumage' (p. 19 of the score), sketched on a tantalisingly unknown date in the Chartres *cahier*, 23051. *Could* this be from 1957, like the rest of the *cahier*, or did Messiaen reuse the *cahier* the following summer once he had decided to enlist jackdaws for the new piece? The richness of the harmony suggests the latter. These magnificent harmonies slowly work up to a ten-note chord with five black notes in the right hand and five white in the left (Ex. 5.14). It is a

---

[56] Characteristically, the fingerings appear completely unchanged in the score several years later.
[57] Perhaps Messiaen also wished to maintain the Alpine chough's status as the cycle's only title bird that is black – the jackdaws being sacrificed for the sake of the team.
[58] Messiaen, *Traité*, Vol. V, Part I, p. 64.

Example 5.13 'Le Merle de roche' p. 9, bb. 1 and 2

Example 5.14 Idealisation of the rock thrush

kinaesthetic climax for the pianist, unravelling earlier 'pouce couché' contortions found on pages 1 to 3.

Messiaen spent limited time in Paris during May and June (a period when he would normally be maintaining teaching commitments), but whilst there his imagination remained active. In early June he sketched what was to become the scene-setting opening and closing music of 'Le Merle de roche'.[59] At this point it was merely an imaginary landscape, yet to include the owls' interjections, and with the heading 'Messiaen' where the location would normally be written, perhaps implying an autobiographical element of some kind. Here in the *cahier* the pentatonic outline of the phrases that rise out of shadowy 'chords of contracted resonance' can be seen clearly. The phrase that alludes to Debussy's 'Clair de lune' was at this point intended to be heard twice, hinting that Messiaen already had a moonlit scene in mind (see Ex. 5.15).

[59] 23060, p. 7.

Example 5.15 *Cahier* 23060, p. 7 (facsimile)

Figure 5.4 'The Sphinx'

Shortly afterwards Messiaen annotated this page 'pour la main levée' ('for the raised hand'), referring to one of the most striking images in 'Le Merle de roche', the 'immense stone hand, raised in a magic sign' (p. 1). It seems likely that Messiaen's second visit to the Cirque at the end of June was the catalyst for all these ingredients coming together. There, in the summer heat, his imagination became more fevered, and prose was dispensed with as his visions proliferated: 'A giant chameleon – columns – pointed towers – an elephant seen from behind – a rhinoceros – a dog – sphinx – a giant hand – a vase – terraces – an Assyrian palace – haloed ramparts – penguins – a hooded monk – a ship's hull – a giant mushroom – an army of two-dimensional elephants ...' In these flights of fancy he was also displaying some local knowledge; the most photographed of the Cirque's many formations is 'The Sphinx', a fitting appellation when viewed head-on (see Fig. 5.4). Its profile, intriguingly, resembles a raised fist, and Messiaen may have noticed this as he moved round the dolomite gallery (the two are adjacent in his description as can be seen).[60]

---

[60] Jean Boivin reports that Messiaen showed pictures of the Cirque to his class: 'Can you make out a hand, forty metres tall? Absolutely, it's a type of hand, though no one has said as much.' The formation's height, and Messiaen's noting that its hand-like aspect had been missed, make him all the more likely to have been looking at the Sphinx. Jean Boivin, *La Classe de Messiaen* (Paris: C. Bourgois, 1995), p. 329.

Table 5.3 The form of 'Le Merle de roche'

INTRODUCTION	owls and stone hand	night
	jackdaws and stone hand	dawn breaking
MEDLEY 1	jackdaws	
	redstart and 'dinosaur' durations	
CENTRAL RONDO	rock thrush	10 a.m.
(ABA¹CA²)	'cortège' durations	
	rock thrush reprise	5 p.m.
	slower 'luminous' rock thrush and jackdaws	
	rock thrush reprise	
CENTRAL CODA	redstart and 'idealised' rock thrush	
MEDLEY 2	'tous de pierre' (dinosaurs, diverse monsters and durations)	
	redstart, jackdaws	
	'stone stegosaurus' durations	
CODA	owls and stone hand	end of twilight
	stone hand, no birds	night

The Cirque is a character in its own right – it has the presence of the Commendatore in Mozart's *Don Giovanni*, coming alive in the passages of 'numbered silences' described in the preface. The final member of the cast to be integrated was the black redstart, another bird featured on the Swedish discs – so its presence on 28 June must have delighted Messiaen. Its registral diversity helps bind the piece together, just like the red-backed shrike in 'La Buse variable'. It has two distinct styles: a glowing, repetitive song heard in the Cirque and, from the Swedish discs, its 'bruitage', which echoes a tremolo figure at the extremities of the instrument in *Ile de feu 1*.[61] This sound is likened to 'the crumpling of paper, or a shower of broken glass'.

Then came the task of arranging these sounds and visions into a convincing design. The piece's musical argument resides in the contrast between the rock thrush's radiant 'orange' song and the dissonance of the surrounding landscapes and calls. The reclusive thrush's limited appearances (all between 10 a.m. and 5 p.m.) create the sense of a piece-within-a-piece: a rondo embedded within an arch form (Table 5.3). The images summoned up in the 'durations' sections support this interpretation of the form, as do the rhythmic sequences employed in these passages. The dinosaurs that inhabit the two medleys are depicted by a free selection of durations

---

[61] Respectively 23062, p. 10; and 23045, p. 8.

between one and thirty-two demisemiquavers.⁶² The 'cortège' sequence, on the other hand, is derived from a permutation series that Messiaen used in many subsequent works, starting with *Chronochromie*. It also sounds different: Messiaen employs a loose 'scissor'-like sequence in the manner of 'Soixante-quatre durées' (the final movement of the *Livre d'orgue*), which causes long durations to congregate round each other. The music is less restless than the 'dinosaur' passages, evoking the stillness at the height of the day in the Cirque. Once again, 'process' music is employed as a telling metaphor.

The arch element of the form features various subtleties: medley 2 both reverses and reprises the order of medley 1, for example, and there are fewer birds in the coda than the introduction. Changes of time do not necessarily correspond with formal boundaries, which makes the form less emphatic. Ambiguity also exists as to whether the 'cortège' section is a compressed seven-hour period connecting the 10 a.m. and 5 p.m. rock thrush calls, or the last event of the morning followed by a sudden temporal leap. The latter interpretation would make for the most extreme of the *Catalogue*'s many splices; either way the pianist has little choice about how to articulate this juncture, which features a sudden but extreme change of texture. The cortège seems the closest passage in the *Catalogue* to a dream sequence, true to the aesthetic of the piece: somnambulism at the height of the day, a deep sleep in which we lose track of time.

Messiaen and Max Ernst

Messiaen's 'cowled stone phantoms, carrying a dead woman whose hair trails along the ground' is the other memorable image from the preface, alongside the raised hand. The mention of Max Ernst in the preface adds intrigue: could Messiaen be referring to a specific picture that had caught his imagination? A strong candidate is *Au rendez-vous des Amis*, Ernst's portrait of the nascent surrealist group painted in 1922 (might Messiaen's reference to a 'group à la Ernst' be a further clue?), with its eye-catching mountain range in the background which could be seen as the apparition Messiaen describes (Fig. 5.5). Two strands of hair certainly seem to be trailing along the valley floor, and the three peaks have the look of hooded figures in profile.⁶³ The raised hands in the painting increase the likelihood that it was in Messiaen's mind.

---

⁶² Cheong, 'Symmetrical Permutation', p. 127.
⁶³ Boivin's extract from Messiaen's in-class analysis of 'Le Merle de roche' is again helpful, confirming that the phantoms are Ernstian rather than the dinosaurs: 'I'm talking about Max Ernst [… Messiaen explains who Max Ernst is]. There was a row of stones, bolt upright, which

168   The Second Wave of Composition

Figure 5.5 Max Ernst, *Au rendez-vous des Amis*

The painting shows seventeen identifiable characters: Ernst himself (with silver hair in the front row) and fourteen contemporaries, joined by Dostoevsky and Raphael. They are identified by numbers in the scrolls on either side of the group. Amongst them are:

René Crevel (seated on the far left, facing left) – poet and writer of *Le Clavecin de Diderot*;
Dostoevsky (front row, next to Ernst);
Paul Eluard (back row fifth from left, with raised fist) – poet; cited in the preface to Messiaen's *Technique de mon langage musical*;
Louis Aragon (back row, sixth from left) – poet and novelist;
André Breton (caped figure between the two rows) – writer, poet and leader of the surrealists;
Giorgio di Chirico (back row, a bust on a column) – painter;
Gala Eluard (back row far right) – wife of Paul, soon to be mistress of Dalí.

Much has been written on this remarkable painting, but one feature that remains unmentioned is the correspondence between the hand gestures and the mountains at the top of the picture – to take one example, Breton's hand raised as if in a blessing mimics the left-hand phantom.[64] The characters' gestures are commonly understood to be derived from sign language; Ernst's father worked with deaf-mutes, and the self-portrait within the picture – he is sitting on Dostoevsky's knee, tugging at his beard – is a clue that the artist is confronting paternal authority.[65]

The dominant theme of both painting and piece, therefore, is silence – the silence of stone – and this may have been what inspired the association for Messiaen. We know that Ernst was a painter Messiaen admired; when visiting Mont Aigoul in the Cévennes the day before his second trip to the Cirque, he likened the effect of the mountains suddenly being lit up to an Ernstian panorama – this narrows his imagination's Ernst collection down considerably.[66] Silence was also something that hung over Messiaen's relationship with his father, Pierre (who had died the previous year, 1957), and it is conceivable that the raised 'main de pierre' had paternal associations for the composer, whatever his interpretation of the painting.[67]

Another similarity between painting and piece is the numbering used – Ernst of his characters, and Messiaen of his durations.[68] In 'Le Merle de roche' the first duration (p. 5, b. 10) is seventeen demisemiquavers, matching the number of characters in the painting. This could of course be

---

looked very much like cowled phantoms. You know, like penitents, a hood which partially hides the face.' Boivin, *La Classe*, p. 329.

[64] It is identified as a 'quasi-benediction' by Cathrin Klingsöhr-Leroy and Uta Grosenick (eds.), *Surrealism* (Cologne: Taschen, 2004), p. 15. Elizabeth Legge also says that Breton appears to be a 'madman who believes he is Pope. Breton wears a red cape and his hand gesture certainly has the overtone of benediction and authority.' Elizabeth Legge, 'Posing Questions: Max Ernst's *Au rendez-vous des Amis*', in *Art History* 10 (June 1987), 227–243 (p. 236).

[65] At the time Ernst had just abandoned his own family and taken off into the Tyrol in a *ménage à trois* with Paul and Gala Eluard. Legge quotes Spies as saying that Ernst considered the painting to refer to 'die Welt des Vaters' (Legge, 'Posing Questions', p. 227).

[66] PH/NS, p. 225: 'The fragments of panorama, suddenly lit up, resemble a picture by Max Ernst – the effect is very surreal!' It is likely that Messiaen would have seen or at least known about the painting for some time before the composition of *Catalogue*. Though it is not featured in Breton's *Le Surréalisme et la peinture*, which we know Messiaen read in the 1940s, it was exhibited at a major Parisian exhibition of surrealist art in 1938.

[67] For more on how Messiaen's relationship with his father had an impact upon his music see Julian Anderson, 'Messiaen and the Problem of Communication', in Dingle and Fallon, *Messiaen Perspectives 1*, pp. 257–268 (pp. 264–268). Legge, 'Posing Questions' also features a long final section on the problematic aspects of language and communication, a preoccupation of the surrealists.

[68] Messiaen had labelled the durations once before, in 'Soixante-Quatre durées'. On that occasion it was to demonstrate the 'opening and closing scissors' technique; in 'Le Merle de roche' it is a performance aid, obviating the need to impose a crotchet or quaver pulse on the music.

coincidental, though if Messiaen did have *Au rendez-vous des Amis* in mind he would certainly have appreciated Ernst's use of a prime number.

Colour is another important feature: the rock thrush's colours (blue, red, black, orange, yellow) are the dominant hues of the painting, whose surreal atmosphere is partly due to its floodlit appearance, the vivid hues against a dark background. The coloured form of 'Le Merle de roche' – the 'day' piece within a 'night' piece – is visible all in one here. More visual correspondences exist in the hand shapes of some of the characters. Eluard's raised fist is uncannily similar to the side-on 'Sphinx', while Breton is showing off the 'pouce couché'. Aragon has the most obvious 'piano-playing' hands; the surrealists were often said to mime the playing of pianos whilst sleepwalking, and Crevel – who had a particular talent for somnambulism – seems to be miming playing a piano in front of a model theatrical stage (both leitmotifs from Messiaen's life).[69] Nearly all the characters could be said to be displaying a 'stone hand, raised in a magic sign', Breton most conspicuously.

In the late 1940s when Messiaen drafted an idea for a ballet about Time he made the following notes:

It is night on stage; a dancer – a man completely still – the creation of Time – an angel with a rainbow halo enters, with a fearsome head, eyes rolled upwards to the beyond, no body, two Greek columns ablaze instead of legs. A hand which emerges from the clouds – the sun and a rainbow surrounding the head – a hallucinatory figure – when it appears, the man dances: it is Time, then the man *stops still*: the end of time. He stands with his arms stretched out, not moving.[70]

The imagery here seems to be a combination of the Book of Revelation and *Au rendez-vous des Amis* (the Greek column Ernst placed beneath de Chirico is a reference to one of his fellow artist's own leitmotifs). And in 'La Nature, les chants d'oiseaux', published in *Guide du concert* shortly before the full premiere of the *Catalogue*, Messiaen quoted the 'magical' words of Rilke: 'Music: the breath of statues, the silences of paintings, the language where all languages end'.[71] 'Le Merle de roche' is a meeting-point for all these concerns: a dramatic landscape populated by petrified beings, where time seems to stop still; a shy bird whose

---

[69] According to Aragon, 'Crevel has never noticed that this planet is solidly fixed with help from meridian and latitudes: he is more of a sleepwalker than anyone.' Louis Aragon, *A Wave of Dreams* (London: Thin Man Press, 2015), trans. Susan Muth from Louis Aragon, 'Une vague de rêves', *Commerce* 2 (Autumn 1924), 11.

[70] PH/NS, p. 169.

[71] Olivier Messiaen, 'La Nature, les chants d'oiseaux', *Guide du concert* 229 (3 April 1959), 1093–1094.

Example 5.16 'Le Traquet rieur', bb. 1–4

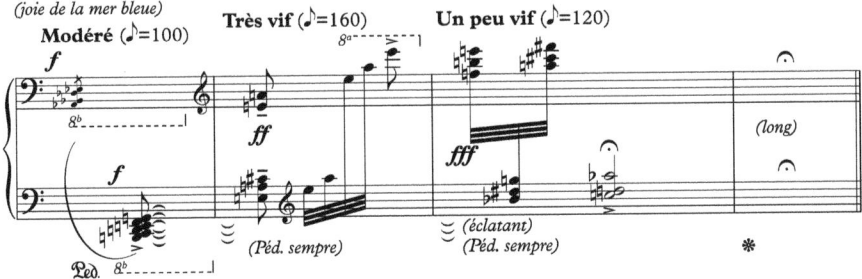

song sounds 'like sun shining on the rocks', just as Messiaen's memories gilded the music he wrote.

'Le Traquet rieur' (Black Wheatear)

Month of May. A beautiful sunlit morning. Cap Béar, above Port-Vendres (Roussillon). A rocky cliff, garrigue, sapphire-blue and 'Nattier'-blue sea, silvered by the sun. Joy of the blue sea. The song of the black wheatear.

Dialogue between the blue rock thrush, more caressing, and the black wheatear, more brilliant, broken up by the barking of the herring gull, the strident cries of the swifts, the short interjections of the black-eared wheatear. Black, with black markings on its white tail, the black wheatear is perched on a point of rock at the foot of the cliff. The spectacled warbler gets excited on the garrigue. A gust of wind passes over the sea, always sapphire- and 'Nattier'-blue, silvered by the sun. Joy of the blue sea.[72]

Messiaen made a further trip to Banyuls – this time alone – in late May 1958. It was rare for him to travel to undertake birdsong research in the middle of a teaching period, but work on the *Catalogue* had now assumed such urgency that any opportunity had to be grasped. His commitment was rewarded with the material for the most celebratory piece in the cycle, 'Le Traquet rieur'. Messiaen's pleasure in returning to the Côte Vermeille is announced straightaway, the 'joy of the blue sea' ('joie de la mer bleue') captured in a three-bar refrain that emphatically announces the piece's home key, A major, and crescendos bar by bar from *f* to *fff* (Ex. 5.16). The wheatear immediately justifies its mirthful French name, mimicking the opening ascent with another rapid crescendo. The music

---

[72] Preface to the score.

that follows is a *jeu d'esprit*: a simple strophic form featuring dialogue between the wheatear and a blue rock thrush, the latter making its first appearance since Book 1.

Book 7 of the *Catalogue* has a recapitulatory aspect to it, suggested by the return to the Dauphiné in 'La Buse variable' and to A major in 'Le Traquet rieur', and the reminiscence of the 'cri du Chocard' in the foghorn blast in 'Le Courlis cendré', amongst other things. In keeping with this, several birds featured in the earlier Banyuls pieces make a return appearance: the swifts and herring gulls in addition to the blue rock thrush from 'Le Merle bleu', and the black-eared wheatear (not to be confused with the *traquet rieur*, the black wheatear) and spectacled warbler from 'Le Traquet stapazin'. Conspicuous by its absence is the Thekla lark: gulls apart, this was the only bird to feature in both earlier pieces, and the only bird Messiaen notated on 29 May 1958 not to be heard in 'Le Traquet rieur'. The spectacled warbler and blue rock thrush are treated differently by Messiaen in 'Le Traquet rieur' (particularly the latter – the other birds are their usual abrasive selves). The spectacled warbler is drawn from an earlier *cahier* notation, 23057 (29 June 1957, when he was collecting material for Books 1 and 2). That day he jotted down a description of the warbler's song, one that is potentially valuable for pianists: 'The spectacled warbler's timbre is charming and sweet. The two opening notes of its strophes are flute-like, *mf*; the other notes recall the hasty twittering of the whitethroat [heard in the previous piece, 'La Buse variable'], but more "attractive", and slightly less rapid.'[73] Messiaen's setting of the two flute-like notes is the main difference between 'Le Traquet stapazin' and 'Le Traquet rieur'; here they become two serious-sounding chords, in a slower tempo than the rest of the call – though the *cahier* shows that they are nevertheless part of the bird's song.[74] And, unlike the E^6 chord that glows constantly beneath the spectacled warbler in 'Le Traquet stapazin', the left-hand chords have a strong diminished flavour, eventually resolving onto a second-inversion A major harmony – an approach chord for the plagal cadence that stretches across the final two pages of the piece.

The blue rock thrush is especially significant in 'Le Traquet rieur'. Messiaen's commentary in the fifth volume of the *Traité* reveals that this

---

[73] 23057, p. 18.

[74] These two chords need to be heard as part of the bird's song, as distinct from the preliminary pair of harmonies in (for example) 'L'Alouette calandrelle', p. 2, which are not part of the bird's song but function as 'colour chords'.

Example 5.17 The last black wheatear solo in 'Le Traquet rieur'

bird was of key importance to his anthropomorphic representation of birdsong:

> In order to offset the radiant colours of the black wheatear's song I wrote the blue rock thrush in an excessively slow tempo, deliberately exaggerated its caressing character, and gave it a tenderness, a passion that it did not have, by way of an almost anthropomorphic transformation! This type of transformative mimicry, renewed, recreated, appears to me to be worthy of interest.[75]

On a broader scale, the main differences between 'Le Traquet rieur' and the earlier Banyuls pieces are twofold: the lack of any 'souvenir' music – with completion of the cycle in sight, Messiaen seemed to want to look forward – and the simplicity of the form: three verses, and a coda that begins when the spectacled warbler starts singing. Nevertheless, Messiaen departs from his usual practice – which has already been in evidence several times in the *Catalogue*, including 'Le Traquet stapazin' and 'La Chouette hulotte' – of repeating 'the same elements in the same order, but with different music'.[76] Here the black wheatear and a blue rock thrush take it in turns to begin the verses – but then the thrush is left out of the third verse, leaving the wheatear to its most extended solo, uninterrupted by the other characters that inhabit the verses: two black-eared wheatears (*traquet stapazin*), a typically belligerent herring gull and some whirling swifts. The black wheatear concludes by singing the same 'laughing' music with which it introduced itself on page 1 (Ex. 5.17).

The main material of the piece, the exchanges between wheatear and blue rock thrush, was gathered at the Cap Béar between 8 and 11 a.m. on 29 May 1958. Messiaen reordered the phrases of both these principal birds; just as

---

[75] Messiaen, *Traité*, Vol. V, Part I, p. 106.
[76] For example several movements of the *Méditations sur le Mystère de la Sainte Trinité*, from which this quotation is taken. 'La Chouette hulotte' is the best example of this type of form in the *Catalogue*.

in 'Le Merle bleu', the order of the blue rock thrush's strophes are specified in the *cahier*, with each phrase awarded a number. Ten phrases are turned into thirteen by numbering some of them twice – 1 and 6; 2 and 7; 5 and 8 – suggesting that the strophic structure was conceived early on. Messiaen's retouchings of the melody are few but significant, and show the way the birds influence each other in spite of their contrasting character. Most radical is the first phrase, where a cadential fourth is broadened to an octave, two tonic As. This eventually leads to the highpoint B (p. 9, b. 8), which is faithful to the *cahier* (B is also the ubiquitous highest note of the black wheatear, until it overshoots by a third in its very last phrase). C♯ and F♯ are often changed to naturals, and vice versa; Messiaen subjects the spectacled warbler to similar treatment, most notably on its two flute-like notes, and the resulting major–minor flux is one of the harmonic features of the piece.

Although 'Le Traquet rieur' is in an emphatic A major, the minor mode impinges on it throughout. C♮ is often present as a colouring in climactic chords (twice on page 1: in bars 3 and 11, where it is sounded against A^6 in the left hand). The two modes combine most tellingly when the blue rock thrush enters its most anthropomorphic phase, its final music at the climax of verse 2 (p. 10). Messiaen twice stretches the tempo to extreme slowness, employing luxuriant harmonies to colour the thrush's song, and marking the phrases 'tender', 'languid' and 'with weariness'. It is one of the moments in the *Catalogue* where the composer steps to the front of the stage as he bids farewell to the bird that has had more varied realisation than any other in the cycle. The third phrase (♪ = 100) is an extra, 'composed' phrase not present in the *cahier*. It is in a black-note pentatonic mode, as if he wished to highlight the oriental character of the bird, in a further reminiscence of 'Le Merle bleu'. The harmonies flux between A major and minor (with major and minor added sixths respectively) in the left hand, before the music comes to rest on A minor (with Lydian fourth, or a combination of A minor and G♯ major as it appears in the score). The spectacled warbler sums up this duality in the coda by spelling out both A major and A minor triads many times over.

The most significant cross-fertilisation between the black wheatear and blue rock thrush is also revealed by studying the climactic passage on page 10 alongside the *cahier* sources. At the thrush's culmination (♪ = 20) the anacrusis–accent–mute pattern (*ff*–*fff*–*mf*) creates a point of contact with the song of the black wheatear. Gesturally, it matches the wheatear's most triumphant moment, which occurs twice: at the end of its first paragraph at the top of page 2, and the first of two outbursts at the top of the penultimate page. These are the only moments when melody from the

Example 5.18 The black wheatear's last call on p. 19 of 'Le Traquet rieur'

cahier crosses to the left hand, and the right hand becomes upper resonance rather than the principal line. There is a further modification from the *cahier*: Messiaen heard many of the wheatear's phrases as tapering away to *piano*, but in this phrase the dynamic is reversed (both times) to a *crescendo* from *ff* to *fff* – the bird has both pre-empted and responded to the blue rock thrush's apotheosis (not only do they share the same top note, A♯, but they are essentially the same chord: D major with added sharpened fourth and fifth) *and* to the 'joy of the blue sea'. The close ties between the birds are sealed at the last: just before a final 'joy' closes the piece, the wheatear selects a prior phrase (from page 1) that most resembles the blue rock thrush's opening motto, with which the latter begins its contributions to verse 1 and verse 2. The wheatear transposes the phrase up a minor third, concluding with two Ds rather than Bs (above an E major triad in the left hand, which means that Messiaen has altered the *cahier* source to create a conventional dominant seventh perfect cadence) (Ex. 5.18): repeated notes that motivically 'explain' the alteration he made to the blue rock thrush's melody (as mentioned above), changing a falling D–A to a falling octave A–A. This falling octave is the 'exaggerated tenderness' Messiaen speaks of in the *Traité* (Vol. V, Part I, p. 106 – see above). So, as well as figuring in the transformation of the blue rock thrush, it is motivically significant and, through its association with the wheatear's apotheosis, becomes embroiled in the piece's harmonic argument too.

Messiaen's Twelve-Note Tonality

For all the integration (or alternation) of tonal and serial practice that Messiaen had already achieved in the composition of the *Catalogue*, he still had the trump card up his sleeve: a piece so radiant that it contains

Table 5.4 The left hand of 'Le Traquet rieur'

'Joy of the blue sea' and verse 1	A, E♭, A⁶, F♯⁶, E⁶, D♭, C⁶, B
'Joy of the blue sea' and verse 2	A, E♭, A♭⁶, B♭⁶, G♭⁶, A⁶
'Joy of the blue sea' and verse 3	A, E♭, B♭, G⁶, A♭, A⁶, G♭⁶, D♭⁶, C⁶, A⁶, F♯⁶

Example 5.19 The 'gust of wind over the sea' (p. 17, b. 3)

all the colours of the rainbow, an entire chromatic spectrum; a coherent piece of music that works towards its goal via a synthesis of tonal and twelve-note means.

'Le Traquet rieur' is that piece. The left hand consistently spells out tonal chords, and as they accumulate one gets the impression that over the course of the three verses Messiaen is working towards a sort of pantonality – coverage of all the keys. Closer inspection reveals that this is indeed his method. In the left hand, major triads or added sixth chords on nearly all the degrees of the chromatic scale are sounded at least once (Table 5.4).

The remaining two tonalities, F and D, have been heard in more complex formations (added second and sixth: p. 14, b. 8 and p. 15, b. 2), but are yet to be sounded with the clarity of the others. The reason is that they have been reserved for a different role. After the spectacled warbler has brought the music round to A major, two passages of twelve-note music flash by: the 'gust of wind over the sea' and 'silvery sun sprinkled over the sea'. The former climaxes breezily on an A and F♮, with a C in very close vicinity (and a pedalled F right at the bottom of the complex); locally, the A and F are a response to the spectacled warbler's slowed-down 'grace notes', just heard (Ex. 5.19).

In the 'silvery sun' passage, Messiaen hangs the passage on a recurring sonority (chords that contain an A and a G♯ along with either a B♭ or G♮) that initially seems to return too soon for all twelve notes to have been exhausted (Table 5.5). He plays various games to create this impression,

Table 5.5 Twelve-note groupings in 'silvery sun sprinkled over the sea'

Bars	Brackets identify twelve-note groupings; chords separated by commas; recurring sonority in bold.
p. 18, b. 3	(B, D–**A**–**G**♯–**G**, C♯–B♭, E♭)–(E
p. 18, b. 4	B♭–**A**–**G**♯–**G**, F♯–D–C♯, F–C–B, (E♭), **B♭**–**A**–**G**♯ [the E♭ is common to both groups]
p. 18, b. 5	D–C♯–G–F♯, F–C–B, E)–**A**–**G**♯–**G**
p. 18, b. 6 (first part)	(C♯–B–A♭–G, F♯–E♭–C, B♭–F, E–D–(A), …)

Example 5.20 'Silvery sun sprinkled over the sea' (p. 18, b. 9)

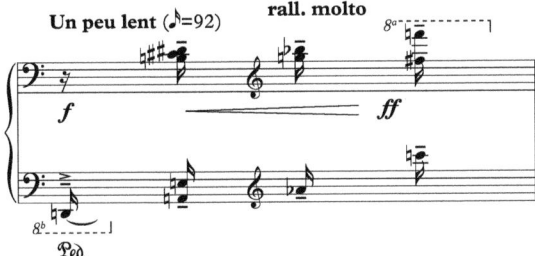

for example by starting in the middle of a row, and allowing sets of twelve notes that overlap (dovetailing occurs on the E♭ in bar 4 and the A in bar 6). By bar 6 the segmentation becomes clearer, and the final bar of the 'poudroiement' is the only one to have all twelve notes stated just once: a rich harmony built on a resounding bass D that is clearly a plagal preparation for the final washes of A major (Ex. 5.20).

This twelve-note subdominant chord is very conventionally approached by the only other low bass note in the 'silvery sun', the E in b. 6, topped by a high treble D and A – a sonority that both activates and summarizes the V–IV–I which occurs across the last two pages. Bar 9 therefore becomes the point where conventional tonal motion, and pan-tonal and serial forces coalesce – and the effect is thrilling.

Who should then intervene but the swifts, whose strident twelve-note sonorities tumble down into the central region of the piano (something that doesn't happen in 'Le Merle bleu'), leading into the wheatear's final exultation and the eleven-note bass cluster of the joyous blue sea, missing an A as always – and clearing the way for this tenacious yet hard-won tonic to be sounded one final time (p. 19, b. 6). Messiaen's compositional renewal was complete, and both he and Loriod knew it.

6 | Performance

I have an extraordinary, marvellous, inspired interpreter whose technical brilliance and playing – by turns powerful, light, moving and coloured – suit my works exactly, an exceptional pianist who understands and knows my music as though she had written it, and who plays it like no one else plays it or ever will play it: Yvonne Loriod.[1]

Yvonne Loriod's Two Complete Recordings

The immediate critical response to the *Catalogue* was enthusiastic, even from former detractors. Claude Rostand – who in the mid 1940s dismissed Messiaen's latest works as 'lies and sacrilege' – captured the significance of the premiere in *Le Monde*:

> The final concert given this season by Domaine musical was a homage to M. Olivier Messiaen who recently celebrated his fiftieth birthday. It was a homage from friends and admirers of every country and also from the public, for someone who, now at the height of his powers, is recognised worldwide as one of the most daring and all-embracing representatives of the musical genius of our time, both through his own music and through his teaching at the Paris Conservatoire.[2]

This success aside, 1959 was what Loriod called an 'année terrible'. Messiaen had been devastated by the sudden death of Claire a week after the premiere, while exhaustion gradually overcame Loriod, and by the summer she was plagued by a slipped disc – so much so that on an Alpine excursion to Pralognan-la-Vanoise in August she begged Messiaen to leave her to die 'alone in the grass, hidden away like a cranefly'.[3]

---

[1] Claude Samuel, *Music and Color: Conversations with Claude Samuel*, trans. E. Thomas Glasow (Portland: Amadeus, 1994), p. 202.

[2] Claude Rostand, review of *Catalogue d'oiseaux* world premiere, *Le Monde*, 18 April 1959. For his earlier comment see PH/NS p. 151, quoting from Jean-Yves Daniel-Lesur, 'Revue de la presse musicale: *Trois petites Liturgies de la Présence Divine* d'Olivier Messiaen', *Revue musicale de la France*, 1 April 1946.

[3] OMR, p. 133.

Loriod had launched herself into recording the *Catalogue* in early May, with the score still in her fingers. This was to be the first of two complete accounts made in relatively quick succession – 1959 and 1970 – as part of two broad 'waves' of solo Messiaen recordings (her *Vingt Regards* date from 1956 and 1973). The later version is the more immediately attractive of the two, mainly because of its sound quality. The 1959 account sounds both muggy and forensically close, but despite this it retains the thrill of the new, and for understanding the *Catalogue* contextually it is a vital document.

Altogether, Loriod and Messiaen spent six days in the recording studio. Maintaining consistent sound proved difficult; one of the most striking moments is the burst of sonority at the beginning of 'La Chouette hulotte', after the rather enclosed 'Le Traquet stapazin'. Here Loriod gives a lesson in low-register playing: each note has its own timbre, resisting the homogeneity of that region of the piano. Elsewhere the occluded sound can be advantageous, such as at the end of 'La Bouscarle': the fragmented music of the poplars, the meandering Charenton, the confident robin and the sudden thrusts of Cetti's warbler, all separated by grainy silences – a painterly effect.

Messiaen adopted the role of producer during the sessions, relishing the opportunity to catalogue Loriod's takes (false starts and all). The editing was spread over the next five months, and by March 1961 the triple LP had received its first accolade, the *Grand Prix du Disque*. The defining feature of the recording is the quickness of Loriod's fingers and her mind – typical of her early recordings. The more rapid passages sound brusque, acrobatic – frenzied even – as if the spirit of Cetti's warbler had infiltrated the other twelve pieces. But they are interspersed with flashes of poetry, like glimpses of a kingfisher.

Loriod's account of 'La Rousserolle effarvatte' epitomises the explosive energy that the post-war avant garde – Messiaen included – drew from the piano. She shows urgency in the long stretch of material between 5 and 6 p.m., exploiting the percussiveness of the instrument, and taking the reed warbler duets at breakneck speed. This is an unusually long passage that threatens to undermine the piece's diurnal simulation; her approach counteracts the problem, by simply playing the material more quickly. The frequent edits during the duets, rather than breaking the momentum, reinforce the 'wildness' of the rhythms; they work well because the passage is a collage of rhythmic cells. The skylark, frogs and water rail that precede the sunset combine the impact of Boulez's Second Piano Sonata (which had been a repertoire piece for Loriod throughout the 1950s) with *Rite*-like rhythms – a 'grande diversité d'attaques', as the score suggests.

Often Loriod's playing is so rapid that adjacent notes in the score are played almost simultaneously. In the final 'vol des chocards' of 'Le Chocard des Alpes' her hands race each other to the top of the keyboard, with seemingly little regard for the number of notes written down. In fact the playing is remarkably accurate, respecting the precise contours of the score even if individual notes are hardly perceptible.[4] The raven's call on page 3, normally a trenchant rhythm, becomes a single rolled sonority.

The most extreme example of this approach is the music for garden warblers in 'Le Loriot'. As each duet progresses the speed picks up, to the point that unrhythmicised (but otherwise accurate) harmonic fields are heard, flecked with accents. Counteracting this mêlée, however, are the sunrise chords, which are impeccably judged both in terms of their individual timbres and of the continuity from one passage to the next. It is a striking counterpoint of earthly chaos and celestial order. Continuity is also a feature of the outer sections, owing to the 'lent' chords (b. 1 and similar) being played approximately twice as fast as the published score indicates (♪ = 60). The tempo of these chords was one of a series of revisions made in October 1959, in advance of publication – a reworking that evidently occurred to Messiaen some time after the recording.[5]

These moments of brusqueness are reflected in the brevity of the whole cycle. The 1959 account is nearly 15 minutes shorter than that of 1970, with nine of the thirteen pieces quicker by more than 30 seconds, and three – 'Le Loriot', 'L'Alouette lulu' and 'La Bouscarle' – shorter by 2 minutes or more.[6] 'L'Alouette lulu' is perhaps the most surprising of these, given its brevity; the discrepancy can be put down to the extreme slowness of the later version, the opening chords being played at approximately 50 semiquavers per minute rather than the marked 63. Interestingly, even though these chords were also slowed down in Messiaen's revisions, by May 1959 Loriod was already playing them a touch slower than 63. Some modifications had already taken place; others (such as the tempi in 'Le Loriot', p. 1) were yet to come.[7]

The woodlark itself is brisk in the earlier recording, but captures beautifully Messiaen's injunction – 'poetic, liquid and unreal (like a voice that falls from the stars)'. Its accented chords (beginning at the top of page 3) are gentle yet persuasive. The descending repeated notes on page 4 are rapid and

---

[4] The effect is quite different from another example of extreme speed in the Messiaen discography, Momo Kodama's 'Regard des hauteurs' (*Vingt Regards*), which is a thrilling display of incisive birdsong.
[5] Details of the October 1959 revisions can be found in PH/NS, p. 235.
[6] The 1970 recording was originally issued by Erato, then by Warner Classics.
[7] PH/NS, p. 235.

neat, and the threads of song in the final bar are truly 'mysterious, rejoining the silence'.[8] This is certainly not the only instance of hushed playing; in the opening right hand of 'La Rousserolle effarvatte', for example, Loriod again produces a delicate *pianissimo*. Though she was sometimes accused of strident playing, these passages are proof of her range.

In spite of its muggy sound, 'Le Traquet stapazin' is the most gripping of all on this first recording. Pianists will be reassured that Loriod found the opening call of the wheatear challenging; it involves a bigger stretch than the others, making coordination difficult.[9] Nevertheless, the incendiary brilliance of this performance demonstrates what a vital member of the 1950s avant garde Loriod was, and why her pianism revolutionised Messiaen's worldview in the early 1940s.[10] The spectacled warbler shows her dexterity (the 'fairy with the magic fingers')[11] – it is voluble, warm, often rapid, and the resonance at the end of each phrase is caught expertly. Above all, the sunrise chords make this a performance of stature. To begin with they sound like a lazy god observing creation, but once they have grown from *mf* to *fff* the power is of nuclear intensity, with inner colours like spots on the sun. The coda is typically unsentimental, with liberated Thekla lark accents, and the *rubato* on the final spectacled warbler 'souvenir' has a drawn-out poignancy.

At its best, then, this recording features fiercely individual accounts, and of course the fascination of sitting close to the moment of creation. Of Loriod's two recordings it gives a clearer impression of the contrast between her sensibility and that of the composer, and thereby the nature of their creative partnership. Though Messiaen had repositioned himself in relation to mainstream modernism in the late 1950s, the youthful Loriod was still fully engaged – she was to give the premiere of *Structures II* with Boulez two years later. The fiery quality that she brings to the work is

---

[8] The dynamic of the woodlark was changed from *mf* to *p* in the October 1959 revisions – again, this decision seems to have already been taken in May.

[9] Her spreading of minor-ninth chords in 'L'Alouette lulu' suggests that her reach was little more than an octave.

[10] Jésus Aguila brackets Loriod as a member of the 'Ensemble du Domaine musical' along with Claude Helffer, before going on to state that 'For some particularly challenging works Pierre Boulez drew from a pool of starry European soloists, who already had the pieces in their repertoire: the pianists Marcelle Mercenier, Paul Jacobs, Aloys and Alfons Kontarsky; the flautist Severino Gazelloni; the percussionist Christoph Caskel; the cellist Siegfried Palm; and above all the singers Marie-Thérése Cahn, Eva-Maria Roquer, Cathy Berberian, Berthe Kal, Helga Pylarczyk and Ethel Semser.' Jésus Aguila, *Le Domaine musical: Pierre Boulez et vingt ans de création contemporaine* (Paris: Fayard, 1992), pp. 148–149.

[11] Suzanne Demarquez, 'Le *Catalogue d'oiseaux* d'Olivier Messiaen', *Guide du concert* 233 (1 May 1959), 42.

sometimes dazzling, and there is a wildness that is certainly not anathema to Messiaen, in particular the Messiaen of *Harawi* and the two *Ile de feu* studies. She sounds like a musician immersed in contemporary trends – electronic music included – but with an extensive core repertoire.[12] Given her influence upon Messiaen's piano writing, and of his piano works upon the Boulez–Stockhausen generation, her role in the development of the new musical language of the 1950s should not be overlooked. The speed of her facility matched Stockhausen and Boulez's quickness of thought, and continually encouraged Messiaen to push boundaries.[13] She was not merely an accomplice, but a driving force behind post-war renewal. Messiaen's admission that '[her] existence transformed not only the composer's way of writing for the piano, but his style, vision of the world, and modes of thought' puts this beyond doubt.[14]

Loriod's Performances in the 1960s

The early performance history of the *Catalogue* suggests that Loriod and Messiaen took a pragmatic approach to programming. A second complete performance took place later in 1959 (on 15 December), but after the turn of the decade such occasions were rare, at least until the mid 1960s. Messiaen's stock was certainly rising worldwide during this period, but *Catalogue d'oiseaux* pieces are absent – except for lecture-demonstrations – from the big tours to Japan, Argentina and the USA that the couple undertook in the early 1960s. It may be that, proud as he was of new developments in his music, Messiaen felt the *Vingt Regards* had more chance of speaking directly to, and being taken up by, audiences and pianists outside Europe (the *Catalogue* was not available in print until 1964, in any case). There is also the physical challenge of practising and performing the complete *Catalogue*. Much of the playing is concentrated in the treble, a possible

---

[12] Schaeffer's *In Search of a Concrete Music* features an unidentified 'YL' – in all likelihood Loriod – who responds positively to his early experiments; Pierre Schaeffer, *In Search of a Concrete Music,* trans. Christine North and John Dack (Berkeley, CA: University of California Press, 2012), p. 22.

[13] Loriod described this, with characteristic modesty, to Irene Tüngler in the liner notes of the Erato/Warner box set: 'Of course, there were differences between us. We had quite different rates of working. He was very, very slow in his work, but he always worked well and exceptionally thoroughly. But while he was doing that, I could have done two things – though possibly badly. But this speed had its advantages … we were two very different, not to say antithetical, characters who complemented each other very well.'

[14] Antoine Goléa, *Rencontres avec Olivier Messiaen* (Paris: René Julliard, 1960), p. 147.

cause of Loriod's back troubles in 1959. Another factor was the sheer commitment of Loriod's playing, even when the performance was a private one. Alexander Goehr recalled Felix Aprahamian's piano being 'covered with blood' after a late-night performance of Boulez's Second Piano Sonata, played straight after the British premiere of *Turangalîla*.[15]

There were, however, abridged performances of the cycle, including a Bordeaux performance in January 1962, where ten pieces were played (leaving out 'Le Merle bleu', 'Le Merle de roche' and 'La Buse variable'). In December 1965 at Metz Conservatory eight pieces were played in the published order ('Le Chocard des Alpes', 'Le Loriot', 'La Chouette hulotte', 'L'Alouette lulu', 'La Rousserolle effarvatte', 'La Bouscarle', 'Le Traquet rieur' and 'Le Courlis cendré'). Though the cycle expanded and contracted the journey from the Alps to Finisterre seems always to have been important; the original LP issue of the 1959 recording has a quite different order of pieces (designed by Messiaen to fit on to six sides of vinyl), but still begins and ends with 'Le Chocard des Alpes' and 'Le Courlis cendré'.

During the same period, individual pieces were integrated into programmes that showed Loriod maintaining her colourful repertoire. In 1965 'La Rousserolle effarvatte' was particularly prominent, featuring in some fascinating recitals:

23 January, Czechoslovakia: Rameau, Suite in E; three movements from Ravel, *Le Tombeau de Couperin*; Debussy, two *Etudes* and a *Prélude*; Messiaen, 'Les sons impalpables du rêve…', 'Regard de l'Esprit de joie', 'La Rousserolle effarvatte'.

29 May, recital for French Radio: Rameau; Mozart, Sonata K. 331; Chopin, *Barcarolle*; three movements from Ravel, *Le Tombeau de Couperin*; Messiaen, 'La Rousserolle effarvatte'.[16]

20 June, Royaumont (the same day as the premiere in Chartres Cathedral of *Et exspecto resurrectionem mortuorum*, which took place in the morning): Mozart, Sonata K. 331; Messiaen, 'La Rousserolle effarvatte'; Mozart, four Fantasias.

---

[15] Christopher Dingle, 'Yvonne Loriod as Source and Influence', in Christopher Dingle and Robert Fallon (eds.), *Messiaen Perspectives 1: Sources and Influences* (Farnham: Ashgate, 2013), pp. 197–212 (p. 200); and Alexander Goehr, *Finding the Key: Selected Writings*, ed. Derrick Puffett (London: Faber and Faber, 1998), p. 44. Felix Aprahamian (1914–2005) was an English music critic based in London who championed Messiaen's music.

[16] This selection of pieces is particularly interesting: it traces the composers with whom Messiaen describes the developing textures, variation by variation, of 'Le baiser de l'Enfant-Jésus' in the Erato liner notes: Rameau, Mozart, Chopin. OMR is unspecific (p. 229) about the identity of the Rameau piece, but it is likely to have been the Suite in E again, as this was in Loriod's repertoire during the first half of 1965.

31 August, Edinburgh Festival: Mozart, Sonata K. 331; Messiaen, 'La Rousserolle effarvatte'; two Debussy *Etudes*; Boulez, Second Piano Sonata.

Thereafter the couple became more adept at weaving pieces from the *Catalogue* into programmes of an appropriate character. 'Le Merle de roche' was a staple of modernist programmes in 1967, being paired with works by Boulez (Second Piano Sonata, first and fourth movements), Holliger, Castiglione and Matsushita, and 'Par Lui tout a été fait' (from *Vingt Regards*). A particularly joyous programme, performed at Jyväskylä in Finland in May 1966, featured Rameau, Chopin, Mozart and Debussy; 'Noël', 'Première communion de la Vierge' and 'Regard de l'Esprit de joie' from the *Vingt Regards*; and 'Le Traquet rieur' and 'Le Loriot' from *Catalogue d'oiseaux*.[17]

Complete performances gradually became more frequent, and the *Catalogue* was heard in its entirety in Britain for the first time at the English Bach Festival in Oxford on 2 July 1967 (along with several other works by Messiaen). Roger Smalley's review in the *Musical Times* painted a vivid portrait of the occasion:

Possibly the most revelatory moment of the whole week came not during one of the performances but when Messiaen introduced the performance of *Catalogue d'oiseaux*. After beginning slowly and factually (presumably out of respect for his audience's lack of French) he gradually became more and more voluble and excited as he enthused over the landscapes, colours, flowers, and birds depicted in his piece. It was as if one of his programme notes had suddenly come to life, and one was completely convinced by the passionate sincerity of what sometimes looks on paper like rather fulsome verbal extravagance.

In his introduction to *Catalogue d'oiseaux* Messiaen mentioned that he considered its most revolutionary aspect was the form. It was a form, he said, based on the passing of the hours of the day. This is another strange idea because the mere passage of time does not in itself constitute a form, only the manner in which it is filled. But once again, in some unfathomable way, Messiaen seems to have distributed the events of these thirteen pieces so intuitively that they fall with amazingly satisfying rightness and coherence on the ear.

Yvonne Loriod's finest moment came in the *Catalogue*, two and a half hours of solo playing during which her individual and consummate technique produced an inexhaustible range of sonority.[18]

---

[17] The following day Loriod took part in yet another conference on music and ornithology, organised by Margareta Jalas, Sibelius's daughter.
[18] Roger Smalley, review of English Bach Festival 1967, in 'Festivals', *Musical Times*, 108.1494 (August 1967), 730–731.

Large parts of the *Catalogue* were also heard in Vienna that year, and at the end of the decade a stunning programme was heard in Shiraz that included Albéniz's 'Lavapiés', five movements from *Vingt Regards*, 'Le Loriot' and 'Le Traquet rieur'. The *Catalogue* was now evidently fit for long-distance travel.[19]

Loriod's Second Recording

By the time of the Erato recording (1970) Loriod was more exclusively a Messiaen pianist.[20] Her last commercial release of music by a composer other than Messiaen – a pot-pourri of works from Mozart to Albéniz (and Messiaen: 'Le Loriot' and 'Par Lui tout a été fait') entitled *Florilège du piano* – was released immediately before the second *Catalogue*, making 1970 a watershed year. The pair's musical development can be seen in parallel up to this point: Messiaen's music had become more monumental, richer in harmony and colour, and punctuated by frequent silences; her performances are similarly more spacious, emphatic, with the balance of chords sounding more premeditated than before. Messiaen had just completed *La Transfiguration*, which frames expansive gestures with ritualistic silences. Loriod, who took part in the first performance in Lisbon, could hardly have avoided its influence. Her birdsong characterisation is more vivid than ever, the colours brighter than before; this translates into a more anthropomorphic outlook, and the 1970 recording of the *Catalogue* is closer to her husband's vision in this respect. It is significant, too, that all the piano recordings of this era took place in an ecclesiastical setting: the Eglise Notre-Dame du Liban in Paris. Messiaen's beliefs, which were partly 'hidden behind the birds' during the 1950s, had reinhabited his music by this point. Stone and stained glass reverberate with the sound of birdsong, in contrast to the earlier unresponsive studio environment.

Loriod's emphatic style of playing is not always an enhancement, but the increased sense of colour invariably is, particularly in the two rock thrush pieces. Her vision of Banyuls is crystal clear in 'Le Merle bleu' (in the first recording it sounds stressed by comparison), and even the dark passages of 'Le Merle de roche' are many-hued.

---

[19] This concert took place three days before Messiaen heard the famous unidentified 'Oiseaux de Persepolis', which graces the seventh of the *Méditations* for organ (which R.D. Etchécopar later confirmed to be a bulbul).

[20] For a detailed appraisal of the extent to which her career gravitated towards Messiaen's piano output see Dingle, 'Yvonne Loriod', p. 200.

'Le Loriot' epitomises the contrasts between the two recordings. It is a stately rendition, where the ♪ = 60 tread of the chords infiltrates other tempi that are much quicker on the page. An extreme example is the robin's solo on page 2, where the demisemiquavers are quick and the longer notes in a much slower tempo. The change in Loriod and Messiaen's personal circumstances since 1959 is hard to ignore – with years of marriage behind them, there is no longer the urgency of 'impossible love' (as Loriod characterised their feelings for one another in the 1950s).[21] The midday chiffchaff is also extreme, twice as slow as the metronome mark and far more gentle than its earlier counterpart, receding rather than cutting off before the oriole bursts back in (p. 9).

A feature common to the two recordings of 'Le Loriot' is Loriod's use of agogic accentuation in the 'souvenir' passage. *Rubato* often occurs after high, accented notes – a powerful and refined effect. Once heard, it is difficult to avoid the influence of these moments – this is truly Loriod's passage.

'La Rousserolle effarvatte' is another high point. Though there are moments where Loriod's pianism sounds under more strain than in previous decades, there is a broader gamut of sounds: blistering outbursts of 'la nuit' next to tender 'bruits dans le marais'. An ongoing characteristic of her playing is that moments that seem – on the page – to be of lesser significance register with unexpected force; the coot's trumpet is so fiercely pointed that it sounds momentarily like the epicentre of the piece. Rather than imitating the bird, Loriod extols Messiaen's fantastical vision of it; she revels in the immediate, as one must in this music.

One hallmark of the 1959 recording of the *Catalogue* that is retained in this version is the avoidance of sentimentality – a feature particularly apparent in Book 7. 'La Buse variable' is especially impressive as a result; the mistle thrush sounds almost upbeat in spite of the left-hand stretches, and the rest of the piece has a stark intensity, and great variation of tone. The anthropomorphised blue rock thrush on page 10 of 'Le Traquet rieur' follows the incremental tempo changes precisely, with transitions completely avoided. 'Le Courlis cendré' is, as one would expect, poetic and powerful (the *profundo* cluster on the bottom line of page 13 is anything but *piano*). Listening to this version of Book 7 one senses the extent to which Loriod both was intertwined with, and protected herself from, the highs and lows of Messiaen's life.

The most significant difference between the two recordings is encapsulated by the 1970 'L'Alouette lulu': Loriod plays it as a 'souvenir' of her

---

[21] PH/NS, p. 229.

earlier reading, capitalising on the acoustic of the church. It is a memory of a bird that they both heard; the 1959 recording, in contrast, was about their life at that time. Extending this notion one might say that Messiaen's later music is a 'souvenir' of his earlier styles: more expansive, and with enriched harmony, like the 'memory of gold and rainbow' in 'Le Loriot'.

Is there a danger of idealising Loriod's performances? Perhaps: but it is important to respect and understand what Messiaen said about her playing. Unlike his anecdotes about events such as the *Quatuor* premiere, these views need not qualifying (whatever one's personal taste), but assimilating into our understanding of the music – as would be the case if recordings of Clara playing Robert Schumann's music were to exist. Messiaen's comments do not, however, imply that his wife had an interpretative monopoly; he simply said that she 'plays it [his music] like no one else plays it or ever will play it'.[22] A composer whose personality 'resembles some great baroque building' (as Boulez memorably suggested)[23] should be viewed from as many aspects as possible; Peter Hill's ensuing account of his own studies with Messiaen, working together on his piano music between 1986 and 1991, reveals many more.

Working with Messiaen

I first met Messiaen in October 1986, at the British premiere of his last organ cycle, *Livre du Saint Sacrement*, performed by Jennifer Bate in the vast acoustic of Westminster Cathedral. Surrounded by members of the audience, he wore the rather gloomy, withdrawn expression he often had in public, which made him a difficult subject for photographers; but he brightened when I was introduced, told me he had heard of my plan to record all his piano works, and invited me to his home in Paris to work on the music. Given the interest Messiaen always took in performances of his music, I had little doubt that he was anxious to make sure I was up to the challenge.

A few weeks later I arrived at the rue Marcadet, in my pocket a handwritten letter from Messiaen with characteristically meticulous directions for finding the apartment. I had with me the first six pieces from the *Catalogue*, which I'd been working on over the past year. During that time I had grown to love the music, and had formed my own view of how

---

[22] Samuel, *Music and Colour*, p. 202.
[23] Pierre Boulez, 'The Power of Example', in *Orientations: Collected Writings*, ed. Jean-Jacques Nattiez, trans. Martin Cooper (London: Faber and Faber, 1986), pp. 418–420 (p. 420).

it should be interpreted. But I was fascinated to know how Messiaen saw a work that seemed to me something of a hybrid, combining the sensuousness of sound and harmony of the music of the 1930s and 1940s with the dissonance and rigour of the more modernist works of 1949 onwards. And being a uniquely detailed piece of musical ornithology made its own demands. Did Messiaen see the birdsong as an abstraction, or should it actually sound like robins or blackbirds? And how should one convey the colours of plumage or landscape that Messiaen so obviously saw and heard in the music? But beyond these was a more fundamental question, namely what kind of musician Messiaen really was. I was deeply curious to find what his natural musical instincts would be, to see how he hummed or whistled a melody, or simply played a chord on the piano. Here was a composer who had created some of the most overwhelmingly emotional music of the twentieth century, from the ecstasies of *Visions de l'Amen* and *Vingt Regards* to the unashamed excess of *Turangalîla*; yet at the other extreme was the Messiaen of the *Quatre études* or *Livre d'orgue*, not to mention huge swathes of *Turangalîla*, obsessed with number and process; and in *Technique de mon langage musical* inclined to describe his techniques in formulaic terms. By contrast, the prefaces to *Catalogue d'oiseaux* have no analysis of this kind, but instead are prose-poems with a dash of operatic stage direction: did this, I wondered, indicate a change of approach?

People often ask me about him. The answer is that Messiaen was both charming and formidable: he was the most courteous person I've ever met, but at first I found the directness with which he made criticisms disconcerting. Such honesty breeds trust, however, and I knew that if Messiaen expressed himself satisfied this was truly the case. I began by playing 'Le Merle bleu', and it was immediately clear that I was under the microscope, with Messiaen, sitting a few feet away with his score, keeping up a blizzard of instructions. I can see myself now, stretched to the limit as – urged on by Messiaen – I struggled to make the music catch fire, perspiring in the small over-heated room, the acoustic deadened by layers of red carpet and by the thick curtains that excluded the sounds of the city. But the ordeal was short-lived: quite suddenly I became aware that Messiaen had fallen silent, and I could sense him listening intently as he allowed me to play without interruption. By the end of the piece it was a relief to feel that I had been accepted.

Later that evening I summarised in my diary my impressions of Messiaen: 'Altogether an absolutely *passionate* (not "abstract") musician: everything has to be 100 per cent vivid, and really *be* the birds, places, etc.' In 'Le Merle bleu' this meant making the piano a resonating cave, engulfing the cries of the swifts in the splintered dissonances of the cliffs and the turbulent waves; above the boom and crash rises the song of the blue rock thrush, eloquent, plaintive, nostalgic. Birds, I quickly found, were differentiated from one another by Messiaen through their character as well as their song. He would imitate the songs and calls, describing to me the 'irascible' black-eared wheatear (in 'Le Traquet stapazin'), the liquid lyricism of the robin or the 'heroic' mistle thrush. In this way Messiaen reinforced the conclusion I'd already come to, that the pieces in the *Catalogue* were miniature dramas, with the birds as actors. One birdsong that I found elusive was the woodlark (from 'L'Alouette lulu'). Set in the upper registers of the piano, I was playing this with a sound and rhythm that were too brilliant and hard-edged. Messiaen also wanted the different layers of the music to be held in a very precise balance that is very difficult to achieve: the octaves gliding in the bass, the shadowy right-hand harmonies, and the woodlark, sounding as if at a great height, 'like a voice falling from the stars', as the score puts it. As well as touch and dynamic, the effect of the rhythm is equally subtle: the demisemiquavers of the descant are within the same tempo frame as the bass octaves, but being grouped in threes they drift away, creating their own independent pulse.

Messiaen spoke for the first time about colour when I played him 'Le Loriot'. As I reached the central cadence on E major (coming after the sunrise, with its accompanying solos for garden warblers) Messiaen interrupted me, and asked me to play the chord so that it sounded like a choir of trombones. How? Very simply, he explained, by emphasising the G♯ in the left hand – a trick that really does make this harmony seem to glow from within, without the brittleness that comes from picking out the E at the top of the chord, as I had been doing. Messiaen wanted a similar approach with the harmonies of 'the river' in 'La Bouscarle', with a slight emphasis on C♯ to make a chord of A major still more 'major'. It was interesting to me that Messiaen was so responsive to major and minor, and indeed to the tonalities of the music; in 'La Bouscarle' he showed me how the design of the piece is built around a modulation to the dominant and to the 'dominant of the dominant' (see 'the river', score, pp. 12–13). Another passage where Messiaen encouraged me to explore the inner balance within harmonies was in the sunset in 'La Rousserolle effarvatte'. Here he explained the use of contrasting modes as giving different colours: mode 2 for the 'rouge et violet' (p. 38), and mode 5 for the darker shades of twilight – he asked me to imagine these were scored for low reed instruments (p. 39, where the score mentions oboe and cor anglais), while the sense of imminent darkness could be enhanced by bringing out the thirds inside the minor chords at the cadences (pp. 40–41). Colour is a difficult subject in Messiaen, made the more difficult by the sheer detail of his explanations (in the *Traité*, for example), and it had worried me that the colours that Messiaen 'saw' in his music were an aspect of the greatest importance to him but inaccessible to the rest of us. However, as we worked at this – always in the very practical ways that I have described – I seemed to feel my way into this part of his imagination, starting (as it were) to 'play blue' or 'play green', or at the very least to feel and project the 'emotion' of the colour.

Messiaen demanded the highest standards of playing, and would spot the slightest confusion. But his advice was always constructive, and he had a pianist's understanding of the technical difficulties; how the music was to be played had been in his mind even in the early stages of sketching a piece, as the fingerings added to birdsongs in the *cahiers* show. Nonetheless, Messiaen disliked precision that sounded mechanical. Some birdcalls, of course, had to be unyielding and ruthless, but birds' *songs* were another matter, always to be melodic, phrased and nuanced, however rapid the tempo: 'never like an *étude*', he would say.

This advice also applied to the quasi-serial passages in the *Catalogue*, which are the work's descriptive set pieces. An example is the darkness in 'La Chouette hulotte'. The pianist needs to be exact, of course, in realising the pointillism of pitch, duration and dynamic (dynamic especially), but at the same time must convey not an abstraction but a vivid descriptive idea, the music a metaphor for the ominous darkness that cloaks predator and prey. With the mysterious passage in 'La Bouscarle' that stands for the reflections of willows and poplars, Messiaen encouraged a misty wash of sound corresponding with the muted greens and greys that he imagined. A similar touch is needed for the left hand in the 'music of the ponds' in 'La Rousserolle effarvatte', in contrast with the xylophone-sharp attacks in the upper strand, which suggest perhaps the prickly plants at the water's edge, the rhythmic process a microcosm of the rhythm of night and day. In 'Le Courlis cendré' the twelve-note permutations ('l'eau') were to be played melodically, not rigorously, and slower than is marked in the score; the hands should feel the undulations, like the tug and pull of the water, almost as if a *glissando* connected each note (a trick I also find helpful in 'La Buse variable' with the slow orbits of the gliding buzzard). The magnificent seascape from 'Courlis' seems to me now to have a passionate gloom that recalls Scriabin (Piano Sonata no. 9 – the 'Black Mass') or even the coda of Chopin's Fourth *Ballade*.

Our rehearsals were conducted in the workshop language of musicians, Messiaen showing no inclination for lengthy explanations. We would pause between pieces and he would offer refreshment suitable for a British visitor: whisky (which I declined) or tea. In conversation Messiaen had a lightness that one would not have guessed from how he seemed in public. He spoke simply, as one colleague to another, in perfect classical French, enunciated with such clarity that I could follow with ease. I soon discovered that there were two topics on which one had to be wary: one was his current work – on which Messiaen was always obsessively secretive – the other any query about notation, since it was a matter of pride to Messiaen that his published scores were free of misprints (almost: the D♯ in the second bar of 'La Chouette hulotte' should be *ppp*, not *pp*.) Otherwise, we talked widely, and I asked him questions about music, literature and architecture. Messiaen had a beautiful speaking voice, and once (at my request) recited a poem by Mallarmé in a way that transcended its obscurities and made it sound sublime. In return he would ask me to recite passages from Keats or Shakespeare, because in English (he knew them in French) 'they sound so much better' – 'La vie n'est qu'une ombre qui passe' – 'Life's but a walking shadow …'

Birds, of course, were his great passion. He would talk about them as individuals, smiling at his anthropomorphism ('I am not a scientist', he would say, by way of excuse), and would describe the places that had inspired the *Catalogue*. I said, rather gauchely, that 'Le Traquet stapazin' was my favourite, and he replied that it was his too, and that he had never forgotten his first sight of the Roussillon coast on a glittering morning in June. He asked me if I knew what the Mediterranean birds looked like, and went to his study to fetch illustrated books on ornithology. To my astonishment these turned out to be extremely modest publications, almost the sort of simple guides that one might give to a young child. On my second visit I decided to make an addition to Messiaen's library by giving him a modern edition of *The Birds of Great Britain* by the nineteenth-century bird illustrator John Gould. It was a good present, I thought, but nothing could have prepared me for the extraordinary effect it had on Messiaen. For several minutes he was speechless, turning the pages slowly in silent wonder. Years later I discovered that part of the explanation for Messiaen's reaction was that Gould's birds were old friends: when Messiaen moved across Paris to join his wife in her apartment in the 18th (Loriod and Messiaen married in 1961) he had his composing studio decorated with a wallpaper based on Gould's illustrations. On all my subsequent visits I always brought with me a book on birds, sumptuously illustrated. The last book I gave him I sent through the post: this was in April 1992 after Messiaen had written postponing the meeting we'd arranged, explaining that he was due to go into hospital for surgery. On the day I heard of his death I received an extraordinarily touching letter from Yvonne Loriod, telling of Messiaen's pleasure at my present, and passing on his thanks and good wishes.

Looking back on my sessions with Messiaen I am struck by what we did and did not discuss. We concentrated on touch, colour, clarity (he disliked over-pedalling) and characterisation; but it surprised me that he made almost no comment or criticism of my choices of tempo (the passage from 'Le Courlis cendré' was a very rare exception). It became clear to me that for Messiaen rhythm and tempo were to be *felt*, not measured metronomically. Indeed, this complete identification with the emotion of the music was, it seemed to me, the essence of Messiaen as a musician, the answer to the question that had puzzled me before I met and worked with him.

I never ceased to be amazed by how generous Messiaen was. He never fixed a time for our sessions to end; we would begin usually in the late afternoon, and finish only we were both satisfied, on more than one occasion as late as midnight. The intensity with which Messiaen listened made playing to him a constant challenge, but he was quick to give praise and encouragement. On one occasion I succeeded in playing an entire piece ('Le Merle de roche') without interruption, and found him at the end visibly moved, a precious memory. Gradually, I came to realise that Messiaen valued my ideas about his music. He might so easily have set out to be possessive, to be dogmatic – as he was, perhaps, in the first awkward minutes of our first meeting – or to refer to Loriod's way of playing as the preferred model. He was quick to point out the slightest lack of conviction, but I found that he listened with an open mind, and accepted and indeed encouraged my own way of playing, enriching my understanding but never imposing any fundamental change on my interpretation. I shall always be grateful for the chance I had of working with this great musician, and of experiencing his imaginative world at first hand.

Performing *Catalogue d'oiseaux*

When playing the *Catalogue* one is constantly reminded that the work was designed for a pianist of irresistible brilliance and panache: given the all but unlimited possibilities Loriod's playing offered Messiaen, it is hardly surprising that the *Catalogue* is so demanding. The virtuosity seems to reflect her immense repertoire, ranging from the avant garde (shown in the twelve-note pointillism of 'La Chouette hulotte', for example) via earlier Messiaen to Ravel and Debussy, even Chopin (as in the cadenza for the kingfisher in 'La Bouscarle').[24] At the same time there is the exceptional inventiveness of the piano writing, its originality driven by Messiaen's search for musical equivalents to the sounds and sights in nature. Individual birdsongs are often mosaics of contrasted fragments; played at speed, they set up a fierce interplay, as in the solos for the reed warbler ('La Rousserolle effarvatte'). Others have rapid tremolos and trills, or the repeated notes that can be so treacherous for the pianist (the wren or garden warbler in 'Le Loriot'). The more lyrical songs are 'coloured' by a quieter descant, moving in near-parallel motion with the principal line. Chords, too, may act as shadowy upper lines ('L'Alouette lulu'), or contain terraced dynamics, as in 'La Chouette hulotte'. The range of touch and dynamic encompasses the tumult of the sea, in 'Le Merle bleu' or 'Le Courlis cendré', down to the merest whisper, the trilling grasshopper warbler ('La Rousserolle effarvatte') or the splinters of crystal ('cassures de cristal') in 'Le Traquet stapazin'. In all this, there is the danger that the *Catalogue* in performance may degenerate into a sequence of events, however spectacular, without inner motivation. The pianist needs to take a path similar to that taken by Messiaen himself when composing the work: one has to characterise each birdsong as vividly as possible, but at the same time find the connections that make the piece an entity, ideally understanding – and communicating – its central idea.

Interpreting the *Catalogue* may be illustrated by considering recordings of three pieces, starting with the shortest, 'L'Alouette calandrelle' (a starting-point for pianists exploring the work for the first time), along with two others, 'La Bouscarle' and 'Le Traquet stapazin', which between them represent many of the pianistic and structural innovations Messiaen made in the *Catalogue*.

The opening of 'L'Alouette calandrelle' uses a three-layered texture that had featured in Messiaen's music since his earliest works, with slow-moving chords in the bass that are sustained by the pedal underneath the song of the lark, in which the melody played by the left hand is harmonised by a softer upper line. (It is worth noting that *mf* and *p* are adjacent to one another in Messiaen's normal scale of dynamics – *mp* is hardly ever used – so that the right-hand line should probably not be too quiet; but even quite slight changes in balance can affect the timbre – more brittle if the right hand is stronger.) Rhythmically, two points need to be considered. The first

---

[24] Chopin's *Etude* in A flat, Op. 10, no. 10.

is the way Messiaen notates the lark's song, dividing it into motivic 'cells' (see Example 4.14 on p. 98) implied by the beaming used to connect the notes: in passages such as this the pianist has to decide whether the groups can be taken for granted, or whether they need to be projected – in this case the first group (of three) could be seen as the upbeat, the second group 'thrown' from the first of the high Bs. The other element that needs the pianist's attention is the tempo connection between the opening pair of chords ($\flat$ = 54) and the lark's song ($\flat$ = 108): the implication is that the lark's song should be one with the landscape, which creates the stillness within which the song evolves.

In recorded performances of the *Catalogue* pianists are divided in their interpretation of this passage. A number play the lark's song appreciably quicker than the opening chords, giving the effect of a spot-lit solo, standing out sharply from a shadowy background, and too fast to articulate the rhythmic groups implied by the Messiaen's notation. Loriod's pioneering recording from 1959 takes this view, the song articulated with diamond-sharp touch, enhanced by the remarkably close recording. The following compares the tempi taken in the opening bars:

Yvonne Loriod (1959): $\flat$ = 54 / $\flat$ = 116–120
Håkan Austbø: 54/120
Robert Sherlaw Johnson: 54/116–120
Momo Kodama: 36/116
Yvonne Loriod (1970): 46/108
Michael Kieran Harvey: 46/108
Carl-Axel Dominique: 54/108
Roger Muraro: 52/104
Peter Hill: 48/98
Anatol Ugorski: 48/96
Paul Kim: 40/98
Martin Zehn: 36/96

In the episode that follows, her 'cicadas' are ferocious, and in the second of the variations the duet with the crested lark is quick and crisp. The recapitulation (a variant of the opening verse) is beautifully poised and balanced, but with no sense of winding down, and the little phrase for the lark at the end of the piece is played not as an afterthought (as a number of pianists do) but simply as a restatement of the opening bar, as if the cycle were recommencing. The stillness in Loriod's performance comes in the silences, which are exceptionally prolonged, unlike other recordings where they are simply breaks between sections.

Muraro (recorded during a live performance) is at the opposite end of the spectrum. Unlike Loriod (1959) he observes the tempo relationship at the opening, his much slower lark's song enabling him to shape the motifs within phrases, the effect being sensitive and even slightly hesitant (see also Hill). The cicadas are suppressed and muted, while the quail is quiet and rather rapid, so that the interruption (for the cicadas–kestrel–quail trio) is played as if in parentheses. Similarly, the second variation (the duet) is so light and quiet that it occupies a different level, set apart from the developments of the lark in the variations on either side. The return of the lark's song is withdrawn and poetic, and the approach continues to the final bar as if oblivious to the interruption by the skylark, which is played very frenetically.

Anatol Ugorski's performance makes an interesting comparison with Loriod's. Like her, he sees the piece as a contrast between energy and stillness, but his way of conveying this is different. With Ugorski the lark's song is taken steadily, its phrases patiently constructed. Within this framework, everything else in the piece is urgent and dynamic: the variations teem with energy – the duet (variation 2) being marvellously quick and precise – while silences are kept to a minimum. The only similarity with Loriod is the skylark, held back and emphatic (as it is in both Loriod's recordings), unlike the frenzied blur of Muraro.

Momo Kodama is one of the pianists who (like Loriod 1959) play the lark's opening song quickly, but with her the effect is more gestural, with variations in tempo and the phrases shaped by *rubato*. The cicadas are *pesante* (as they are in Loriod's later recording), the kestrel piercingly fast and intense. Like Ugorski's, Kodama's central variations are alert with nervous energy, the duet with the crested lark played very quickly. Austbø takes a different view of the duet, steadier than most, revealing details such as the tiny silences that create a gapped, lacework texture.

With Hill the lark's song is unusually remote, shaped by a slight *rubato* and by articulating the motivic groups. In the middle part of the piece the first variation flutters delicately, as a prelude to a gradual increase in impetus, made possible by playing the duet steadily, and like Muraro he makes much of the contrasts in dynamic and tempo in the climactic third variation. As with Loriod, Hill's silences are very marked, especially (and unusually) during the recapitulation; and his final line (after a very quick skylark) has a hint of *allargando* and *diminuendo*, suggesting a curve to the piece, with the lark approaching and receding.

The Australian composer-pianist Michael Kieran Harvey plays with much more freedom than the other pianists, producing extremes of contrast: at the opening, for example, the lark's song is exceptionally distant, its phrases shaped tenderly by *rubato*, with the cicadas making a bizarre interruption, played almost twice as fast as (for example) Loriod's later version. Harvey's approach makes an important point: for him these are birdsong *impressions* – imitations of birdsong, not a stylisation – and he is the only pianist to include Messiaen's prefaces in the recording, where they are spoken by a ornithologist.

'La Bouscarle' also uses a variant of the double structure in 'L'Alouette calandrelle', but in a more complex way, and with a far greater variety of material. The challenge for the pianist is to characterise each element of the music, but also to give a sense of the different strands woven together, each continuing even when absent from the surface of the music.

The most significant difference among pianists is found in the way they view the music of the river. The first appearance (p. 4) of the river follows immediately after the blurred colours of the 'reflections', the music stepping into the light in one of the *Catalogue*'s most eloquent moments – 'calme, chantant, bien timbré'. With Loriod (1959) the river is brightly lit, flowing briskly, very much in the foreground, and in complete contrast to the 'reflections', which are quiet and unusually clear, with pedalling kept to the minimum. The 'reflections' section elicits a variety of responses: Muraro slightly emphasises the chords in the left hand, perhaps to underline the rhythmic counterpoint; Kodama shapes it melodically, so that the effect is less 'random' than other pianists.

Earlier, Loriod plays the opening of the piece (Cetti's warbler) as a furious tirade, rather overriding the indicated contrast in tempo between the bird's two motifs, with angrily snatched phrases, followed by the first kingfisher cadenza, fearlessly speedy and precise (where some pianists show a degree of caution). Muraro is again very different from Loriod. The opening page is played wittily, the staccato upbeats to the kingfisher's cadenza being deliciously pointed and placed (see also Ugorski and Austbø). With the 'river' Muraro shapes its opening statement (pp. 4–6) as a single paragraph, by treating the first two phrases as upbeats, with the more extended third phrase growing in confidence. Loriod too makes this third phrase the apex (in both recordings), in her case by accenting the harmony on the subdominant (D^6) followed by a pronounced diminuendo.

Several of the pianists favour a full sound for the river (following Loriod's example), the most successful avoiding hardness of tone (Ugorski, Martin Zehn, Austbø, for example). Hill, in contrast, plays the river quietly and inwardly, making it the still centre at the heart of the piece. Ugorski's river is slower than most, and like Muraro he observes deftly the nuances within birdsongs (the codettas for the blackbird, for example, which punctuate the phrases of the chorale).

Austbø's 'reflections' are so quiet as to be on the edge of silence; the harmonies of the river are warm, and almost nostalgic in the final phrase of each verse. Birdsongs are quick (as they were in his performance of 'L'Alouette calandrelle'), and the cadenzas (the kingfisher) light and dazzlingly swift. At the development of the river (pp. 12–13) Austbø gives prominence to the tenor line in the falling phrases (p. 13, bb. 2–4) and with a *dolce* return to the E^9 chord at the cadence. Martin Zehn's 'river' is faster than Ugorski's, but held back at the climactic passage (p. 13) as a way of avoiding forcing the sound at the *forte*; Hill in this passage marks the modulation (from E to B) by a change of colour; the reiterated falling phrases (p. 13, bb. 2–4) are played calmly and quietly, before warming the sound as the music steps back to E.

Muraro again projects the music as a series of co-existing levels. His versions of the flights of the kingfisher are like momentary interjections, flickering across the surface of the piece (Robert Sherlaw Johnson is the only pianist to achieve exactly what Messiaen wanted in the fourth cadenza, with minimal hesitations on the barlines: see p. 16). Muraro's account highlights a difference among pianists in the way the birdsong is played. With some the birdsong is generally rapid (Loriod, Austbø, Carl-Axel Dominique), forming the foreground to the backdrop of the chorale. Muraro belongs to the group who employ greater variety of tempo (see also Kodama, Hill, Zehn): he creates a mosaic of fragments not only between birdsongs but also within the same song (his robin, for example). Few of the pianists observe the long, precisely measured silences on the final page. With Austbø the silences are if anything elongated, but they are ideally 'expectant', thanks to the slight urgency with which he plays the pairs of chords.

'Le Traquet stapazin' illustrates Messiaen's structural inventiveness in the *Catalogue*, with a kaleidoscope of strongly contrasted fragments that are woven into a huge span. In one sense the piece is like a sonata form, with an exposition setting out the principal birdsongs in three subsections or verses, a development (the sunrise), and a recapitulation, headed by the music of the terraced vineyards with which the piece opens, to which the fading colours of twilight act as coda. This sectional design is misleading, however: no other piece in the *Catalogue* depends so much on the play of memory and premonition. Individual songs follow their own life cycle of development and decline. So, the goldfinch, initially just a brief gesture (p. 2) develops in the second verse (pp. 3–4) and again in the recapitulation (as a duet, pp. 21–22); the ortolan bunting also develops in the second verse, thereafter heard as a fragmentary recall, while the spectacled warbler threads its way through the piece, developed in the second verse, but with its longest solos in the coda; at the end its song, in slow motion, is heard as a 'souvenir', in the memory. The constant interweaving of songs in different stages of development goes hand in hand with the strategic use of premonitions. The harmonies of the sunrise, for example, are previewed in the music of the goldfinch in verse 2 (pp. 3–4); the interjection from the Orphean warbler near the end of the exposition introduces the song that will dominate the second phase of the development (pp. 15–17), while its exchanges with the corn bunting are anticipated (p. 11) within the section given to the sunrise.

In performance quite subtle changes to tempo or dynamic, or to the feel of individual birdsongs, twitch the kaleidoscope, colouring the piece as a whole in new ways. Decisions taken in the first verse prove to be crucial. Loriod (1959), for example, plays the first two bars quietly and mysteriously, announcing a reading that will give full value to space and stillness. Others are more flowing (Sherlaw Johnson, Austbø and Hill, for example),[25] while some find a weightier sound (Zehn, Kodoma, Harvey). Another key difference comes with the song of the spectacled warbler: Loriod (1959) is quick and light; in 1970 her decision to play the song more steadily and lyrically accords with her view of the sunrise, which is more sustained than in her earlier recording. Sherlaw Johnson opts for the first of Loriod's approaches to the spectacled warbler. Overall, he takes a witty, fleet-fingered view of the piece, creating a sense of events ricocheting off one another in the opening exchanges; later his sunrise is more flowing than either of Loriod's versions, but like her he plays the final solos for the spectacled warbler (in the coda) lightly and swiftly. Muraro, too, feels free to interpret Messiaen's markings of *mf* as quiet or very quiet: the hallmark of his performance is its feeling of fantasy, with the spectacled warbler and goldfinch given a secretive, quirky charm.

Ugorski, in complete contrast, is fiercely dramatic, making the maximum of the opposition (on the first page) between the soloist (the wheatear) and his very withdrawn way of playing the repetitions of the ortolan bunting. Characteristically, he views the phrases for the Thekla lark in the

---

[25] Peter Hill has recorded 'Le Traquet stapazin' twice, in 1987 and 2014.

final chorale as not within the mood but sharp interjections. A feature of his performance is the balancing of the chords, with a quiet but rich sound to the start of the sunrise (which Ugorski plays, very effectively, with a gradual *crescendo* in place of Messiaen's terraced dynamics); in the final chorale he slightly picks out the lowest note of each left hand chord in order to enhance the doubling of bass and treble.

The second phase of the development (pp. 15–17) creates a difficulty in some performances, seeming to mark time between the end of the sunrise and the cadenza for the Thekla lark. Here both Austbø and Hill (2014) adopt the same solution, keeping the momentum going with a lively, springy Orphean warbler, checked by the 'cassures de cristal' of the corn bunting (Loriod, in 1959, is unmatchable in these, her trills entrancingly quiet and crystalline). During the earlier part of the development Hill (1987) creates a perspective between the foreground (the sunrise) and the solos for wheatear and rock bunting, which he plays exceptionally quickly, as subordinate to the main line. The same is true of his Thekla lark, which ends the development (pp. 17–19), played *prestissimo*, and shearing off abruptly into the silence at the end of the section, with no hint of *allargando*. Others follow Loriod in articulating the gestures within the song, in particular holding back the cadences.

The way pianists handle the transitions is especially revealing. The passage preceding the sunrise (p. 8), for example, transforms hyperactivity into stillness; the music here seems to rebalance itself, with three phrases in quick succession for the spectacled warbler, with a fourth and final phrase isolated from the others by the interjection from the Orphean warbler that previews the middle part of the development. In three of the recordings the spectacled warbler is played lightly and quickly: Loriod (1959), Sherlaw Johnson and Hill (1987). Of these, Loriod's is the most straightforward: in the final phrase of the spectacled warbler there is no *diminuendo* or *allargando*, without Messiaen's 'tendre' (a number of changes were made subsequent to the recording when the *Catalogue* was prepared for publication), and the sunrise begins firmly and sonorously, simply as a new event. Sherlaw Johnson plays the Orphean warbler as a surprise, suddenly brisk and weighty; Muraro achieves a similar effect by exaggerating the rhythm of the slurs, the calls elbowing in among the elegant shapings of the spectacled warbler. Hill, unlike most, starts the sunrise quietly, thereby eliding the sonority of one section into the next. Muraro goes further, beginning *pianissimo*, the sunrise a mysterious swell growing against the bright chattering phrases of the wheatear. Compared with the strong contrasts of Sherlaw Johnson or Muraro, Zehn allows the music to flow into the development. His spectacled warbler is unhurried, the Orphean warbler marked but unexaggerated, and in the sunrise he finds a sound that manages to be both rich and remote.

At the other end of the piece sunset declining into twilight is counterpointed by the sharp cries of birds, briefly recalled (see pp. 22–25). Loriod (1959) keeps the contrasts firmly etched, her melody at *Lent* (p. 24) dreamily singing but with the Thekla lark piercing and soloistic. Others blur the boundaries, perhaps seeing Messiaen's very compressed sunset (pp. 22–23) as the step into unreality. With Austbø, Sherlaw Johnson and Ugorski, the end of the sunset is played quietly, almost as if the end of the piece, and the birdcalls that follow are slightly suppressed, as though looking to the past. Austbø plays the *Lent* very inwardly, with slight hesitations at the cadences, while Sherlaw Johnson's sound is remote, almost fragile. Hill (2014) keeps the birdcalls alert and active, creating a long line whose end point is not the *Lent* but the chorale marked *Très lent* (p. 25). Zehn achieves a similar result through different means. His sunset starts more flowing than most, but sinks rapidly towards quietness, aided by an *allargando*; thereafter he keeps the birdsongs within the mood he has created, judging the dynamics so that the Thekla lark, for example, is 'present' but in parentheses.

Summarising these impressions, it seems that pianists divide between those who largely follow in the tradition established by Loriod (in her teaching as well as her playing) and those who see the work in new ways. The division is a simplification, of course, since all the pianists included in this survey have valuable insights, and given that a number of them worked with Messiaen or Loriod (or both) it is reassuring that they sound so different: the idea of a single 'authentic' way of playing the *Catalogue* was certainly not what Messiaen would have wanted (nor Loriod, who was notably generous to pianists playing what she might have considered as 'her' repertoire).

In terms of how the *Catalogue* is interpreted, the challenge to pianists is to see the music as multi-dimensional, weaving foreground and background, solo and commentary, continuities and interruptions – with even quite subtle changes of emphasis opening fresh perspectives. In the opening of 'L'Alouette calandrelle', for example, are the chords an accompaniment to the lark's song? Or are they themselves the principal line (with the lark as descant or commentary)? The most intriguing of such ambiguities is between different modes of experience. One could, for example, view the middle section of 'L'Alouette calandrelle' as an imaginary development of the lark's song, framed by 'reality' in the outer sections. Alternatively, one might see the lark's song itself as an undercurrent of dream (as Muraro, for example, seems to do), within which reality intrudes in the sharper-edged cries and songs (the trio of cicadas–kestrel–quail, the crested lark and the skylark). Such fascinating possibilities may explain why the *Catalogue* appeals to new generations of pianists, so that a work that was once played only by specialists is increasingly an integral part of the twentieth-century repertoire.

7 | Postlude

> It is some thirty years now since I began noting down birdsong. My first transcriptions are scattered through my earliest works. Unfortunately I had no experience at the time and did not always know to which bird I should attribute this or that song. Subsequently I asked the advice of specialists in the field and learnt a great deal in the course of guided walks ... Once I had done that, I was able (no transformation or pun intended) to fly with my own wings. And so each spring, armed with pencils, erasers, manuscript paper, drawing paper and an enormous pair of binoculars, I visit a different province of France in search of my teachers. This is how I wrote the *Catalogue d'oiseaux* for solo piano ... It is an open-ended work. If death does not put an end to my activity, this first catalogue will be followed by a second and perhaps by a third.[1]

Messiaen's prediction, made in the introductory essay published before the first performance of *Catalogue d'oiseaux*, is confirmed by notes made during the summer of 1957, with plans for fifteen further birdsong pieces.[2] Several of these are outlined in some detail. The 'Linotte des vignes' (linnet) would have had three different settings, corresponding to the time of day (morning, afternoon, evening); the 'Rouge-gorge' (robin) includes the church at Saint-Amant de Boixe (in the Charente), 'terrifying and austere'; and the 'Grive musicienne' (song thrush) takes place in the evening at Gardépée, with 'the poetry of twilight and of the growing darkness'. Most intriguing is the piece for jackdaws mentioned earlier against a backdrop of the cathedral at Chartres, with the twelfth-century tower, the sculpture of the Angel of Time, the Jesse window and the sounds of bells. None of these was composed, although eventually the robin, blackbird and song thrush would each be the subject of pieces in Messiaen's last work for piano, *Petites Esquisses d'oiseaux* (1985). Certainly there was no let-up in Messiaen's birdsong researches following the completion of the *Catalogue* in September 1958. Two *cahiers* from the early months of 1959 record a trip to the Jura in March, as well as notations made in and around Paris, including the

---

[1] Olivier Messiaen, 'La Nature, les chants d'oiseaux', *Guide du concert* 229 (3 April 1959), 1093–1094.
[2] 23056(2), p. 9.

garden of the nursing home at Bourg-la-Reine where Messiaen's wife was a patient.[3] Claire's sudden death, so soon after the triumphant premiere of the *Catalogue*, must have seemed like a cruel irony.

By now Messiaen had received a commission for an orchestral work for the 1960 Donaueschingen Festival. His initial working title was 'Postlude', suggesting a pendant to the *Catalogue*, finishing with a solo for a nightingale.[4] Although *Chronochromie* developed very differently from these first thoughts, the example of the *Catalogue* remains. The form of *Chronochromie* follows the design for the 'mountain' sections in 'Le Chocard des Alpes', based on the triad of Greek drama, with a Strophe, Antistrophe and contrasting Epode (in *Chronochromie* the design is enlarged so that there are two pairs of Strophe and Antistrophe, as well as the introduction and coda); and the device of chorales to close the introduction and coda may be traced back to the chorale that closes 'Le Traquet stapazin'. Although *Chronochromie* has no piano part – the piano and ondes Martenot were excluded at the request of Donaueschingen's director, Heinrich Strobel – the experience of several years composing for solo piano caused Messiaen to rethink the way he notated birdsong for orchestra. Prior to *Chronochromie*, he had solved the problem of coordinating the asymmetrical rhythms of birdsong by using a regular pulse and metre (as in the opening movement of the *Quatuor*, for example, or the central medley of *Oiseaux exotiques*); now Messiaen began the practice of notating birdsong a-metrically, in its natural rhythm.

The most important influence from the *Catalogue* is the technique of permutations ('interversions'), applied to the scale of thirty-two chromatic durations, which Messiaen borrowed from the music of the cortège in 'Le Merle de roche'. The way these are clarified and 'coloured' by harmonies and birdsongs gives the work its title, from the Greek *chronos* (time) and *chrôma* (colour). In asserting the primacy of number and calculation Messiaen seems to be going back to the music of the years 1949–1952 (especially *Livre d'orgue*); an alternative explanation is that he was now fulfilling his original conception for the *Catalogue*, which had been hinted at in the Brittany *cahier*.[5] In the event, as we have seen, the plan for basing the *Catalogue* on a unifying numerical or serial scheme was abandoned, with passages based on twelve-note permutations confined to descriptions of mountains, water or darkness; now in *Chronochromie* permutations form the backbone of the piece.

---

[3] 23013 and 23014.
[4] PH/NS, pp. 233–234.
[5] 23044.

This should not be taken as implying a subordinate role for the birdsong, however. The birdsong in *Chronochromie* comes in many forms. In the introduction and coda the cries of two Swedish species, the osprey and white-tailed eagle, are magnified massively by the resources of the full orchestra. In the Strophes individual songs are assigned to woodwind instruments or tuned percussion, creating medleys of birdsong reminiscent of *Réveil* or *Oiseaux exotiques*, while in the Antistrophes (as well as in the introduction and coda) Messiaen uses generally single birdsongs or calls, centred on the brief incantatory rhythms of song thrush and skylark. Birdsong at last flies free in the Epode, a tangled medley of birdsongs scored for eighteen solo strings. The significance of the Epode is that birdsong is no longer in 'translation', but uncompromising in its truth to nature.

The French premiere of *Chronochromie* (at Besançon on 13 September 1961) sharply divided critical opinion, and the first performance in Paris (13 February 1962) created what Messiaen called 'an unimaginable scandal'. Nonetheless, Messiaen had become a public figure, widely known through recordings of his music (including the complete works for organ, which he himself had recorded at the Trinité in 1956), with further recognition in the award of the *Grand Prix du Disque* for Loriod's recording of the *Catalogue*. In June 1961 Messiaen received the invitation to tour Japan the following summer, which would be his first trip outside Europe since the premiere of *Turangalîla* in Boston in 1949. Despite these successes 1961 was a strangely fallow year. The only composition was a short organ work, *Verset pour la fête de la Dédicace*, commissioned by the Conservatoire the previous autumn and completed rapidly, since on 24 January 1961 Messiaen was able to note in his diary that he had reviewed the first proof, which had been corrected by Loriod.

Verset apart, the completion of *Chronochromie* saw Messiaen temporarily without a commission. Lacking a deadline, he turned his attention (just as he had in 1954, a similarly fallow year) to birdsong. The focus for his research was an area of central southern France, the Hérault, which had featured once in the *Catalogue*, in the rock formations of the Cirque de Mourèze – the setting for 'Le Merle de roche'. Messiaen now planned a dictionary of the birds of the Hérault (probably a collaboration with his friend the ornithologist François Hüe, who lived near Pézenas), and he outlined in his diary plans for a triple concerto – for flute, xylophone and piano – based on the birdsongs of the region.

Messiaen's notations in the Hérault were made near the village of Nizas. He and Loriod spent several days there in May 1960, revisiting the area the following April as part of a three-week trip across southern France that began in the Camargue and finished with a visit to the caves of Lascaux in the Dordogne. Returning to Paris, Messiaen seems to have been in the grip of a creative idea, since he lost little time in returning to Nizas, abandoning his teaching duties at the Conservatoire to spend several days (4–9 May) notating birdsong.

The result was a work for piano, *La Fauvette Passerinette*, composed at Petichet, during the summer break of 1961, and unknown until its discovery by Peter Hill in 2012.[6] The draft score, though not a fair copy, is in an advanced state of completion. The outer sections consist of duets for the *fauvette passerinette*, or subalpine warbler. These were difficult to decipher, being scribbled in Messiaen's untidiest handwriting. However, what at first glance appeared to be a rough draft proved to be complete in every detail, including articulations, pedalling and even fingering (Ex. 7.1). This hard-to-read but at the same time very finished draft has a precedent in (for example) the page from the Brittany *cahier* where Messiaen sketched the harmonies for 'L'Alouette lulu'. Even so, it is puzzling; and the answer must be that by 1961 notating birdsong and composing with birdsong had become almost indistinguishable activities: hence the subsequent composition into piano score would have occurred rapidly and with considerable certainty.[7]

The music of the middle part of the piece consists of fragments, placed in order by Messiaen using an alphabetical scheme, a method familiar from the sketches for 'La Bouscarle' and 'Le Traquet stapazin'. The section that presented the most difficulty was for a flock of six *coucous geais* (great spotted cuckoos) that existed only as block harmonies; fortunately, it was possible to find the corresponding passage in the *cahier* and to transfer the rhythms, dynamics and articulations. The result is a passage of extraordinary violence, with brutal reiterations of dissonant chords and refrains.

Very probably *La Fauvette Passerinette* was the start of a new birdsong project, perhaps the second 'catalogue' that Messiaen always said he had intended to write. If so, it is clear that his thinking had moved on in the two years since the *Catalogue* was premiered. The opening duet, for example,

---

[6] The discovery was made by Peter Hill in the pages at the back of one of the *cahiers*, 23023. The birdsong sources for the music are notations found in the same *cahier* and in two others, 23020 and 23072. A note in the margin of one of the pages of the draft score dates composition to August 1961 at Petichet. The score is published by Faber Music.

[7] It is worth noting that Messiaen was on honeymoon. He and Loriod were married in Paris on 3 July (the civil ceremony took place two days earlier). That summer a garage was constructed at Petichet with enough space for the car (a Renault 4) and an upright piano for Loriod to practise on. See PH/NS, p. 241.

Example 7.1 *La Fauvette Passerinette* (facsimile)

is more integrated than duets in the *Catalogue* (like the reed warblers in 'La Rousserolle effarvatte'), a true counterpoint between equal voices, with witty exchanges, and with melismas knocked off balance by syncopated accents. The only non-birdsong music is a sequence of chords that introduces the first episode, cadencing on a chord of B^9, and later (at the exact midpoint of the piece) 'resolved' by the E major of a golden oriole. The oriole is joined in the episodes by other birds familiar from the *Catalogue* – woodlark, Orphean warbler, red-backed shrike and nightingale: all are recognisable, but varied and clearly reimagined.

As well as these differences, it is evident in other ways that Messiaen was not content to follow the model of his earlier cycle. As we have seen, the *Catalogue* had been made possible by bringing the natural surroundings of the birds into the music, a solution to the problem of composing birdsong music within the limitations of solo piano: as a result the *Catalogue* became as much about the landscapes of France as about its birdsongs. In *La Fauvette Passerinette*, on the other hand, Messiaen dispenses with scenery, time of day, darkness, sunlight – all key features of the *Catalogue*. The precedents for this were *Oiseaux exotiques* (which was birdsong pure-and-simple, without programme, and without even an accurate order of events), and more recently *Chronochromie*, with the birdsong embedded in the abstract rhythmic scheme.

Instead, in *La Fauvette Passerinette*, Messiaen juggles various kinds of musical opposition: active/passive, fluid/static, near/far – plus the expected vivid contrasts of character. These are all features of the *Catalogue*, of course, but in *La Fauvette Passerinette* they come with two innovations. One is that the birdsong has to harmonise itself, as we can hear in the second duet for the passerinettes, where the dialogue is increasingly infiltrated by cadences (using Messiaen's chords of 'contracted resonance'). Harmony is then one of the ways in which the music of the passerinettes undergoes a transformation. The way this is done seems to be purposeful, reflecting the other birdsongs encountered in the piece; in particular, the richness of harmony in the final section draws on the hard-edged 'vertical' writing in the episodes for the cuckoos and for the Orphean warbler. As a result the chordal style of the closing section is particularly exciting because it makes a genuine climax to the trajectory of the piece.

The use of harmony within birdsong (as opposed to accompanying birdsong) would become an essential feature in *La Fauvette des jardins* (1970). The difference is that the birdsong in *La Fauvette Passerinette* is self-sufficient, while in *La Fauvette des jardins* it is part of a lovingly detailed evocation of the vista of lake and mountain opposite Messiaen's summer retreat in the French Alps. But the example in *La Fauvette Passerinette* of birdsong in the abstract was not forgotten, and Messiaen would return to it many years later in *Petites Esquisses d'oiseaux*.

La Fauvette Passerinette therefore forms a missing link between the *Catalogue* and Messiaen's later birdsong works. But if the piece was indeed the start of a second birdsong cycle, it was overtaken by events. By the end of 1961 Messiaen was occupied with plans for an orchestral work for Debussy's centenary in 1962, and soon afterwards three more important commissions came his way, for *Couleurs de la Cité céleste* (1963), *Et exspecto resurrectionem mortuorum* (1965) and *La Transfiguration de Notre-Seigneur Jésus-Christ* (1969). Given the pressure of work, it is easy to imagine how *La Fauvette Passerinette* became sidelined and forgotten.

La Fauvette des jardins and *Petites Esquisses d'oiseaux*

To them [the warblers] I've dedicated 'La Rousserolle effarvatte' in my *Catalogue d'oiseaux*, a piece I've long considered my greatest success in bird songs, but which

I now think has twice been surpassed, by *La Fauvette des jardins* for piano and 'The Sermon to the Birds' from *Saint François d'Assise*.[8]

What were the likely criteria behind this statement? Composers will naturally want to create the impression of progress, but there seems more to it on this occasion. Perhaps the richness of the birdsong writing – as opposed to broader compositional matters – was Messiaen's main criterion; this would reflect his exalted view of birds, of course. But others shared his opinion. Harry Halbreich, in his 1980 book on his former teacher, praised the synthesis of colour and time in *La Fauvette des jardins*, which intensifies throughout the piece's vast expanse (it is fifty-five pages long and lasts over half an hour).[9] Whatever the reason, *La Fauvette* is similar enough to the *Catalogue d'oiseaux* to offer a useful reverse perspective, and illuminate his working process still further.

Nearly a decade elapsed between *La Fauvette Passerinette* and this latest piano work, during which time Messiaen's compositional style had become more grandiose. It began to expand in *Et exspecto* (1965), commissioned by André Malraux, the Minister of Cultural Affairs, and premiered in the Sainte-Chapelle, culminating with the vast *La Transfiguration* (1969). Completed six weeks before the Apollo moon landing, this latest work seems to be tapping into a great historical sense of ambition.

With the changes of scale these works entailed, the method of almost instant realisation from *cahier* to composition had to be left behind. The *cahiers* of the 1960s are superbly vivid and sophisticated, some as many as 100 pages long. One of the richest, 23101, contains an encyclopedic collection of French birds that could have filled a second *Catalogue*. Collected during two summers at Petichet (1965 and 1966), and springtime trips to the Sologne, Charente and Quercy-Rocamadour in 1970 (plus recordings by Roché and Tesson) it features birds both familiar (great reed warbler, blackcap (Ex. 7.2), redstart) and novel (common redpoll, red crossbill and several species of woodpecker), as well as the inevitable frogs. There are fewer harmonised sketches – possibly because of the prevalence of field notations over commercial recordings – but also a growing presence of mellifluous songsters such as the garden warbler. Articulation, expression and dynamic markings, however, are abundant, Messiaen's gift for characterisation becoming increasingly ingrained.

---

[8] Claude Samuel, *Music and Color: Conversations with Claude Samuel*, trans. E. Thomas Glasow (Portland: Amadeus, 1994), p. 92.

[9] Harry Halbreich, *Olivier Messiaen* (Paris: Fayard, 1980), p. 261.

Example 7.2 The blackcap, from 23101, p. 18

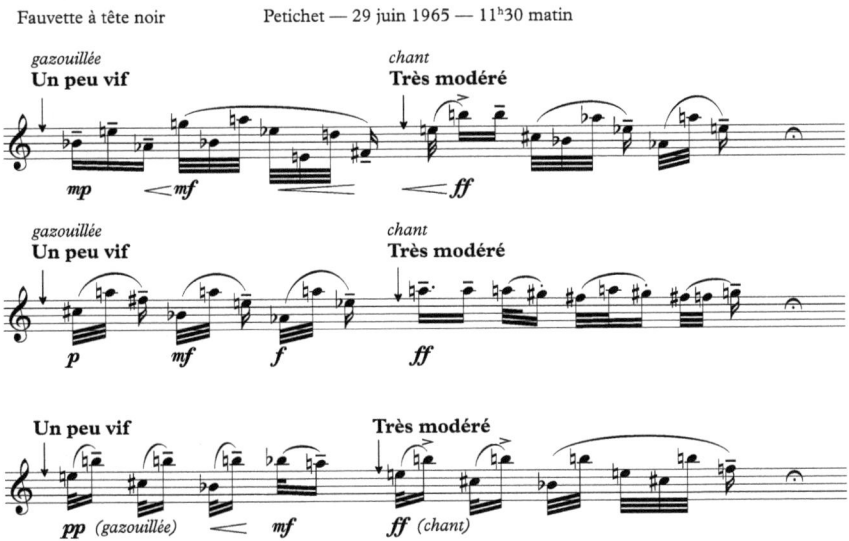

Prose descriptions and diagrams are also plentiful. A delightful page written at Les Baux during the Easter vacation in 1965 compares the mistral, which blew fiercely for a day and two nights, with a wrestler ('Il s'agit plutôt d'un "catcheur"') and analyses its sound into two layers: a succession of low, continuous swellings, and a rhythmicised series of *sforzandi* in a higher register.[10] Perhaps the idea to use a wind machine in an orchestral work – *Des Canyons aux étoiles …* (1974) – took seed while Messiaen lay awake that night.

An extraordinary amount of song was collected during the summer months at Petichet, with garden warblers the undisputed stars. Full pages are devoted to their song, the result being a remarkable cache of melodic inspiration. The impulse for Messiaen to depict this bird and its landscape in sound must have grown each summer until, with his most demanding commission finally fulfilled, there was time available for a new project; the result, completed in the summer of 1970, was *La Fauvette des jardins*.

Messiaen always seemed to regard garden warblers as having a special quality – as he describes in the preface to 'Le Loriot': 'Tirelessly, and at length, the garden warblers pour out their soft virtuosity' ('Longtemps, sans se lasser, les Fauvettes des jardins déversent leur virtuosité douce').

---

[10] 23098, p. 17.

The ability of these duetting birds to suspend time, a trait spelled out in *La Fauvette des jardins*, is implicit here, as is the allegory with the lovers of the 'Tristan' trilogy, whose rendezvous in the garden (where 'Le Loriot' is also set) stands outside time, or so they would wish. Their indirect association with the *Cinq Rechants* melody 'Tous les philtres' in turn lends sense to the 'Tristan' trilogy melody (from the 'slow movement' of *Turangalîla*, 'Jardin du sommeil d'amour' – see Ex. 4.19 on p. 114), which Messiaen uses to represent night at the opening of *La Fauvette des jardins*.

Late in life Messiaen used the garden warbler as an example of his approach to transcription: 'I've heard ten thousand warblers and only written one of them, the epitome of all the others. I've used the best passages of all the others' (a statement that is only partly borne out by the *cahiers* for *La Fauvette des jardins*, as we shall see).[11] This is a bird whose song belies its appearance. Its spectacular phrases contrast with unremarkable grey-brown plumage and a tendency to keep itself to itself (despite its name, it is usually found at the edge of woodland rather than in domestic gardens). In *La Fauvette des jardins* this triumph of song over appearance is celebrated; half an hour of music is dominated by twelve of the bird's solos. 'La Rousserolle effarvatte' and *La Fauvette des jardins* both trace the hours of a single day, but whereas 'La Rousserolle' is a magisterial arch, *La Fauvette* is a ritornello form, underpinned by grandiose tonal motion that was not part of Messiaen's musical language in the 1950s. It marks a new way for him to depict the earth turning beneath the sun, and this alignment with the circle of fifths is what gives the new piece its emotional as well as gravitational pull; the final pages of *La Fauvette des jardins* contain two climaxes that sit alongside his most impassioned (such as 'Regard de l'Eglise d'amour'). The first, occurring at 'the most beautiful hours of the afternoon', when 'the sun radiates light and warmth', lands on a D major chord with added triadic resonances inspired by the deep blue sky and gilded green of the imposing mountain, the Grand Serre, which overlooks the Lac de Laffrey and the meadows around Petichet (Ex. 7.3). The second, on the final page, is more intimate, turning on an unusual (for Messiaen) augmented-sixth harmony that is left to resonate rather than resolve, so that it merges with the silhouettes of trees in the night. The final word goes to the

---

[11] Olivier Messiaen, 'Entretien avec Claude Samuel: réalisé à Paris en Octobre 1988', liner note to Erato/Warner CD, trans. Stuart Walters, p. 8.

Example 7.3 *La Fauvette des jardins*, p. 49, bb. 10–12

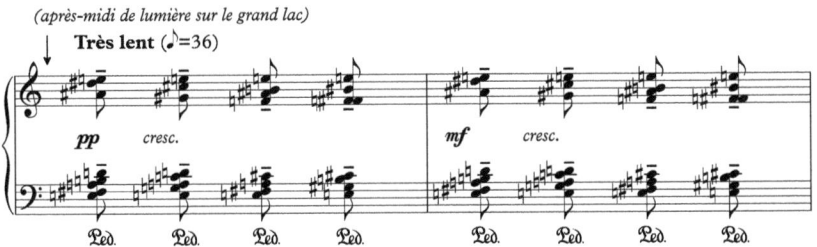

Example 7.4 *La Fauvette des jardins*, p. 55, bb. 14–17

ever-present Grand Serre as the bass strikes an A, the lowest note on the piano (Ex. 7.4).

This extensive canvas never failed to enthuse Messiaen, and once the *Catalogue* had been completed (and Claire laid to rest) its possibilities seemed to open up again. On 15 August 1960, after a day's ascent to Notre-Dame-de-Vaulx (overlooking the lakes of Laffrey and Petichet from the opposite side to the Grand Serre), Messiaen made a study of the evening scene, rich with allusions:

7.15 p.m.: the Grand Serre, green and bald, is gilded all over by the end of the day. 8 p.m.: extraordinary sunset! A *huge* pink cloud bathes the sky in its horizontal vicinity, like a *reclining cloak of red and pink* – underneath this pink cloud, the sky is lightly tinged with blue, yellow and pale green – the pointed Valkyrie helmet of Chamechaude is *mauve* – the Lac de Laffrey is divided into mauve and pink strips (pointillist!).[12]

Seven years later, on 23 September 1967, he was still enraptured by 'zones' of blue, orange, green, red, grey-blue, blue-violet and yellowish green. That summer brought numerous studies of the surface of the lake – including whilst bathing – later translated into the chorale-like refrains that punctuate *La Fauvette* and illustrate the day's progress: colour and time in a simple, evocative conjunction. The day of 21 July was so energy-sapping it only produced two words: 'chaleur terrible!!!'; the ensuing storm overnight, however, produced watery harmonies and melodies of droplets. The next day Messiaen was woken early by the abating storm, and in the 'sombre but cleansed' scene he heard a new 'réveil des oiseaux' initiated by the cretic rhythm of a quail, the first bird to be heard in *La Fauvette*.

Following the precedent of the *Catalogue d'oiseaux*, the garden warbler's song is an integral part of the landscape; Messiaen writes in the preface that its song is 'an emanation of nature's display'. He achieves this by harmonising it luxuriantly; even the warbler's early morning 'preliminary trials' feature chords of transposed inversion with further added notes, a composing-out of the bird's timbre.

New ground rules needed to be set to in order to fashion the song. In 'Le Loriot' the notes tumble out at a suggested rate of 640 per minute, with up to ten consecutive repetitions of an individual note militating – for the pianist – against the impression of 'sweet virtuosity'. The warbler is also heard in the second and ninth movements of the *Méditations sur le Mystère de la Sainte Trinité*, Messiaen's major cycle for organ of 1969, which forms a companion-piece to *La Fauvette des jardins*. Here, full pages from *cahier* 23104 (pp. 6 and 9, notated on 20 July 1967, the day before the 'chaleur terrible') are quoted verbatim without a break, testing the organist's repeated-note technique with up to four iterations at a

---

[12] 23022, p. 2.

time. The approach changes as the bird takes centre stage in *La Fauvette des jardins*. The song has slowed considerably to 528 notes per minute – although Messiaen was never one to place a premium on speed, always requesting that the lyricism and character of a bird take precedence over the metronome.[13] The opening measures of solos 2, 3, 7, 9 and 10 are cherry-picked from another long solo notated at 4.50 a.m. on 21 July, a piecemeal approach that suggests he did indeed select 'the best passages' when it came to writing a portrait of the bird (as opposed to its more symbolic role in the *Méditations*) – although it could equally suggest that he composed, rather than transcribed, the remainder of each solo himself, such was his familiarity with the warbler's inexhaustible invention. Crucially, any repetition of more than two notes that appears in the *cahier* is modified – either by removing or by changing a note – so that the pianist never has to face multiple repetitions, which would be impossible to achieve given the fullness of the texture (Ex. 7.5).

The metronome mark certainly indicates rapidity ($\eighth = 132$), but there is a balance to be struck; and colour, character and contour are more important than dogged adherence to a tempo. Under the first warbler solo there is the instruction 'well-pronounced, clear and melodic'; for good measure this is repeated under solos 3, 5, 9, 11 and 12. A footnote to the performer under solo 6 reminds them that 'all the demisemiquavers are equal'. These instructions may lead to a chiselled, crystalline account, though the description in the preface of the warbler's song modifies this, urging a gentler approach: 'the garden warbler sings again, with its limpid voice … its rapid vocalises, its tireless virtuosity, the regular flow of its discourse seems to arrest time …'. There is something of Loriod's recorded account about the former, and perhaps Messiaen's own 'hearing' of the piece in the latter.

The evidence from the *cahiers* and the score suggests that Messiaen came up with a variety of ways to create the warbler's material, beyond a simple pick-and-mix approach. The most stunning passage comes at the end of the ninth solo, a stream of 121 uninterrupted demisemiquavers (the average length of the warbler's 'phrases' is roughly 20 notes) that gives the strong impression of a climax. Could the bird have performed this feat? The answer is yes, three times at least: twice in succession on 23 July 1967 (117 and 114 notes), and at 8.45 p.m. on 17 July 1960 (109 notes) the Petichet warblers managed to complete a century, and Messiaen somehow kept pace. Whatever their respective inputs into the finished work,

---

[13] This was confirmed in conversation with Peter Hill.

Example 7.5 (a) *Cahier* 23104, p. 13; (b) *La Fauvette des jardins* p. 26, line 2

the notion of man and bird combining to produce such joyous music is exhilarating (Ex. 7.6).

Whilst much of the raw material for the piece was collected in 1967, detailed structural plans had to wait until summer 1969, by which time Messiaen had fulfilled the commission for *La Transfiguration* and was immersed in writing the *Méditations*. *La Fauvette* is a breath of summer air after this intense work, but the 'lake' passages gain power if heard after *La*

Example 7.6 Long garden warbler solo, 23 July 1967 (23022, p. 12)

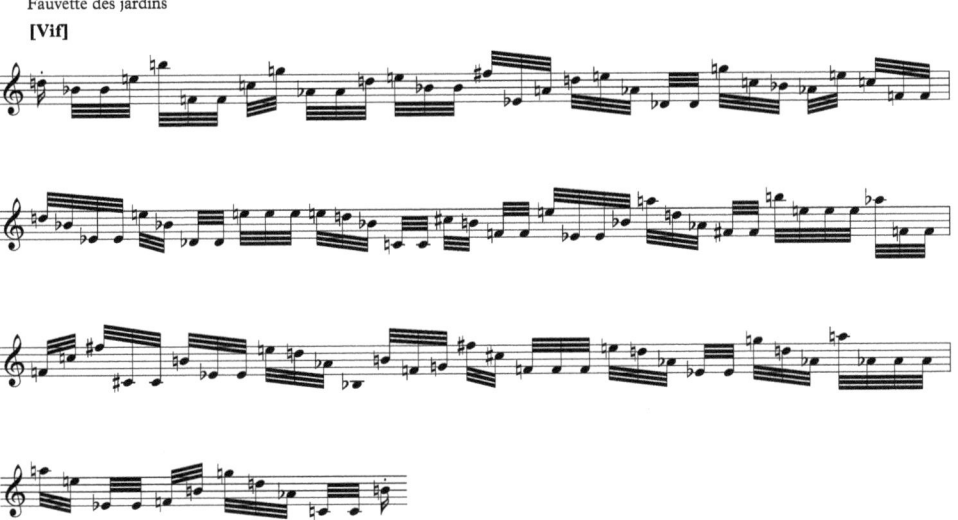

Transfiguration's chorales, which they resemble harmonically.[14] It was not simply a case of bolting together pre-gathered material. The birds influence each other: the height of the day in *La Fauvette* is greeting by a golden oriole, 'gilded, rich in harmonics', and snippets of the oriole's material can be found in a long solo in 23101 (this was July 1966, again in Petichet), implying an editing process similar to that of the garden warbler. The warbler responds to this new voice, echoing both key and contour in a sudden ascent to a high C♯ in its eighth solo (p. 23) – mimicry more pronounced than between these two species in 'Le Loriot'.

The most important of Messiaen's footnotes to the warbler solos appears under solo 4: 'Adhere to the duration of chords at the ends of phrases, so that the colours may be perceptible.'[15] The warbler's harmonies reflect its surroundings (they include chords of transposed inversion and of contracted resonance, and ones derived from the modes of limited transposition); it sings about what it sees. Above all, the chords reflect the colours of the Lac de Laffrey, and as these change throughout the day the progressions

---

[14] According to Olivier Messiaen, *Traité de rythme, de couleur et d'ornithologie: en sept tomes* (Paris: Alphonse Leduc, 1994–2002), Vol. V, Part II, p. 614, the great reed warbler on p. 24 was notated 'sur le plateau de la Matheysine, au pied du Grand Serre, 7 Juillet 1967'.

[15] This is a more useful instruction than Messiaen's advice to the conductor to 'transmit' the colours in *Couleurs de la Cité céleste*. He advised Peter Hill to linger on these chords.

intensify, dynamically and through the addition of tritone-based harmonies that recall the sunset passage of 'La Rousserolle effarvatte'.

Though the warbler's song may seem a barrage of colour-chords, its evolution reflects the structure of the piece. The short-lived 'preliminary trials' and early solos match the minimalism of the early morning scene: the quail's simple, non-retrogradable rhythm; the waving of the alders; and the lapping of the lake. As the warbler gathers momentum later in the morning, its silences become more telling; solo 6 precedes an especially long one, a structural division before a *forte* 'lake' refrain that circles round E major (it cadences on A and B before a series of *ff* chords that establish E as a focal point, rather like the dominant preparation for the 'hunt' music in 'Regard de l'Esprit de joie'). This new key is shared by the golden oriole and skylark, which 'coils itself round a dominant' (B), in Messiaen's memorable phrase.

The fauvette's virtuosity is in full cry in the next few solos. Solo 9 concludes with the 121-note melisma. Solo 10 reaches a new high point (F♮), and 11 is the longest of all: six pages that correspond to the following six, the most extended passage of unbroken scene-painting in the piece, where the music of the alders, the lake and the spiralling flight of the black kite – a new element – is all shown to be part of the same family of undulating music. As the composer cranes his neck to track the kite the music winds up to a peak of chromatic saturation with one immense bar that spans the entire piano, and a succession of cluster-like, black-on-white chords, before unwinding through the piece's only *ritenuto*. Enter the yellowhammer, a symbol of closure whose cousin featured in the *Méditations* (and an ancestor in 'La Buse variable').

The pages that follow are rich with modal harmony with triadic resonance (recalling 'La Colombe'), and the climax on a low bass D (p. 49, b. 12) is, in combination with the twelve-note black kite, an expansion of the 'silvery sun' passage in 'Le Traquet rieur'. The final two-page solo of the garden warbler, conversational in tone, leads into a coda that winds up the tonal strands expertly, and movingly, striking the bottom A of the piano for the first time in the last line and echoing the foghorn of 'Le Courlis cendré' in the process.

Though there are echoes of *Catalogue d'oiseaux*, there is more focus upon the sound of the principal bird in *La Fauvette des jardins*, and at the same time Messiaen's response to the landscape is more rhapsodic. To achieve this he draws more colour out of the piano than he had done at any time, at least since *Vingt Regards*. None of the astringencies of the post-war period remain; *La Fauvette* is a harbinger of other great pianistic soundscapes of the 1970s, such as Tristan Murail's *Territoires de l'Oubli* and Michael Finnissy's *English Country-Tunes*.

Petites Esquisses d'oiseaux (1985)

The finality of *La Fauvette*'s closing gesture heightens the sense that Messiaen's last solo piano work, *Petites Esquisses d'oiseaux*, is an elegant coda to his solo piano output. These 'little sketches' were a tentative road to recovery from the profound low that followed the opera *Saint François d'Assise* and *Livre du Saint-Sacrement* for organ. Coolly refreshing, they have the refinement of Japanese art, and in their delicacy and brevity perhaps celebrate transience more than any other of Messiaen's works.

Yvonne Loriod was once again the stimulus, luring Messiaen back to composition in 1985 by asking why he had not yet written a portrait of the robin. The plan worked; Messiaen put pen to paper and fashioned a suite of pieces featuring, alongside the robin, three other great songsters (blackbird, song thrush and skylark) who were supporting cast in the *Catalogue*. The robin is nevertheless the hero, its patience rewarded with three separate pieces (which Messiaen, according to the *Traité*, regarded as a single piece divided into three):[16]

1 Le Rouge-gorge (robin)
2 Le Merle noir (blackbird)
3 Le Rouge-gorge
4 La Grive musicienne (song thrush)
5 Le Rouge-gorge
6 L'Alouette des champs (skylark)

The six 'sketches' are arranged in a familiar manner: an interleaved design that harks back to *Turangalîla*.[17] The combination of a 'constant' character and a changing or developing one is an aspect of *personnages rythmiques* and *agrandissement asymétrique* (see for example the opening of 'Les Mains de l'abîme', the third movement of *Livre d'orgue*, where some chords lengthen and others stay the same length); in keeping with these techniques, the other birds become increasingly distinct from the robin in both the nature of their songs and the way they are presented.

In the robin pieces the harmonies of Messiaen's 'decorative theme' (three chords of transposed inversion that begin the work and are later varied) are skilfully integrated with the bird's song.[18] Hand in hand with musical

---

[16] Messiaen, *Traité*, Vol. V, Part I, p. 171.
[17] If the four 'individual' movements (1, 5, 6 and 10) of *Turangalîla* are removed, the same alternating design (between three 'amour' and three 'Turangalîla' movements) remains.
[18] Christopher Dingle comments that this is 'like a painting where the boundary between subject and background is deliberately blurred' – like one of Fragonard's sketchier portraits, perhaps; Christopher Dingle, *Messiaen's Final Works* (Farnham: Ashgate, 2013), p. 67.

sophistication comes realism. The technique of inexact doubling (one part not quite following the other) and constant changes of metre render the bird's liquid timbre vividly; and the uninterrupted song – without any need for broader architecture – is a more faithful representation of this voluble character. There is no need for any adjectives in the score: anthropomorphism is completely banished, Messiaen opting instead for a stripped-down style that is not wholly unlike the asceticism of his early 1950s works (*Le Merle noir*, *Réveil des oiseaux*), though with more charm and wit.

The 'thème de décor' is longer and more impassioned in the second piece, 'Le Merle noir' – appropriately so, given the gaps between its strophes tend to be longer than a robin's. From time to time this piece is punctuated by a tam-tam-style cluster, a sonority particularly associated with merles (see for example the 'Balinese' gongs in 'Le Merle bleu' and a quieter, more ceremonial version in *Le Merle noir*). The song thrush has a life-like pearly clarity – this bird has perhaps come the furthest since its comically wooden utterances in *Livre d'orgue*.

Like the last two pages of *Le Merle noir*, the *Petites Esquisses* culminates with *éclatant* music in the upper reaches of the piano. The skylark continues its tradition of 'coiling itself round a dominant' (though this is a misleading phrase – it never goes higher than the 'dominant', B) in a continuous display of frenetic activity that is a struggle to play fast enough. This is another kind of realism: an acknowledgment of the true speed of birdsong. On the surface, this music is as different as can be from the *Catalogue* – it marks a return to birdsong on its own, without the frame of landscape, and it is a paradox that pieces so sophisticated and stylised in fact make the experience of birdsong very real.

Perhaps the most pertinent comparison with the *Catalogue* is between the whole set of *Esquisses* and 'L'Alouette calandrelle'; both are built around repetitious harmonic progressions and inexact doubling in the treble, and topped off with a solo for the skylark. In 'L'Alouette calandrelle' the skylark simply breaks off, but in the *Petites Esquisses* it completes proceedings by tumbling to earth – a concluding visual gesture, the bird plummeting through a series of black-and-white cluster chords, a sudden reminiscence of the *style Loriod* of the *Vingt Regards*. And then, with a soft thud, the sketchbook is shut for good.

The best contemporary source on Messiaen in the 1950s is Antoine Goléa, who conducted lengthy interviews with the composer between 1956 and 1960.[19] When (in 1957) their conversation turned to birdsong Messiaen

---

[19] Antoine Goléa: *Rencontres avec Olivier Messiaen* (Paris: René Julliard, 1960). See the chapter on birdsong, pp. 217–235.

began with a glance at his critics – 'I must ask you to show respect for my bleeding wounds.' Goléa recalled Messiaen's nervousness before lecturing on birdsong at Darmstadt in 1953; since then he had become accustomed to the tittering of his more irreverent students. Seen in this light what Messiaen said to Goléa reads like a carefully constructed defence. Birds are the supreme musicians ('my foremost and greatest teachers'), their music justifying the most painstaking and arduous research, early in the morning or late at night, and in every discomfort ('rain or sun, cold or heat, mosquitoes …'). The method of transcription is equally rigorous, the songs transposed to the range of human hearing and musical instruments, with micro-intervals enlarged to fit with the chromatic scale but always according to a consistent calibration. Two years later, at the time of the first performance, Messiaen felt justified in claiming that the birds were the true composers of *Catalogue d'oiseaux*:

> Everything is accurate: the soloist's melodies and rhythms, those of its neighbours, the counterpoint between the two, the responses, ensembles and moments of silence, and the correspondence between the song and the time of day … The birds alone are great artists … If at times the musical quality drops, it is because the composer out in the countryside has broken cover clumsily, or made a disturbing noise by crunching his feet on the gravel, turning a page, or snapping off a dry branch.[20]

The spontaneity of the notations in the *cahiers* casts doubt on Messiaen's claim that his method of transcription was an exact science. Moreover, although some birdsongs exist in a register too high for human hearing to discriminate accurately – and certainly too high for musical instruments – many birdsongs are within the range of human hearing, and many (like the woodlark, for example) can be adjusted to the tempered scale of instruments without much difficulty. And Messiaen's account contains a glaring omission, the lack of any mention of recordings. No doubt Messiaen felt that drawing attention to them might give ammunition to his critics, who, while they could object to the music or to the idea of working with birdsong, were not in a position to question Messiaen's methods. In reality, it was the work on recordings, starting with *American Bird Songs* for *Oiseaux exotiques*, that had transformed Messiaen's birdsong language and the way he used it. No longer limited to the memory of a bird heard fleetingly in the wild, the multiple notations of each song that Messiaen was able to make were subject to all sorts of imaginative interventions. Messiaen himself might have said that recordings enabled him to be more accurate, except

---

[20] Messiaen, 'La Nature, les chants d'oiseaux'.

that when one listens to a birdsong recording used by Messiaen and compares it to his notations, accuracy seems beside the point. One realises that though the notations were based on the closest observation, it was observation of a very personal kind: one can always see what Messiaen meant, but there is never the slightest doubt that we are hearing an imaginative response, not a transcription.

In *Oiseaux exotiques* each birdsong was either from a recording or from a live notation.[21] The difference in the *Catalogue* is that birdsongs were collected from both; indeed, Messiaen began the practice of preparing his visits to unfamiliar locations (as he would do later before trips abroad) by studying the local birdsongs in advance from recordings. During the course of composing the *Catalogue* there were subtle changes in approach from piece to piece, as birdsongs assumed different roles. More broadly, in the first wave of composition (up to 'La Rousserolle effarvatte') Messiaen worked like a painter who makes sketches from nature that are worked into a finished landscape in the studio; not surprisingly, all these pieces (with the exception of 'L'Alouette calandrelle') contain a high proportion of birdsongs from recordings. Thereafter, from the summer of 1957 (in 'La Bouscarle, 'Le Traquet stapazin' and 'Le Merle bleu'), Messiaen worked *en plein air*, composing as he notated, with recordings playing little part. Then, in the last pieces, description is pared to a minimum in a way that looks forward to *La Fauvette Passerinette*. In 'La Buse variable' the vastness of the Alpine setting is implied by the orbits of the buzzard's flight, while in 'Le Traquet rieur' the Mediterranean is simplified to a gesture, 'the joy of the blue sea'. In 'Le Merle de roche' the progress of night and day is signalled not by the sun but by the choice of birdsongs; description is limited to the weirdly sculpted rocks, represented by the permutations of durations that link back to *Livre d'orgue* and forward to *Chronochromie*.

After the *Catalogue* birdsong remained central to Messiaen's music. Change came from two directions. First, there was the widening of his researches to include birds from all over the world, often experienced at first hand as increasingly he received invitations from abroad; and then the return of birdsong, now greatly enriched, to its role in his earlier music within the symbolism of his faith. Messiaen had spoken of the similarities between birdsong and plainchant, and the two combine in the short *Verset pour la fête de la Dédicace* for organ (1960) – a minor work, but one, like *Cantéyodjayâ* and *Le Merle noir*, that was to signal a change of direction. In

---

[21] The Virginia Cardinal is the one exception, its song notated from *American Bird Songs* and heard live in an aviary.

Japan, in 1962, Messiaen found birdsongs new to him in landscapes dotted with Buddhist temples or wayside shrines. This conjunction of nature and the numinous is reflected in *Sept Haïkaï* (1962), the birdsong set in complex rituals, embedded in rhythmic process (as in *Chronochromie*); typical also are the introduction and coda inspired by the 'guardian kings that frame the entrance to Buddhist temples'.[22] *Couleurs de la Cité céleste* (1963) incorporates birdsong into a work inspired by the colours of the Book of Revelation, recalling the *Catalogue* in its structures, like a play (as Messiaen described it) with different characters and subplots superimposed.[23] The cast of birds is international, with the New Zealand bell bird chiming against a backdrop of bells, cencerros and gongs, and with the shriek of the Brazilian araponga expressing the Apocalypse, 'extraordinary, extravagant, surrealistic and terrifying'.[24]

In the 1960s Messiaen's *cahiers* reach a peak of virtuosity and richness. Thereafter, the number diminishes, Messiaen tending to concentrate his researches on his visits overseas. A decade after Japan Messiaen repeated the experience with ten days in May 1972 in Bryce Canyon, Cedar Breaks and Zion Park, supplemented by the exhaustive study of recordings of the birdsongs of the American south-west. *Des Canyons aux étoiles …* exhibits an integration between birdsong and tonality that can be traced back to 'L'Alouette lulu' at the start of his composing of the *Catalogue*, the songs here complementing the brightness and blueness of A major, or the red-orange E major of the rocks. A number of the birds heard in *Oiseaux exotiques* recur, among them the wood thrush, which gives its name to the tenth movement ('La Grive des bois'); but the list of birds is international, from Asia, Africa and Australia, and including the Indian shama, again from *Oiseaux exotiques* (in the eleventh movement, 'Omao, leiothrix, elepaio, shama').

By the early 1970s Messiaen was already contemplating an opera. *Saint François d'Assise* (first performed in 1983) was to be his *magnum opus* in every sense, birdsong included. Many of the birds from the *Catalogue* recur, Messiaen's huge orchestra enabling a fresh scrutiny of their timbres. As in the *Catalogue* the blue rock thrush has the sound of Balinese music, but 'with triumphal accents and a whole dusting of trills in the strings and cymbals'.[25] The blackcap which features in the first part of St Francis's sermon to the birds ('Le Prêche aux oiseaux'), is descended from its exquisite treatments in 'La Bouscarle' and was the product, Messiaen told Samuel,

---

[22] Footnote in the score of *Sept Haïkaï*, p. 1.
[23] Preface ('Première note de l'auteur') to the score.
[24] Samuel, *Music and Color*, pp. 138–139.
[25] Ibid., p. 219.

of thousands of notations: 'I had to invent chords on each note in order to translate the special timbre, which is very joyous and very rich in harmonics.'[26] The tawny owl signals the start of Scene 7 – 'Les Stigmates' – and comes not only with the pointillism of 'La Chouette hulotte' but also with Messiaen's original discarded idea for the *Catalogue* of low clusters (for darkness), here hummed by the chorus. 'The Sermon to the Birds' contains an innovation, when various birdsongs, played by solo instruments, are permitted to co-exist independently, each starting after a signal from the conductor. The device was continued in Messiaen's last works, in *Un Vitrail et des oiseaux* (1987) and most beautifully in 'Plusieurs Oiseaux des arbres de Vie' from *Eclairs sur l'Au-delà …* (1987–1991). The effect is to allow birdsongs to be shaped naturally, and with the flexibility that Messiaen always wanted (and recommended for the *Catalogue*) but that in his earlier music had ceded priority to the need to keep ensembles and orchestras together.

The odd thing about what Messiaen told Goléa is that his position took no account of the changes that had occurred since the premiere of *Réveil* in 1953, a position that was to remain essentially unmodified in Messiaen's later accounts. The private documents, however, in particular the notations and sketches in the *cahiers*, tell a story that is far more fascinating, showing the struggle between opposing sides of Messiaen's character, which reveal themselves in the *Catalogue* perhaps more vividly that in any other work: the passion for detail and the passion for the sublime. On the one hand there is Messiaen as he describes himself, the selfless observer sparing no effort to achieve truth to nature; on the other is the rampant imagination revealed in the notes in the *cahiers*: the high Alpine peaks that are home to a race of giants, the rocks that assume monstrous forms, or the call of a bird that is like a child shrieking in terror.

There is method, of course, in Messiaen's myth-making. With *Quatuor pour la fin du Temps* his story of the cello with three strings may have been untrue but it illustrated the difficulties in which the first performance took place; while enlarging the audience to 5,000 (always a suspiciously biblical figure)[27] acknowledged the support and admiration Messiaen received from his fellow prisoners. The power of the imagination to reveal truth, and to make real what is known only through faith, had been the driving inspiration of Messiaen's religious music up to 1945. In the birdsong works of the 1950s he used the close observation of something real (but to most of us largely unknown) for imaginative ends; at the same time he used

---

[26] *Ibid.*, p. 237.
[27] See PH/NS, p. 100. Etienne Pasquier, the cellist in the first performance, remembered the audience as numbering about 400.

imagination as the means to communicate the truth as he saw it. In this respect one must say that he succeeded: the fourth version of the American wood thrush (as in the finished score of *Oiseaux exotiques*), when compared with the first literal notation sounds much more convincing and authentic.

Messiaen was further liberated by his decision to set birds in landscapes and at different times of day. At first he turned to the unlikely source of the quasi-serial writing pioneered in *Cantéyodjayâ* and the *Quatre études de rythme*, but this was quickly superseded by a willingness to admit tonal and modal harmonies (for darkness or sunlight, or a river in April) following the example of *Oiseaux exotiques* but brought to glorious fruition in the *Catalogue*. The result (as we have seen in the commentaries on the pieces) was an entirely original approach to musical form, a world away from the repetitions and accumulations in his music up to *Turangalîla*, and which seemed capable of reinvention from one piece to the next.

Central to Messiaen's experience of birdsong was anthropomorphism – the 'old fault of mine', as Messiaen told Claude Samuel half apologetically.[28] In *Saint François d'Assise* the Pacific birdsongs act as leitmotifs: so Brother Elias, the worldly administrator, at odds with the ideal of poverty, is caricatured by the 'gloomy' New Caledonian pigeon and by the 'fitful rhythms' of the reed warbler.[29] This sort of characterisation begins in the *Catalogue*: one only has to compare the bright but somewhat rambling solos in *Réveil* with the sharply differentiated robins, nightingales and blackcaps of the *Catalogue* to appreciate the change. No wonder the pieces in the *Catalogue* become like miniature dramas, resonating with references to the operas that Messiaen loved.

There was a deeper reason for this, however. Although Messiaen had played an important part in avant-garde music from 1949, by the mid 1950s he had become disillusioned, as one of his students recalled:

Face to face with his sometimes obstreperous students and opinionated hangers-on, he was even reduced to tears. We sat in silence for long periods, especially after an aggressive attempt by one of us to argue with him. Here we were, before one of the most perfect musicians of our times, combative and argumentative, in tense, unbroken silence. And he would say, 'Gentlemen, let us not argue like this. We are all in profound night, and I don't know where I am going; I'm as lost as you.'[30]

But he did know. Music needed to be not some hothouse plant but deeply rooted in the ancient and eternal. Birdsong was one element of this, 'the

---

[28] Samuel, *Music and Color*, pp. 88–89.
[29] Ibid., p. 218.
[30] Alexander Goehr, *Finding the Key: Selected Writings*, ed. Derrick Puffett (London: Faber and Faber, 1998), p. 56.

true face of music' as Messiaen claimed it to be, having the same role in his music as Hungarian folk music had in Bartók's.[31] At the same time there was the rapprochement with the past, his own, and with the music of other composers. Vital to the *Catalogue* as the developments since 1949 were, it is the revival of the past that signalled the really important change. After years of experiment Messiaen was now ready to write music based on the widest possible means of expression open to him. Colour pours back into his music, as the new Messiaen (of the works since 1949) joins with the old. In this sense the *Catalogue* is not just *a* turning-point but *the* turning-point, the hinge connecting the two halves of Messiaen's long composing life, and the start of the synthesis that made possible the masterpieces of his later years.

---

[31] Interview in *Le Figaro littéraire*, 15 February 1958, p. 13.

Bibliography

Aguila, Jésus, *Le Domaine musical: Pierre Boulez et vingt ans de création contemporaine* (Paris: Fayard, 1992)

Anderson, Julian, 'Messiaen and the Problem of Communication', in Christopher Dingle and Robert Fallon (eds.), *Messiaen Perspectives 1: Sources and Influences* (Farnham: Ashgate, 2013), pp. 257–268

—— 'Olivier Messiaen and the Notion of Influence', *Tempo* 247 (January 2009), 2–18

Aragon, Louis, *A Wave of Dreams (Une vague de rêves (1924))*, trans. Susan Muth (London: Thin Man Press, 2015)

Boivin, Jean, *La Classe de Messiaen* (Paris: C. Bourgois, 1995)

Boulez, Pierre, 'The Utopian Years', in *Orientations: Collected Writings*, ed. Jean-Jacques Nattiez, trans. Martin Cooper (London: Faber and Faber, 1986), pp. 411–417

Brent Murray, Christopher, 'Olivier Messiaen's *Timbres-Durées*', in Christopher Dingle and Robert Fallon (eds.), *Messiaen Perspectives 1: Sources and Influences* (Farnham: Ashgate, 2013), pp. 123–142

Broad, Stephen *Olivier Messiaen: Journalism 1935–1939* (Farnham: Ashgate, 2012)

Cheong, Wai-Ling, 'Symmetrical Permutation, the Twelve Tones, and Messiaen's *Catalogue d'oiseaux*', *Perspectives of New Music* 45.1 (Winter 2007), 110–136

Cœuroy, André, 'Manifeste et concert des "Jeune France"', *Beaux-Arts*, 5 June 1936

Daniel-Lesur, Jean-Yves, 'Revue de la presse musicale: *Trois petites Liturgies de la Présence Divine* d'Olivier Messiaen', *Revue musicale de la France*, 1 April 1946

Delamain, Jacques, *Why Birds Sing*, trans. Ruth Sarason and Anne Sarason (London: Victor Gollancz, 1932)

Demarquez, Suzanne, 'Le *Catalogue d'oiseaux* d'Olivier Messiaen', *Guide du concert* 233 (1 May 1959), 42

—— 'Premières auditions … Domaine musical (Gaveau 30.3)', *Guide du concert* 151 (12 April 1957), 893

Dingle, Christopher, and Robert Fallon (eds.), *Messiaen Perspectives 2: Techniques, Influence and Reception* (Farnham: Ashgate, 2013)

Dingle, Christopher, *The Life of Messiaen* (Cambridge: Cambridge University Press, 2007)

Messiaen's Final Works (Farnham: Ashgate, 2013)

'Sacred Machines: Fear, Mystery and Transfiguration in Messiaen's Mechanical Procedures', in Christopher Dingle and Robert Fallon (eds.), *Messiaen Perspectives 2: Techniques, Influence and Reception* (Farnham: Ashgate, 2013), pp. 13–32

'Yvonne Loriod as Source and Influence', in Christopher Dingle and Robert Fallon (eds.), *Messiaen Perspectives 1: Sources and Influences* (Farnham: Ashgate, 2013), pp. 197–212

Dingle, Christopher and Robert Fallon (eds.), *Messiaen Perspectives 1: Sources and Influences* (Farnham: Ashgate, 2013)

Dingle, Christopher and Nigel Simeone (eds.), *Olivier Messiaen: Music, Art and Literature* (Aldershot: Ashgate, 2007)

Fallon, Robert, 'The Record of Realism in Messiaen's Bird Style', in Christopher Dingle and Nigel Simeone (eds.), *Olivier Messiaen: Music, Art and Literature* (Aldershot: Ashgate, 2007), pp. 115–136

Freeman, Robin, 'Courtesy towards the Things of Nature', *Tempo* 192 (April 1995), 9–14

Goehr, Alexander, *Finding the Key: Selected Writings*, ed. Derrick Puffett (London: Faber and Faber, 1998)

Goléa, Antoine, *Rencontres avec Olivier Messiaen* (Paris: René Julliard, 1960)

Griffiths, Paul, *Olivier Messiaen and the Music of Time* (London: Faber and Faber, 1985)

Halbreich, Harry, *Olivier Messiaen* (Paris: Fayard, 1980)

Hill, Peter, 'From *Réveil des oiseaux* to *Catalogue d'oiseaux*: Messiaen's *Cahiers de notations des chants d'oiseaux*, 1952–59', in Christopher Dingle and Robert Fallon (eds.), *Messiaen Perspectives 1: Sources and Influences* (Farnham: Ashgate, 2013), pp. 143–174

(ed.), *The Messiaen Companion* (London: Faber and Faber, 1995)

Hill, Peter and Nigel Simeone, *Messiaen* (New Haven and London: Yale University Press, 2005) [PH/NS]

Olivier Messiaen: Oiseaux exotiques (Aldershot: Ashgate, 2007)

Howat, Roy, *The Art of French Piano Music* (New Haven and London: Yale University Press, 2009)

Hüe, François and R. D. Etchécopar, *Les Oiseaux du Proche et du Moyen Orient* (Paris: Boubée, 1970)

Jameux, Dominique, *Pierre Boulez*, trans. Susan Bradshaw (London: Faber and Faber, 1991)

Klingsöhr-Leroy, Cathrin and Uta Grosenick (eds.), *Surrealism* (Cologne: Taschen, 2004)

Legge, Elizabeth, 'Posing Questions: Max Ernst's *Au rendez-vous des amis*', *Art History* 10 (June 1987), 227–243

Loriod-Messiaen, Yvonne, 'Olivier Messiaen: Relevé des concerts, des classes et des évènements de la vie d'Olivier Messiaen notées au jour le jour sur ses agendas depuis 1939' (unpublished) [OMR]

Louvier, Alain, *Messiaen et le concert de la nature* (Paris: Cité de la musique – Les Editions, 2012)

Macfarlane, Robert, *The Wild Places* (London: Granta Books, 2008)

Marks, Dennis (executive producer), 'Messiaen at 80', TV programme, BBC, 10 December 1988

Massin, Brigitte, *Olivier Messiaen: une poétique du merveilleux* (Aix-en-Provence: Editions Alinéa, 1989)

Messiaen, Olivier, 'Autour d'une parution', *Le Monde musical*, 30 April 1939

Catalogue d'oiseaux, 7 vols. (Paris: Alphonse Leduc, 1964).

'Entretien avec Claude Samuel: réalisé à Paris en Octobre 1988', liner note to Erato/Warner CD, trans. Stuart Walters

'La Nature, les chants d'oiseaux', *Guide du concert* 229 (3 April 1959), 1093–1094

Technique de mon langage musical, 2 vols. (Paris: Alphonse Leduc, 1944)

Technique de mon langage musical (Paris: Alphonse Leduc, 1999)

The Technique of My Musical Language, trans. John Satterfield, 2 vols. (Paris: Alphonse Leduc, 1956)

The Technique of My Musical Language, trans. John Satterfield (Paris: Alphonse Leduc, 2001 [1956])

Traité de rythme, de couleur et d'ornithologie: en sept tomes (Paris: Alphonse Leduc, 1994–2002)

Rößler, Almut, *Contributions to the Spiritual World of Olivier Messiaen* (Duisberg: Gilles and Francke, 1986)

Rostand, Claude, review of *Catalogue d'oiseaux* world premiere, *Le Monde*, 18 April 1959

Saint-Jean, Robert de, 'C'est le merle noir et non le rossignol qui inspire Olivier Messiaen: à quarante ans, le musicien se prépare à écrire l'opéra dont il rêve depuis son enfance', *France-Soir*, 28–29 March 1948

Samuel, Claude, *Music and Color: Conversations with Claude Samuel*, trans. E. Thomas Glasow (Portland: Amadeus, 1994)

Sauvage, Cécile, *Œuvres complètes* (Paris: La Table Ronde, 2002)

Schaeffer, Pierre, *In Search of a Concrete Music*, trans. Christine North and John Dack (Berkeley, CA: University of California Press, 2012)

Sherlaw Johnson, Robert, *Messiaen*, 2nd paperback edn, updated and with additional text by Caroline Rae (London: Omnibus Press, 2008 [1975])

Smalley, Roger, review of English Bach Festival 1967, in 'Festivals', *The Musical Times* 108.1494 (August 1967), 730–731

Weller, Philip, '*L'Ame en Bourgeon*: Translation and Afterword', in Christopher Dingle and Nigel Simeone (eds.), *Olivier Messiaen: Music, Art and Literature* (Aldershot: Ashgate, 2007), pp. 191–278

'Messiaen, the *Cinq rechants* and "Spiritual Violence"', in Christopher Dingle and Robert Fallon (eds.), *Messiaen Perspectives 1: Sources and Influences* (Farnham: Ashgate, 2013), pp. 279–312

Xenakis, Iannis, *Arts/Sciences: Alloys. The Thesis Defense of Iannis Xenakis*, trans. Sharon Kanach (New York: Pendragon Press, 1985)

Index

Albéniz, Isaac, 185
   Lavapiés, 185
American Bird Songs, 30–32, 219, 221
Aprahamian, Felix, 183
Aquinas, St Thomas, 59
Aragon, Louis, 168, 170
Austbø, Håkan, 194–200

Barraqué, Jean, 67
   Piano Sonata, 67n. 24
Bartók, Béla, 224
Bate, Jennifer, 187
Baudelaire, Charles, 64
Benjamin, George, 94n. 44
Berberian, Cathy, 181n. 10
Berg, Alban, 14, 95
   Lyric Suite, 67
   Wozzeck, 94–95, 141
Bergson, Henri, 59
Berio, Luciano,
   Serenata I, 112n. 65
Bernard-Delapierre, Guy, 17n. 3
Bernstein, Leonard, 11
Billot, Mme, 29–31
Birtwistle, Harrison,
   Silbury Air, 154
Boston Symphony Orchestra, 11
Boulez, Pierre, 12, 31, 48, 66–68, 73, 111–12, 181–82, 187
   Marteau sans maître, Le, 158
     'Bourreaux de Solitude', 158
   Orientations, 112n.64
   Second Piano Sonata, 179, 183–84
   Sonatine for flute and piano, 112n. 65
   Structures Ia, 67
   Structures II, 181
Breton, André, 168, 170
   Surréalisme et la peinture, Le, 169n. 66

Cahn, Marie-Thérése, 181n. 10
Caskel, Christoph, 181n. 10
Castiglioni, Niccolò, 184
Char, René, 158
Cheong, Wai-Ling, 69

Chopin, Frédéric, 61, 184, 193
   Ballade no. 4 in F minor, Op. 52, 190
   Barcarolle, Op. 60, 183
   Etude, Op. 10, no. 10, 132
Couperin, François, 112
Crevel, René, 168, 170
   Clavecin de Diderot, Le, 168
Crumb, George,
   Vox Balaenae, 58
Crunelle, Gaston, 17n. 4

Da Vinci, Leonardo, 82
Dalí, Salvador, 168
Dante Alighieri (Dante), 71, 161
Darmstadt Ferienkursen, 79n. 18
De Chirico, Giorgio, 168, 170
Debussy, Claude, 14, 62, 64, 80, 87–88, 110, 184, 193, 207
   'Clair de lune', 65 Example 3.9, 163
   Etudes, 112, 183–84
   'Hommage à Rameau', 61
   Mer, La, 58, 152n. 35
   Nocturnes: 'Sirènes', 152
   Pelléas et Mélisande, 61, 63–64, 65 Example 3.7, 80, 80 Example 4.5, 153
   Préludes, 183
Delamain, Jacques, 12, 22, 23f. 2.1, 23–25, 27, 126
   Why Birds Sing, 23, 24n. 12, 83
Delbos, Claire, *see* Messiaen, Claire
Delvincourt, Claude, 29
Demarquez, Suzanne, 110
Domaine musical, 8, 31, 67, 111, 158, 178, 181n. 10
Dominique, Carl-Axel, 194, 197
Donaueschingen Festival, 26, 28, 203
Dostoevsky, Fyodor, 168–69
Ducretet-Thomson (record label), 47
Dukas, Paul, 2, 155
Durand et Cie, 47, 125
Dupré, Marcel, 75n. 9

Eglise de la Sainte-Trinité, 12, 29
Eluard, Gala, 168

Eluard, Paul, 168, 170
Présence, 158
Emmanuel, Maurice, 75n. 9
Ensemble du Domaine musical, *see* Domaine musical
Ernst, Max, 160, 167, 169–70
Au rendez-vous des Amis, 167, 168f. 5.5, 168–70
Etchécopar, R.D., 160n. 53 *see also* Hüe, François and R.D. Etchécopar, *Les Oiseaux du Proche et Moyen Orient*

Fauré, Gabriel, 79
Finnissy, Michael,
English Country-Tunes, 216
France-Soir, 1, 3, 19, 26

Gazelloni, Severino, 181n. 10
Goehr, Alexander, 183
Goehr, Walter, 111n. 63
Goeyvaerts, Karel, 66
Goléa, Antoine, 218–19, 222
Gould, John, 191
Birds of Great Britain, The, 191
Griffiths, Paul, 90, 116

Halbreich, Harry, 208
Harvey, Michael Kieran, 194–96, 198
Helffer, Claude, 181n. 10
Henry, Pierre, 22
Hill, Peter, 6, 120, 187, 194–200, 205
Holliger, Heinz, 184
Hüe, François, and R.D. Etchécopar,
Les Oiseaux du Proche et Moyen Orient, 160, 204

Jacobs, Paul, 181n. 10
Jalas, Margareta, 184n. 17
Jameux, Dominique, 67
Jeune France, La, 70
Jolivet, André, 112
Cinq danses rituelles, 99n. 46

Kal, Berthe, 181n. 10
Keats, John, 191
Kim, Paul, 194
Knappertsbusch, Hans, 62n. 17
Koch, Ludwig, 35, 52, 128
More Songs of Wild Birds, 35, 36 Example 2.6, 36–37, 38 Example 2.8, 48, 104, 105 Example 4.17, 105–6
Songs of British Birds, 35, 36 Example 2.7, 36–37, 104

Kodama, Momo, 180n. 4, 194–97
Kontarsky, Aloys, 181n. 10
Kontarsky, Alphonse, 181n. 10

Lavignac, Albert,
Encyclopédie de la musique et dictionnaire de la Conservatoire, 75n. 9
Leduc, Alphonse, 23
Lekander, Gunnar, and Sture Palmèr, *Radions fågelskivor* (the 'Swedish discs'), 41, 52, 86, 115, 129, 166
Ligeti, György,
Etudes, 2
Loriod, Yvonne, 2, 6, 8, 10–13, 18, 27, 30, 39–41, 46, 50, 68, 71, 78, 80, 83–84, 90–91, 96, 103, 109–12, 115, 117, 124–26, 150, 156, 158–60, 162, 177–78, 191–92, 194–200, 204, 213, 217–18
Louvier, Alain, 74, 79

Mallarmé, Stéphane, 191
Malraux, André, 208
Matsushita, Shin-ichi, 184
Mercenier, Marcelle, 181n. 10
Messiaen, Alain, 2
Messiaen, Claire (*née* Delbos), 11, 19, 29, 40, 124, 157–59, 178, 203, 211
Messiaen, Olivier,
1971 Erasmus address, 61
anthropomorphism, 4, 173–74, 191, 223
ballet on the subject of Time (sketched), 19, 66, 170
Cas Messiaen, Le, 58
compositional techniques,
agrandissement asymétrique, 217
Greek and Hindu rhythms, 26, 48, 68, 75, 97, 129
Personnages rythmiques, 75–76, 217
'scissor' scheme of durations, 167
style oiseau, 6, 22, 68, 116–17, 150
impressionism, 48
Piano Concerto (sketched), 26
plainchant, 26
serialism, 1, 9, 11, 13, 19, 22, 48, 66–70, 72, 93, 103, 111, 130, 175, 190, 203
tonality, 16, 49, 57, 90, 101, 145, 149, 156, 174–75
winning Grand Prix du disque, 179, 204
WORKS:,
Ascension, L', 16
Cantéyodjayâ, 9, 11–12, 20 Example 2.2, 19–21, 27, 33, 69, 93, 104, 220, 223

Catalogue d'oiseaux,
  'Alouette calandrelle, L'' (short-toed lark), 5, 8, 10, 14, 46, 52, 96, 109, 124, 172n. 74, 193, 196–97, 200–1, 218, 220
  'Alouette lulu, L'' (woodlark), 5–6, 9, 37, 47–49, 60, 81–82, 85, 92, 95–98, 109, 180, 183, 186, 189, 193, 205, 221
  'Bouscarle, La' (Cetti's warbler), 5–6, 8, 10, 14, 42, 43 Example 2.11, 48, 60–61, 125, 140, 157–58, 179–80, 183, 189–90, 193, 196, 205, 220–21
  'Buse variable, La' (buzzard), 5–7, 10, 14, 42, 69, 153, 166, 172, 183, 186, 190, 216, 220
  'Chocard des Alpes, Le' (Alpine chough), 5, 9, 48, 59, 66, 68–69, 71, 82, 103, 109, 147, 152–53, 158, 180, 183, 203
  'Chouette hulotte, La' (tawny owl), 5, 9, 15, 46–49, 60, 69, 82, 91, 109, 131, 141, 173, 179, 183, 190–91, 193, 222
  'Courlis cendré, Le' (curlew), 5, 9–10, 15, 46, 48–49, 62, 62 Example 3.2, 63 Example 3.5, 63–64, 66, 69–70, 74, 79–80, 102, 109, 141, 157, 172, 183, 186, 190, 192, 216
  'Loriot, Le' (golden oriole), 5, 9, 39, 49, 56, 58, 64, 64 Example 3.6, 80, 82, 97, 103, 109, 140–41, 143, 147, 150, 152–53, 156–57, 180, 183–87, 189, 193, 209–10, 212, 215
  'Merle bleu, Le' (blue rock thrush), 5–6, 9, 56, 82, 97, 103–4, 134, 145, 157, 172, 174, 177, 183, 185, 188, 193, 218, 220
  'Merle de roche, Le' (rock thrush), 6, 9–10, 44–45, 58, 64, 65 Example 3.8, 69, 126, 159–60, 183–85, 192, 203–4, 220
  'Rousserolle effarvatte, La' (reed warbler), 5–6, 8–9, 19, 20 Example 2.2, 35, 40, 42, 44–45, 45 Example 2.12, 58, 60, 63, 82, 109–10, 143–44, 147, 157, 179, 181, 183–84, 186, 189–90, 193, 206–7, 210, 216, 220
  'Traquet rieur, Le' (black wheatear), 6, 10, 103, 134, 157, 159, 171, 183–86, 216, 220
  'Traquet stapazin, Le' (black-eared wheatear), 5–6, 9, 14, 16, 25, 56, 60, 69, 82, 87, 97, 99, 133, 157, 159, 172–73, 179, 181, 189, 191, 193, 197, 203, 205, 220
Des Canyons aux étoiles …, 209, 221
  'Grive des bois, La', 221
  'Omao, leiothrix, elepaio, shama', 221
Chants de terre et de ciel, 3
Chronochromie, 57, 67, 69, 73, 167, 203–4, 207, 220–21
Cinq Rechants, 12, 19, 83, 90, 124, 210
  'Mayoma kalimolimo, mayoma kalimolimo', 124
Corps glorieux, Les, 116
Couleurs de la Cité céleste, 57, 207, 221
Eclairs sur l'Au-delà …, 69
  'Plusieurs Oiseaux des arbres de Vie', 222
Et exspecto resurrectionem mortuorum, 183, 207–8
Harawi, 18–19, 26, 182
  'Bonjour toi, colombe verte', 18
Fauvette des jardins, La, 6, 57, 114, 114 Example 4.19, 153–54, 157, 207, 217
Fauvette Passerinette, La, 7, 42, 205–8, 220
Livre d'orgue, 3, 11, 21, 70, 75, 81, 188, 203, 220
  'Chants d'oiseaux', 21
  'Mains de l'abîme, Les', 217
  'Soixante-Quatre durées', 21, 167
Livre du Saint Sacrement, 187, 217
Méditations sur le Mystère de la Sainte Trinité, 212–14, 216
Merle noir, Le, 11, 19, 20 Example 2.2, 22, 25, 154n. 38, 218, 220
Messe de la Pentecôte, 3, 11, 21
  'Communion', 21
  'Offertoire', 21
  'Sortie', 21
Oiseaux exotiques, 1, 12–13, 19, 29–30, 32–33, 34 Example 2.5, 47–48, 70, 97, 203–4, 206, 219–21, 223
Petites Esquisses d'oiseaux, 7, 202, 207, 217
Poèmes pour Mi, 3, 87, 158
Préludes, 16, 87
  'Chant d'extase dans un paysage triste', 16
  'Colombe, La', 16, 50, 216
  'sons impalpables du rêve, Les', 183
Quatre études de rythme, 11–12, 19, 21, 27, 33, 93, 188, 223
  Ile de feu 1, 21, 166, 182
  Ile de feu 2, 69, 93
  Mode de valeurs et d'intensités, 9, 19, 66–67, 69, 93–94
  Neumes rythmiques, 72, 72n. 3
Quatuor pour la fin du Temps, 11, 17–18, 24, 26, 70, 117, 187, 203, 222
  'Abîme des oiseaux', 18
  'Fouillis d'arcs-en-ciel, pour l'Ange qui annonce la fin du Temps', 72n. 3

Messiaen, Olivier (*cont.*)
  'Liturgie de cristal', 17–18, 21, 24, 73, 117
  'Louange à l'Immortalité de Jésus', 18
  'Vocalise, pour l'Ange qui annonce la fin du Temps', 117
  Réveil des oiseaux, 1, 4, 12–13, 18–19, 21, 25–29, 31–33, 35, 39, 44, 48, 58, 60, 84, 87, 97, 204, 218, 222–23
  Saint François d'Assise, 8, 61, 116, 217, 221, 223
    'Lauds', 93
    'Prêche aux oiseaux, Le', 208, 221–22
    'Stigmates, Les', 222
  Sept Haïkaï, 221
  Technique de mon langage musical, 80, 168, 188
  Thème et Variations, 158
  Timbres-Durées, 22, 26, 67–68
  Traité de rythme, de couleur et d'ornithologie, 47, 58–59, 80, 111, 115, 146–47, 151, 172, 175, 190, 217
  Transfiguration de Notre-Seigneur Jésus-Christ, La, 114, 114 Example 4.19, 185, 207–8, 214
    'Christus Jesus, splendor Patris', 120
    'Perfecte conscius illius perfectae generationis', 120
    'Quam dilecta tabernacula tua', 114
  Trois Mélodies, 87
  Trois Petites Liturgies de la Présence Divine, 26, 152
    'Séquence du Verbe', 26
  Turangalîla-Symphonie, 1, 3, 11, 18–19, 22, 33, 66–67, 75, 87, 114 Example 4.19, 123, 183, 188, 204, 217, 223
    'Jardin du sommeil d'amour', 18–19, 20 Example 2.2, 145, 210
    'Turangalîla 2', 19
  Verset pour la fête de la Dédicace, 204, 220
  Vingt Regards sur l'Enfant-Jésus, 2–3, 8, 18, 87, 97, 179, 182, 184, 188, 216, 218
    'Noël', 184
    'Par Lui tout a été fait', 184–85
    'Première communion de la Vierge', 184
    'Regard de l'Eglise d'amour', 210
    'Regard de l'Esprit de joie', 183–84, 216
    'Regard des Anges', 3
    'Regard des hauteurs', 18, 180n. 4
    'Regard du silence', 73
    'Regard du Temps', 59, 97
  Visions de l'Amen, 18, 99n. 46, 188
    'Amen de la Création', 118
    'Amen des Anges, des Saints, du chant des oiseaux', 18

  Un Vitrail et des oiseaux, 222
Messiaen, Pascal, 3, 11
Messiaen, Pierre, 2, 169
Milhaud, Darius, 30, 35
Monde, Le, 178
Moreux, Serge, 67
Mozart, Wolfgang Amadeus, 184–85
  4 Fantasias, 183
  Don Giovanni, 93, 166
  Piano Sonata in A, K. 331, 183
Muraro, Roger, 194–201
Murail, Tristan,
  Territoires de l'Oubli, 216
Murray, Alex, 17n. 4
musique concrète, 27, 67–68, 70

Ohana, Maurice,
  Douze études d'interprétation, 37n. 35
Opéra Garnier, 62n. 17

Palm, Siegfried, 181n. 10
Palmèr, Sture, *see* Lekander, Gunnar, and Sture Palmèr, *Radions fågelskivor*
Paris Conservatoire, 2, 12, 22, 83, 178, 204
Pasquier, Etienne, 222n. 27
Perrault, Charles, 61, 93
Pylarczyk, Helga, 181n. 10

Rameau, Jean-Philippe, 183–84
  Suite in E, 183
Raphael Sanzio (Raphael), 168
Ravel, Maurice, 14, 79, 193
  Gaspard de la nuit, 26, 111
  Tombeau de Couperin, Le, 183
  Miroirs, 26
    'Oiseaux tristes', 62, 63 Example 3.4
Reverdy, Pierre, 159n. 51
Rilke, Rainer-Maria, 170
Roland-Manuel, Alexis,, 67
Rößler, Almut, 61, 63
Roquer, Eva-Maria, 181n. 10
Rostand, Claude, 178

Samuel, Claude, 4, 57, 72, 221, 223
Sauvage, Cécile, 2, 61, 93
  Ame en Bourgeon, L', 65
Schaeffer, Pierre, 27, 68
  Oiseau RAI, L', 68n. 29
  Orfée, 68n. 31
Schumann, Clara, 187
Schumann, Robert, 187
  Novelettes, 112
Scriabin, Alexander, 190
  Piano Sonata no. 9 (the 'Black Mass'), 190

Semser, Ethel, 181n. 10
Sibelius, Jean, 184n. 17
Shakespeare, William, 2, 61, 191
Sharngadeva, 75n. 9
Sherlaw Johnson, Robert, 150, 194, 197–200
Smalley, Roger, 184
Stockhausen, Karlheinz, 48, 66, 68, 182
    Klang: Die 24 Stunden des Tages, 58
    Kreuzspiel, 67
Strauss, Richard,
    Alpensinfonie, Eine, 58
Stravinsky, Igor, 80 Example 4.5
    Rite of Spring, The, 80, 179
Strobel, Heinrich, 26–27, 203
surrealism, 12, 70

Tanglewood, 19
Traber, Hans,
    So singen unsere Vögel (the 'Swiss discs'), 41, 128

Tremblay, Gilles, 63
Turner, J. M. W., 13

Ugorski, Anatol, 194–200

Wagner, Richard, 14, 62, 73–74,
    93, 153
    Götterdämmerung, 62, 74
    Rheingold, Das, 74, 153
    Siegfried, 93, 116
    Tristan und Isolde, 62, 63 Example 3.3, 74,
    74 Example 4.1
Weller, Philip, 157
Winged Victory of Samothrace, 108

Xenakis, Iannis, 70

Zehn, Martin, 194, 196–98, 200
Zilgien, Line, 29

For EU product safety concerns, contact us at Calle de José Abascal, 56–1°, 28003 Madrid, Spain or eugpsr@cambridge.org.

www.ingramcontent.com/pod-product-compliance
Ingram Content Group UK Ltd.
Pitfield, Milton Keynes, MK11 3LW, UK
UKHW050108230326
469255UK00020B/445